IRISH MOVES

IRISH MOVES

An Illustrated History of Dance and Physical Theatre in Ireland

Deirdre Mulrooney

The Liffey Press

Published by
The Liffey Press
Ashbrook House
10 Main Street
Raheny, Dublin 5, Ireland
www.theliffeypress.com

A catalogue record of this book is
available from the British Library.

ISBN 1-904148-92-1

RIVER PRODUCTIONS LTD

Research for this book was kindly
sponsored by River Productions Ltd.

Design and origination by The Liffey Press

Printed in Ireland by Colour Books.

Contents

About the Author

Deirdre Mulrooney is a writer, specialising in dance, a lecturer in drama, and a director. Her five-part radio series *Nice Moves*, out of which *Irish Moves* grew, was broadcast on RTÉ Radio One with the Second International Dance Festival Ireland in 2004. Deirdre has been published internationally in dance publications including *Dance* Magazine, and has contributed to *Rattlebag, Artszone, Sunday Miscellany, The Irish Times, The Sunday Business Post, Magill, IT Magazine* and more. She has also written a book on *Pina Bausch's Tanztheater Wuppertal* (her PhD). Among other shows, Deirdre has co-directed *ShesaWhore*, based on an idea by Angela Carter, at Project Cube in 2001, and co-curated South Africa Week at the Helix in 2002. She is curating *Achtung:Dance*, a programme of events on the dance connections between Germany and Ireland for CoisCéim Dance Theatre in November 2006.

Acknowledgements

Jennifer O'Connell for the initial editing; Mella Travers for the photographs; June Fryer and Walter Kuhn; Antony Farrell of Lilliput Press; Paula Burke at Abhann Productions; Moya Doherty; John Scott of IMDT; Robert Connor and Loretta Yurick of DTI; Colin Dunne; Jean Butler; Tom Hickey; Liz Roche of Rex Levitates; Joanna Banks; David Bolger and Jenny Traynor at CoisCéim; Mary Nunan; Jade Travers; Patrick and Mary Mulrooney; Pat Laffan; Stephanie Lamache at IMEC; Cormac Cuffe; Clodagh Dooney; Dorothy McCormack and all respondents to the *Irish Times* letter of 31 Dember 2003; Sophie Gélinier; Katy Hayes; Catherine Foley; Declan Kiberd; Ashley Taggart and IES; Mairead Delaney at the Abbey Theatre Archive; Bernadette Divilly; Bernadette Comerford (producer of *Nice Moves* series on RTÉ Radio One); Seamus Hosey; Lorelei Harris; Paul Johnson; Breda Quinn of the Joan Denise Moriarty School of Dance, Cork; Marguerite Donlon of Donlon Dance Company; Olivia McCormack at Irish Theatre Archive (Pearse street library); Gaye Tanham; Doreen and Percy Lovegrove; Padraig and Markie Tarrant; James Coyle; The Horgan Family of Furbo, County Galway; Geraldine Leonard; Maggie Byrne; Blanaid Travers; Robert Mulcahy; Cathy Delaney; Dance Research Forum Ireland; all contributors to *Irish Moves*; Heidi Murphy and Brian Langan of The Liffey Press; Sinead McKenna; and a very special thanks to David Givens of The Liffey Press for committing to this project with or without Arts Council funding. If I have left anybody out, I beg your forgiveness in advance!

Photographic Credits and Thanks to:
Maurice Gunning; Chris Nash; Maureen Bourke; Ursula Kaufmann; Bettina Stoess; Todd Rosenberg; www.inpho.ie; *Irish Examiner;* Fáilte Ireland Photographic Department; Irish Traditional Music Archive; Abbey Theatre photographs courtesy of the Abbey Theatre; Gate Theatre photographs courtesy of Gate Theatre; *Riverdance* photographs courtesy of Abhann Productions. All other photographs are as credited, and copyright for all photographs remains with the photographer or organisation named. Every effort has been made to determine copyright holders; omissions or errors will be rectified in any future editions.

Acknowledgements

Captions and credits for photos on chapter title pages are as follows:

Introduction (page 1):   Olwen Fouere as Salomé in the 1988 Gate Theatre production of the eponymous play (courtesy Gate Theatre)

Chapter 1 (page 25):   Champion Irish dancers, 1930s, Cork (courtesy *Irish Examiner*)

Chapter 2 (page 49):   Front page of programme for Abbey School of Ballet production of Yeats's *The Dreaming of the Bones* (courtesy Dublin City Archive)

Chapter 3 (page 83):   June Fryer practising poses (courtesy June Fryer)

Chapter 4 (page 115):   CoisCéim production *Swept* (2003) (courtesy CoisCéim Dance Theatre)

Chapter 5 (page 173):   Alan Stanford as Pozzo in *Waiting for Godot* at the Gate Theatre (courtesy of the Gate Theatre)

Chapter 6 (page 205):   Joanna Banks and Sebastiao Mpembele Kamalandua in *(Like) Silver* (Irish Modern Dance Theatre) (photo by Chris Nash)

Chapter 7 (page 225):   Colin Dunne publicity still (courtesy of Colin Dunne)

Chapter 8 (page 255):   Cheryl Mann, Tobin DelCore and Sebastian Matthias Gehrke (face hidden) perform Marguerite Donlon's *Strokes Through the Tail* for Hubbard Street Dance, 2005 (photo: Todd Rosenberg/Hubbard Street Dance Chicago)

For my Parents, Mary and Paud

Foreword

Declan Kiberd

In the old world, every telling of a tale was enlivened not just by the voice but by the motions of the teller. The body, in effect, stood as guarantor for the movements of the mind. Without the spoken voice, the hand gestures and other signals, the word would have been little or nothing; with them, the word became a deed, an action.

Even in late medieval texts, the body was celebrated as a metaphor for the community. In repressive societies, the orifices were closed and as strictly patrolled as the borders of the territory; but in a state of freedom they were opened, as people in perpetual circulation took pleasure in the shared movements of different persons and types. The very rhythms of poetry were linked to the delight which people took in the act of walking or riding, as their bodies moved through the world.

The tradition lasted much longer in Ireland than in many other parts of Europe. Changes in clothing in western Europe of the seventeenth and eighteenth centuries suggest a new desire to deny or greatly conceal the movement of the body, a development which had its source in the rise of puritan forms of religion. The "free movement" clothing promoted by the French republicans of 1789 was based on a felt need to unshackle the human form. Brian Merriman's *Cúirt an Mheán Oíche* (c. 1781) was written to some degree under these continental influences: but it is on an even deeper level a critique of the objectification of the female body in a recently anglicised culture. The few English loan-words in the poem are satiric references to such new-fangled apparel as "cover", "púdar", "starch", "húda" and the "screw" in the stiletto heel. Merriman felt nothing but contempt for those women willing to reify their own bodies for the pleasure of a jaded puritan male imagination: and his work was an honest appeal for the rights of the human body on an equal basis with the rights of the mind.

An astonishing number of the major poetic statements about the Anglo-Irish confrontation of the colonial period found a focus in the female body. In the aisling poems, a sighing wilting woman lay on her bed in a weak condition — not unlike that of a centrefold of today's *Playboy* magazine — awaiting deliverance from a male saviour who might prod her back to life.

All of these disparate treatments maintain the medieval tradition of equating the health of the country with that of the body. As late as the 1860s, that still held true in political discourse, when James Stephens and the Fenians found Ireland "like a corpse on a dissecting table". Two generations later, the young James Joyce, writing in a Triestine newspaper, re-worked the image, saying that if the body was capable of reviving, it should do so at once, or else lie down decently and die.

Joyce himself would go on to construct his masterpiece *Ulysses* as a version of the body, with a distinctive organ assigned to each of the eighteen episodes. He did this as a deliberate revival of those medieval modes which had, he told Pádraic Colum, been blocked off by the colonial intervention and by the prim, bourgeois Catholicism which replaced the old vernacular folk traditions in the second half of the nineteenth century. He wrote his book as an "epic of the body", in a Europe whose young men were maiming and killing one another's bodies. He used the book to depict not the old Victorian "body beautiful" — which was really just another abstraction — but the actual, flawed but fascinating human form. Leopold Bloom was shown shitting and pissing in order to dramatise a man who had no silly pretensions. Joyce was unpretentious himself. When a young admirer in Paris asked whether he might kiss the hand that wrote *Ulysses*, the Irish writer laughed and said "you can if you want to, but before you do, remember one thing — that hand has done many other things as well". Whenever people talked to Joyce about romantic love, he would twit them by declaring that "the seat of the affections is lower down".

One of the most moving moments in *Ulysses* occurs when the winsome Gerty McDowell is revealed to have a limp. In statuesque pose, she was a rare beauty with eyes of the bluest Irish blue, but once in movement, she surprises Leopold Bloom: "Tight boots? No. She's Lame! O!"

The words stop and start four times in half a line, as if in fellow-feeling with her difficult movement. Joyce was a musician, who knew how to make sounds match sense, but he was also a graceful mover, whose own peculiar "spider-dance" was a noted entertainment of Zurich beer-halls and Parisian restaurants. A typical modernist, he preferred to dance in improvisational style in his own personal space rather than consort with a partner. In his younger days, as a student in Dublin, he was often unpopular with girlfriends, because of a maddening habit of breaking away in the middle of a dance to jot down notes of what they had been saying. His partners, left to their own devices on the dance-floor, might well have seen this ungallant behaviour as an all-too-direct illustration of the primacy of the word over dance in revival Ireland.

Deirdre Mulrooney is right to say that in twentieth-century Ireland the word became privileged over any bodily form of expression. But that is generally true of western civilisation ever since René Descartes diagnosed a split between mind and body, a split which later writers presented as an ever-widening gap between thought and feeling. In part, the problem is one of synchronisation over the life-cycle: the young knew how to feel but not how to express, whereas the old learn how to express but often only after they have begun to forget how to feel. At the end of his life the poet W.B. Yeats could lament having lived for seventy years "and never have I danced for joy". Only rare people, at rare moments in life, achieve such a congruence between expression and feeling.

Yet, for that very reason, the pleasure and problem posed by the dancing body are ever-present to Yeats. A child dancing on a windy seashore, or a Helen of Troy practising a tinker-shuffle, become for him images of pure self-concentration, of an art uncorrupted by knowingness. Yet Yeats was also shrewd enough to note that the professional dancer is far from such insouciance, bruising knees and twisting ankles in the attempt to create a moment of pure stillness. "How can we know the dancer from the dance?", he asks, but deep down he knows that we all do. As a fellow-artist, he recognises only too readily the distinction between the artist who suffers in rehearsal and the one who creates a beautiful image. That image is sustained for only a moment, but at a cost of a lifetime of sacrifice. When Yeats writes plays for dancers, or when he says that all men are dancers, he means to show that all art is implicated in real pain.

The dance performed by Lucky in Beckett's *Waiting for Godot* seems a further illustration of the point; but so, in a more surprising way, is the famous stomp of the five Mundy sisters in the first act of Brian Friel's *Dancing at Lughnasa*. There is a sense of release in their self-expression, but it comes also with a bitter anger at their frustrated condition. For the outbreak is furtive, conspiratorial, a forbidden act in a private space after the Public Dance Halls Act of 1935, the year previous to that in which the play's main action is set. Worse still, the dance is over all too soon, as the music from the radio peters out, failing to deliver the promised moment of ecstatic orgasm. Far from leading to a scene of golden pastoral, the stage directions insist that "the movements seem caricatural", "the sound is too loud", and "the beat is too fast". The sisters are expressing themselves but the mask of happiness is "crude". Deeper still, they are protesting against their condition, much like those Brazilian slaves who performed capoeira.

Friel's play leaves us in no doubt that the new Irish state and the Catholic Church used the Public Dance Halls Act to police sexuality, to drive dance out of kitchens, haysheds and barns into a public space where it could be more fully controlled. This hardly suggests that most Irish people were embarrassed by the body — merely that their authorities, like lords and masters the world over, felt some need to police it. The literature of the 1930s is filled with jibes by free-spirited artists against the new restrictions, which of course had parallels in autocratic countries elsewhere in

Europe. For example, Flann O'Brien in *At-Swim-Two-Birds* mocks earnest discussions as to whether waltzes were genuinely Irish dances or not.

However the "cold, fanatical character" of Irish dancing, described so accurately by Kate O'Brien, cannot just have been a result of clerical and nationalist programming. For all its sense of liberation and outbreak, Friel's scene has the same coldness and fanaticism, qualities which seem to be coded into the Irish somatic system, as a way through which a people might protest against the given conditions. Those priests who preached denial of the body were not necessarily Jansenists, but the sons of stout farmers who feared the subdivision of the family holding into fewer and fewer economic units and who advocated sexual continence as a form of social survival.

All the evidence from rural Ireland, from Merriman to McGahern, suggests a people at home with their bodies. But, after the Great Hunger of the 1840s, a problem is revealed, which Micheael Keegan-Dolan astutely calls "a fear of intimacy". This may arise less from a fear of sexuality than from a distrust of nature itself. After all, before 1847 the people had put their trust in nature, and nature had failed them. The loss of the Irish language, and the confident self-expression which it allowed, may be a further element in this story, for the explosion of brilliant writing in English at the end of the nineteenth century was, among other things, a myth of compensation. A people who had hobbled themselves by going dumb in their native language now sought to console themselves by proving that they could write the new language even more eloquently than its official owners. Perhaps the taut arms and controlled waists of the Irish dancer tell us more of our secret cultural history than we wish to know? The worst wounds in any culture are the self-inflicted ones and it may not be fanciful to see in pre-*Riverdance* forms a kind of self-denial or even self-punishment.

History is always written on the human body. Deirdre Mulrooney, an astringent critic, knows this better than most and has suggested that the "invented Irish body" needs our urgent study. She is correct and her chapters advance a lively and telling indictment of narrow-gauge nationalism and a triumphalist Catholicism. My own suspicion is that these were themselves symptoms rather than causes of the modern reticence within official Ireland about the body. The roots of the problem may lie further back in the sufferings of an impoverished people. But further back still in the writings of Gaelic Ireland may be found the authentic voices of a medieval and late-medieval people who lived most fully in their bodies and never for one moment wished to be out of them. The attempt by the current generation of artists to reconnect our theatre of the word with those experiences buried deep in our bodies is one of the glories of our current culture.

Declan Kiberd
March 2006
Dublin

Introduction

Introduction

How did we get from the naked man galloping bareback across Kilkee Strand in celebration of the festival of Lughnasa, to the alarmingly strait-jacketed movements of our "national" dance? From Síle-na-Gig to the prohibition of shiny shoes in girls' schools? How was it that second position *plié* came to be banned from dance class in 1940s convent schools? Should we blush and attribute it to a fecund national erotic imagination? Spurious theories on this subject matter abound, but — rather revealingly — the facts are few and far between.

1. "That's Not Us" – Inventing Irish Bodies

In the beginning, let us presume that we, like all ancient peoples, were barbarians. Some time later prudish Victoriana and Puritan Catholicism landed, and in some paradoxical, unlikely way put their backs behind the nationalist project. Fanatic nationalism was born. If, as sociologist Norbert Elias explained, "the formation of 'civilised' comportment is very closely connected to the organisation of Western societies into states",[1] then physicality was hijacked in the mission to create the new Irish nation-state. This was the first nation to decolonise in the British Empire, and it took a Herculean psychic effort. Our wild, free (there is no evidence to disprove it) physicality was co-opted to the national cause.

Tracing out our physical trajectory towards nationhood ("civilised" comportment), from our original barbaric state in which we were unfettered by the so-called rules (for example of the Irish Dance Commission), may help to shine light on this unexplored, untold area.

Of course, shaming of the body is rooted in fear — fear of our bodies and the expression, through physicality, of our true psychic impulses. Admittedly, the potential anarchy of innate physical impulses can be terrifying indeed. So what did we

3

do? We simply looked the other way, towards literature. We became a celebrated nation of storytellers — witty, cerebral, entertaining. But, as Noam Chomsky said, if you are told to look in one direction (by the powers that be), the real story and crux of the matter is surely happening elsewhere.

As a people we are comfortable with literature and its words, words, words. We have produced acres of words. That's our comfort zone. Ingenious Hiberno-English, outwitting the colonisers. No need, then, to face our insecurities, the area we are so uncomfortable with that we ignore it outright — physicality and the body. Where was the logic in paradoxically adopting imported Victorian values while declaring out the other side of the mouth "we are Irish" (meaning, in particular, "not British")?

Take the 1907 *Playboy* riots. The nationalists in the audience at the first performance of J.M. Synge's *Playboy of the Western World* were uncomfortable with the portrayal of such "uncivilised" barbaric folk as Synge had evoked with his pen. "That's not us!" they protested, breaking into a rather barbaric riot. The mere suggestion that we might be uncivilised made that eager, inchoate "Irish" audience see red. We were, after all, in the process of over-civilising ourselves, over-compensating, swinging too far in the opposite direction.

Simply documenting something validates it, and assigns it value. We can document things into existence. The absence of documentation on dance and movement speaks volumes. This book is an attempt to map out the territory, fill in the gaps, and open out a debate on this most neglected (and therefore most interesting) area in Irish social, cultural and historical life — our bodies, and how we move them. Why have we been averting our eyes, and putting the lid on our pens whenever the body, unfettered by words, words, words, has presented itself?

> *The absence of documentation on dance and movement speaks volumes. This book is an attempt to map out the territory, fill in the gaps, and open out a debate on this most neglected (and therefore most interesting) area in Irish social, cultural and historical life — our bodies, and how we move them.*

More than just about pirouettes, there is also a dark underbelly to our problematic physicality. Clerical abuse (think The Ferns Report); shaming and mistreatment of unmarried mothers (the Magdalen Laundries/Good Shepherd phenomenon); horrific incest (given voice and body in plays like Marina Carr's *On Raftery's Hill*), were, it now seems, systematically ignored until tragedy dictated we look away no more. Finally there was no choice — for all the worst reasons, we had to, and still have to face our problematic physicalities.

There is a hidden narrative here waiting to get out. It is the shadow narrative of our renowned literary narrative. That literary narrative is great indeed — who would argue with that? The body is to be found there too, taking its rightful pride of place in the work of writers like Joyce and Beckett. As movement therapist Bernadette Divilly pointed out in an interview with me, these writers "write from many layers of being", to produce "the embodied word".

Well may we boast of the likes of Wilde, Joyce and Beckett, but in their time they were censored in Ireland and forced into and/or chose exile. Dublin-born Beckett was so beyond any kind of narrow nationalism that he chose to write in French and German, thus elegantly sidestepping the whole issue. Indeed his plays of stage directions and breath can be regarded as the work of our first true modern choreographer, producing the most eloquent Irish body of all time on stage — if we have the right to really claim such a passionate internationalist as Irish at all. Though we certainly would like to.

Since its independence in 1922, and in the conjuring trick that led up to that moment, Ireland has been, and still is, a country in which literature, poetry and theatre maintain an absolute hegemony at the expense of non-verbal artforms. Besides the acres of literature itself, there are wall-to-wall critical books on Irish literature. Words, words, words. But not one book on what lies between the words — the physicality, the unsaid. Maybe because as Emily Dickinson said:

> Could mortal lip divine
> The undeveloped freight
> Of a delivered syllable
> 'Twould crumble with the weight

Yes, dance, physicality, and the stuff that's in between the words are ephemeral, and do not lend themselves to recordings for posterity in the annals of history. There is no script, as in a play, or even the transcription of oral poetry, like the eighteenth century *Cúirt an Mheán Oíche* or *Caoineadh Airt Uí Laoghaire*.

It is understandable that in the eighteenth and nineteenth centuries the documentation of dance was not a priority. But what is the excuse for the lack of records on that 20th century innovation — one that was aeons (well, at least 30 years) ahead of its time: the Abbey School of Ballet? Neglected, forgotten, shoved under the carpet — why? There is plenty of evidence, both written and photographic, of the plays that happened simultaneously under the same Abbey theatre roof. Yet not even one photograph of this significant cultural moment in Irish history (1927–1933) could I procure in any archive or private collection in Ireland, despite the 50 or so enthusiastic replies I received to a request for such photographs on *The Irish Times* letters page. The failure to value this visionary project, which dreamed up a miniature *Ballets Russes* for Ireland, physical training for actors and dancers, and choreographers collaborating on play production, is inexcus-

Imagine the beautiful poetry of the fact that it was an Irish woman, Ninette de Valois (born Edris Stannus in Blessington, County Wicklow, a transformation Oscar Wilde would no doubt relish), who invented the British Ballet.

able. Here, despite the fact that it has practically been erased from memory, we undertake to salvage what we can.

Imagine the beautiful poetry of the fact that it was an Irish woman, Ninette de Valois (born Edris Stannus in Blessington, County Wicklow, a transformation Oscar Wilde would no doubt have relished), who invented the British Ballet. If, as Declan Kiberd suggests in *Inventing Ireland*, Ireland functioned as England's unconscious, it is almost unbearably fitting that the English National Ballet sprang directly from the loins of its unconscious. Who has even given this juicy fact a passing thought? But I digress.

Then, a full half millennium after the mid-fifteenth-century advent of the printing press, while the Second World War was raging throughout Europe, came yet another lost chapter of contemporary dance in Ireland. Comprising many a Bohemian war refugee, including its part-Irish founder, Erina Brady's Irish School of Dance Art could be called the "Emergency Chapter of Contemporary Dance in Ireland". Erina Brady's Mary Wigman-inspired Harcourt Street Irish School of Dance Art has been so overlooked that even key figures in contemporary dance in Ireland today — including the seminal Joan Davis — had never heard of it.

We only know of it because one of its star pupils, Jacqueline Robinson, here as a war refugee from Paris during the aforementioned "Emergency", took the trouble to write a memoir of her time in Dublin entitled *Modern Dance in Dublin in the 1940s*. Published here for the first time, it was written in 1999, the year before she died. The memoir outlines how Robinson, already a trained pianist, began her dance training here with the "mysterious" Erina Brady in 1939. She went on to perform with her co-star, and Ireland's first modern dancer, June Fryer, at the Peacock Theatre in productions by the likes of T.C. Fitzmaurice, T. Sturge Moore, and with Austin Clarke's independent Lyric Theatre Company. They also performed in Brady's own choreographies like Tennyson's *The Voyage of Maeldune*, at the Peacock, and the Irish Red Cross-sponsored *TB Ballet* at the Mansion House (opened by de Valera himself).

Yet we are led to believe there is no legacy of modern dance in Ireland? The real story is not just that there was a considerable, and a cosmopolitan, modern dance movement here, linked in with the most important practitioners on mainland Europe, but that nobody considered it worthy of documentation.

Inspired by her experience of modern dance in Dublin, when she returned to Paris after the war Robinson opened Paris's first professional school of modern dance, *L'Atelier de la Danse*. Passing on Brady's passion for her art form, Robinson subsequently translated Mary Wigman's writings into French. Meanwhile, her co-star, fellow student and fellow teacher, June Fryer, went on to study the Jooss-Leeder method in London, and subsequently taught at Oxford Theatre School for many years. Yet we are led to believe there is no legacy of modern dance in Ireland?

The real story is not just that there was a considerable, and a cosmopolitan, modern dance movement here, linked in with the most important practitioners on mainland Europe, but that nobody considered it worthy of documentation.

What's more, the same dramatic antipathies were played out in Ireland between ballet and modern dance as everywhere else in Europe. Dublin was right at the vanguard, with balletomanes here making fun of Erina Brady's freer, Wigmanesque movements once they caught sight of them at variety programmes in the Gaiety Theatre. Indeed, poor Brady ended up the butt of many a balletomane's joke. (This is not a criticism of the balletomanes, who were, after all, just being proper balletomanes). Brady, meanwhile, in her bohemian Harcourt Street studio, which was frequented by the likes of Basil Racoszi of the White Stag Art Group and the writer John Betjeman, was no doubt none too fond of them either. In this mutual antipathy, some balletomanes, according to my sources, would send Erina Brady up as their party-piece/charade, indicating that the thriving 1940s dance scene in Dublin was a party to precisely the same robust debate as every other European capital. To allow these happenings to vanish into obscurity is to impoverish the Irish cultural heritage, and to put dance at a disadvantage as an art form. So happily, here with Jacqueline Robinson's memoir, and June Fryer's interview, we can salvage at least some of it.

> *What's more, the same dramatic antipathies were played out in Ireland between ballet and modern dance as everywhere else in Europe. Dublin was right at the vanguard, with balletomanes here making fun of Erina Brady's freer, Wigmanesque movements once they caught sight of them at variety programmes in the Gaiety Theatre.*

Because of this lack of documentation, each new dance movement, thinking they were the first, wasted a lot of its precious energy re-inventing the wheel, instead of building on what was already there. Yet again it seems those who do not learn from history are condemned to repeat it. It became a fated cycle as hopeless as Yeats's system of gyres — but never reaching the apex of sublimation. Not yet anyway.

When I set out to write this book, I did not have to get very far into my research to realise the dearth of material — not least the absence of any primary source material — on many eras. So I had to change tack, and assemble the primary source material first, hence sketching out a sort of map of "what happened" and "who did what" by the protagonists, in their own words. I have made discoveries along the way. For starters (see above and below), dance, movement, the body have been *persona non grata* in Irish theatre history. On the one hand, it was fantastic that RTÉ Radio took up my proposal to do the radio series, *Nice Moves*, on this history of dance and physical theatre in Ireland, to run in tandem with the Second International Dance Festival Ireland in May 2004. But on the other, it is disheartening that The Abbey School of Ballet is generally deemed not worth the trouble of documentation in any archive in

Ireland, beyond a few programme notices. That's the state of affairs at the time of writing. But hopefully this will change as people begin to realise how important the body, and our attitude to it, is in terms of social history.

Reflecting on the ensuing first-ever map of contemporary dance and physical theatre in Ireland this book also aims to provide a meditation on our attitude to the body as a nation and the body-journey we are still on. Looking also at the body as a metaphor for nation, it contains revelations about Irish society seen from a fresh perspective, which, while often illuminating and celebratory, are sometimes disconcerting too.

Now that Ireland's first centenary as an independent nation is just within reach, the time is nigh to look back, upon mature recollection, at a nation that had to be conjured into existence out of thin air. This act of creation took a lot of mental, political and psychic energy from everyone involved. In some cases the actions were extreme. Politicians, clergy, zealots, insurgents, visionaries and those in power sometimes over-shot the mark — as manifests itself most eloquently in their over-zealousness with regard to the body.

> *Looking also at the body as a metaphor for nation, [this book] contains revelations about Irish society seen from a fresh perspective, which, while often illuminating and celebratory, are sometimes disconcerting too.*

But let's rewind to the outset of the twentieth century. On the road to nationhood, number one on the inchoate nation's to-do list was to establish the fact that we were "not British", even before establishing what we actually were. Nonetheless (as if things needed to be any more complex), we were already well advanced in the process of adopting those aforementioned imported Victorian values in terms of physicality, sexuality and the body — the ones where even a piano leg had to be covered in case it would give rise to sinful thoughts. Then layer on that Puritan Catholicism. And to make a truly potent cocktail, throw in a dash of Eoin O'Duffy-style misguided fascist goose-step marching to visit, in one fell swoop, Mussolini and the pope. Talk about confused. What after all, was it to be "Irish"? It seems there hadn't been much progress made since Shakespeare's Irish character Captain MacMorris responded to Fluellen in *Henry the Fifth*:

> Of my nation? What ish my nation? Ish a villaine, and a bastard, and a knave, and a rascal. What is my nation? Who talks of my nation? (Act 3, Scene 2)

Physical poet Tom Mac Intyre picks up the question in his 1987 poem, "Appalachia"[3]:

> What ish my nation?
>
> My nation is Appalachia, Appalachia,
> Worn trail of eye for hand, tooth
> For claw, scalp for cup and saucer,

Busted telly in the bog-hole,
Washing-machine sneezing rust
On the uninsurable bargain-line

Irish Moves attempts to work out how physicality fuelled and expressed this identity crisis by first salvaging, and then allowing us to ponder, a new map of dance and physical theatre in Ireland.

For the project of "inventing Ireland" manifested itself most eloquently in the National Project Part Two, the unspoken one of "inventing Irish bodies". Central to the events that shaped the future of Irish dancing and the curtailment of Irish bodies at the turn of the century was the foundation in 1892 of Conradh na Gaeilge, or the Gaelic League.

Tellingly, and not a little paradoxically, the first ever céilí was held in, of all places, London. Organised by Fionán Mac Coluim, it was held by the Gaelic League in London's Bloomsbury Hall, near the British Museum on Saturday, 30 October 1897.[3] Thirty years later, hot on the heels of the 1929 advent of *An Coimisiún Le Rinnci Gaelacha* (The Commission for Irish Dance) and the intensification of the project to invent Irish bodies, came the 1930s ban (known as "the Ban"), prohibiting its members from dancing any other dances than Irish dances. This xenophobic knee-jerk impulse was, ironically enough, most un-Irish, given what Kiberd describes as:

> the extraordinary capacity of Irish society to assimilate new elements through all its major phases . . . taking pleasure in the fact that identity is seldom straightforward and given, more often a matter of negotiation and exchange . . .[4]

So, instigating a programme tantamount to cultural cleansing, "the Ban" propelled Irish dancing down a *cul de sac* that went against the grain of Irish tradition's tendency to amalgamate foreign influences, which in turn made it flourish and grow. We had to wait for *Riverdance* to reverse it out of that blind alleyway in the 1990s, loosening up the stultified form by re-introducing some arm movements, and juxtaposing it with flamenco, American tap and Russian folk dance. Previous to that, in the 1970s, Fr Pat Aherne had also nurtured what Irish dancing damage control he could with Siamsa Tire, the National Folk Theatre, in Tralee, County Kerry.

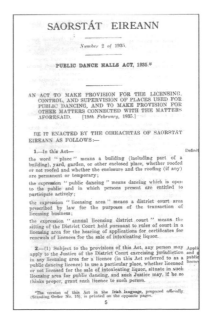

The 1935 Public Dance Halls Act

Part of the xenophobic anti-jazz movement, the fact that "social and recreational dance became a symbolic border to be vigilantly patrolled"[5] was however common throughout Europe and the United States in the 1930s. As for the rigid upper body though, which is unique to Irish dancing, it must have had something to do with the fact that, as sociologist Barbara O'Connor tells us, "for elite cultural nationalists . . . the ideal Irish dancing body was an asexual body". In set dancing of the day, the clergy could rest assured that "the nearest approach to contiguity is the joining of partly out-stretched hands".[6]

> As for the rigid upper body though, which is unique to Irish dancing, it must have had something to do with the fact that, as sociologist Barbara O'Connor tells us, "for elite cultural nationalists . . . the ideal Irish dancing body was an asexual body".

O'Connor continues, enlightening us further on our dance heritage: "what appears to be unique to Ireland was the decision by the government of the day to row in behind the Movement in the early 1930s" — culminating in the 1935 Public Dance Halls Act. This act was a social turning point in Irish society, controlling where, when and under whose supervision dancing could take place. It effectively doused out dance as an informal leisure time activity in kitchens, backyards, on doors, living room tables, etc. In 1998 the burgeoning, repressed sexuality of this era (a wonderful topic for a play) became the subject of the first dance-theatre piece at the Peacock Theatre for years in *Toupées and Snare Drums*, by Gina Moxley and CoisCéim Dance Theatre.

The personal, as always, is political, and vice versa. As O'Connor intimates below:

> It was seen as necessary . . . to mould individual bodies to reflect the body politic of the new state. The State's interest in dance can also be seen as part of a broader concern with the moral state of the nation and with the conduct of its youth in particular. So the combined anxieties resulted in public social dancing becoming an object of scrutiny and a site of struggle over identity politics.

Meanwhile, leaving no stone unturned, out on the far-reaches of the Blasket Islands the long arm of the clergy was instilling shame into the hearts and minds of the locals, as across all of Ireland. Here Eilís Ní Súibhleabháin describes the new imported rules of bathing on the Great Blaskets in her 1936 diary:

> Great changes have come on the island lately with the visit of two Redemptorist Fathers. No mixed bathing is allowed. No dancing in any house, day or night. And no-one out later than half-past ten.[7]

However, while these control-freak tendencies — the 1935 Dance Halls Act, the xenophobic "Ban", the nurture of shame — appear alarmingly idiosyncratic when considered in isolation, they make more sense when you stand back and take in the big picture. From a wide angle, they can be seen more clearly as knee-jerk reactions, symptomatic and an expression of our national identity crisis:

> Most nation-states existed, so to speak, before they were defined, and they were thus defined by their existence: but states emerging from occupation, dispossession or denial had a different form of growth. . . . There was (and is) a lot of strain attending this artificial process by which an abstraction is converted into reality . . .[8]

We were after all an inchoate nation coming into being, and the 1930s and 1940s was just our gawkiest, sullenest, most non-communicative adolescence, a common phase for all teenagers establishing who they are in the adult world. Teenage Ireland was no exception.

2. Our Gawky Adolescence — Everyday Irish Moves

Having made it through what must be the gawkiest adolescence ever experienced, the time is nigh to look back at the family photograph album, and enjoy the adolescent attire and the bad hair-dos. But while we're at it, we can learn something from it. This important, if cringeworthy, phase in our development manifested itself most eloquently in our sense of physicality. As teenagers tend to, we stuck our heads in the sand, censoring anything to do with the body and physicality. Instead we focused purely on our formidable brain power, and our intellectual prowess. This type of Descartian mind/ body dualism pertains to the entire western world, and is not at all unique to Ireland. But in this case it is Ireland that is in question.

As Kate O'Brien's 1941 County Limerick character, Martin Kernahan, conceded to his new-found French cousin Angèle on her first encounter with Irish dancing: "We're a prim, stiff-backed lot!" We didn't do our national adolescence by halves, as this outsider's perspective, seen through the aforementioned Angèle's half-Irish half-French eyes, confirms:

Champion dancers, Cork, 1930s

> Two men danced a very complicated jig. They were champions, and wore medals which danced with them. The old fiddler who sat on a stool to accompany them wore medals too. The dancers were rigid, serious, and skilful.

Angèle wondered how the rickety little platform bore their force, but they were very agile. She had never seen dancing like this; it had a cold, fanatical character all its own. She could not say she liked it; in any case it was too entirely novel for hasty acceptance, but it was extremely severe; formal and beyond compromise. It had none of the sentimentality or sensuousness of other folk dancing; it was simply a very difficult exercise, skilfully executed. When it was ended, she looked at Martin for interpretation.

"It's amazing", she said to him. "It's so austere that it's almost shocking".

He laughed. "That's well observed", he said. "This national dancing blows the guff on us, I always think. If you like it proves why Dev is making a success of us."[9]

What were we trying to prove with this tightly regulated, quasi-militaristic form? We sidestepped the more holistic form of Irish dancing, that is *sean nós* dancing, in which the impulses flowing up from the feet continue unimpeded through the upper body, and arms are waved about freely, in favour of a sort of body fascism. Not in the sense of the body-beautiful, but the body-controlled, repressed, ignored — the body non-grata.

Winding back further towards our nebulous genesis, in the absence of images and written records, all we can do is speculate. Dance historian Catherine Foley and folklorist Dáithí Ó hÓgáin do that below. It may not be unusual that there is no written record of dancing or movement until the sixteenth century, but what is remarkable is that there is no indigenous Irish word for dance. *Rince* comes from the English "rink", meaning "to skate", and *Damhsa* from the French "danse" — both imported words.

> *We sidestepped the more holistic form of Irish dancing . . . in favour of a sort of body fascism. Not in the sense of the body-beautiful, but the body-controlled, repressed, ignored — the body non-grata.*

So what we've got to work with are absences: absent dancing, absent moving, and the absence of words to even describe these innate human actions. Ó hÓgáin points up Cuchulainn's physical prowess of lore and legend, the recurrent posture of standing on one toe, leaping back and forth across a fire, and spells being cast by walking in left-handed circles. Additionally, he asserts that "the expression of one's emotions ritually through body movements . . . is undoubtedly very ancient in Ireland". So, even if there wasn't a word for dance, physicality and movement were powerful forces in that cosmogony. Catherine Foley is also optimistic that dance was so important to ritual, and so integrated into everyday life, that the ancient Irish didn't need a word for it. The jury is out, and I hope that this book, an initial map of dance and physical theatre in Ireland, will kick-start the debate, and draw out new information. What follows is food for thought — an *amuse-bouche*, opening out the topic, encouraging anyone who has a piece of the jigsaw to come forward with it, and help piece together this giant public puzzle depicting ourselves.

The time has come to re-imagine Ireland, this nation of verbose storytellers, in terms of how we moved, physically, and look for the stuff in between the words. For our true history, our psyche, is embedded in our bodies. According to Neropa Institute-trained movement therapist Bernadette Divilly, our relationship to physicality, and to our bodies, is a complex one. The variables are myriad: from spiritual, sensual, sexual and religious to social. In Divilly's trained eyes, we carry our eight hundred years of oppression literally on our backs. Since the famine, Irish bodies have been carrying a "sense of poverty, shame and hunger", she attests.

Looking back to the apocalyptic moment that was the 1845–47 Famine, all we can do is imagine the impact that trauma would have on what may well have been (there is no documentary evidence to refute it), a more free-flowing, uninhibited sense of physicality and movement up to that point.

But, can we say that there is a way of moving that is unique to the Irish? Apparently, yes. On the one hand Divilly offers an example of the "in being" quality of *sean nós* singers, a phenomenon that is certainly at the other end of the scale to the "above-the-knees epidural effect" of twentieth-century Irish dancing. But more prevalently today, "there is an enormous amount of tension in our bodies and how we move," remarks Divilly.

In her eyes, Irish bodies have a tendency to "contract", and to "feel unsafe about expressing". Divilly sees "a huge contradiction between what is given value and spoken about, and what is actually felt" in Irish people. According to her, "this de-synchronisation is a real sign of trauma". She

> *In her eyes, Irish bodies have a tendency to "contract", and to "feel unsafe about expressing". Divilly sees "a huge contradiction between what is given value and spoken about, and what is actually felt" in Irish people.*

adds that "a common Irish body is totally outside of itself". However she does concede that this need to work on other levels than just the cognitive is something that all Westerners have in common — it is not exclusively Irish.

Physical theatre practitioner Raymond Keane, of Barabbas the Company, muses, "we have the tipping of the cap, or the apologetic nature of our physicality — the eight hundred years of oppression if you like". Growing up in Ireland of the 1970s, Keane reminisces how (unconsciously) his American cousins made him feel physically inadequate with their innately more strident, confident physicality: "I always felt that while the Americans were there taking up space in the kitchen, I was cowering in the corner."

However, this Irish tendency towards physical cowering, and feelings of inadequacy, has shifted on more levels than one, Keane believes. "With Irish society coming of age, finally shedding the colonial past, new riches, Celtic tiger, success, arts, sport, whatever, I think we have straightened up as a society. We're heading on into the world saying 'take us seriously'."

But tensions seem to linger still in our bodies, fuelling some of the most interesting contemporary dance and theatre practice. Taking himself as an example, Irish choreographer Michael Keegan Dolan of Fabulous Beast Dance Theatre recently said:

> I'm personally very "tied up" physically and not good with touching and being too close to people. That creates all sorts of tension in the body. A lot of the work I do is based on the huge levels of tension you find in Irish people because of that fear of intimacy and fear of sensuality and sexuality.[10]

The dark side to this phenomenon can be seen in the all-too-recent Magdalen Laundries era as depicted in Peter Mullan's eponymous film. Divilly draws the link between how this "shaming women for being sexual" in twentieth-century Ireland "led to a lot of sexual abuse". We can't simply blame the coloniser either. It was probably just that potent cocktail of uptight Victorian morality, Puritan Catholicism and misguided fanatic nationalism imploding again. As Kiberd

The dark side to this phenomenon can be seen in the all-too recent Magdalen Laundries era as depicted in Peter Mullan's eponymous film. Divilly draws the link between how this "shaming women for being sexual" in twentieth century Ireland "led to a lot of sexual abuse".

points out with an apposite quote by Patrick O'Farrell from *Ireland's English Question: Anglo-Irish Relations, 1534–1970,* it has always been down to ourselves, ourselves alone:

> No proposed external solution could ever satisfy the Irish, calm their troubles, for they as a people neither knew who they were nor what they wanted — these were problems they would have to solve for themselves, themselves alone.[11]

Calibanesque, all colonised people are good at the white lie, within the coloniser's tongue. But when this aptitude tips over into lying to yourself, trouble is at hand. Bodies, not fully within the remit of cognitive control, however, do not lie so readily. Unbeknownst to ourselves, Ireland was working out its complex identity in our bodies and at the level of our physicalities.

As Norbert Elias points out, nations configure themselves in movement. The unspoken notion that dancing, and the patrolling of Irish bodies, was important to the project at hand, of inventing Irish bodies, was quite real. Similarly in 1930s Germany the rise of Nazism found physical expression in the co-option of choreographer Mary Wigman and the implicit aesthetics of her Movement Choirs (as seen in Leni Riefenstahl's propagandistic films *Olympiade* and *Triumph of the Will*) — nation-state mentality in motion. We had our own "fascinating fascism", to borrow a phrase from Susan Sontag — albeit on a smaller scale — with Eoin O'Duffy's Blueshirts.

But this area is riddled with paradoxes. Ironically, Mary Wigman's disciple Erina Brady set up Ireland's first modern dance school in 1940s Dublin. Brady, one of many bohemian refugees here in 1939, was escaping the same rise of Nazism that was to co-opt Wigman's unwitting work to its cause. But Brady encountered a different kind of resistance here to her free-flowing, almost hippy aesthetic of the body and of life. This revelatory resistance is embodied in the prudish case, described below by Jacqueline Robinson, of the banning of second position *plié* (legs in a wide stance) in a dance class in a Brigidine convent school in 1946:

> For my first class I wore a long fluid skirt, which was a customary garment for dancing at the time. The class went very well, with one of the Sisters attending. Afterwards, I was summoned by the Mother Superior: "Miss Robinson, I hear that you lifted your skirt, revealing your legs, which furthermore were in a wide stance." (We were doing second position *pliés*). "No question of your doing that here!"
>
> What should I wear the following week? In order not to have to lift my skirt I wore a short one, a tunic. Would this be considered decent? Before giving the class, I had to appear before an Areopagus of Sisters. They looked shocked and it was pronounced that there could be no exhibiting bare legs under any conditions. So what was I to do? "Give your class in your coat and skirt", said Mother Superior. Which I did, and for the whole term; at the end of which the Bishop declared that there were to be no more dancing classes of that type at the Convent.[12]

If only they had heard of the burka, we would surely have all grown up wearing one.

It is against this social background of shame, fear, immense ferment and tension, both personal and political, that we must consider the trajectory of performing bodies in Ireland. These were troubled bodies, annexed as an unofficial battleground for identity politics, and the impetuous hammering out of a burgeoning nation state.

> *It is against this social background of shame, fear, immense ferment and tension, both personal and political, that we must consider the trajectory of performing bodies in Ireland.*

3. Performing Irish Bodies

HEROD: Salomé, Salomé, dance for me. I pray thee dance for me. I am sad tonight. Yes; I am passing sad tonight. When I came hither I slipped in blood, which is an evil omen; and I heard, I am sure I heard in the air a beating of wings, a beating of giant wings. I cannot tell what they mean. . . . I am sad tonight. Therefore dance for me. Dance for me Salomé, I beseech you. If you dance for me you may ask of me what you will and I will give it you, even unto the half of my kingdom.

You could say, severed head in hand, that it all goes back to Salomé's strange, cold, erotic dance before Herod. Conveniently for my theory, Frank Whelan suggests the first mention of dance in early Irish was the translation of the words *cleasaíocht*, *léimneacht* and *hopaireacht* from Irish into Latin to describe Salomé dancing before Herod.[13] How apt then, to take Salomé's strange sensual dance with her trophy severed head of John the Baptist in Oscar Wilde's banned play *Salomé* (and its notions of female agency), as the point of departure for dance in Irish theatre.[14] Noreen Doody gives an account below of how Yeats was hugely influenced professionally, as well as infatuated personally, by Wilde, who was thirty years his senior, and his oddly enchanting idiom. "Yeats first started thinking seriously about dance as a useful symbol for his own work after seeing Wilde's play *Salomé* in 1905 in London", says Doody. It inspired him to re-write earlier works, she notes, including his 1906 production of *Deirdre* at the Abbey. The result was denounced by Lady Gregory and Synge as "a degradation of our stage" and by Joseph Holloway for having "sensuality all over it".

Pitched against the prevalent Abbey "stand and deliver" acting style — which was, after all, the perfect vessel for their predominant fare of "peasant plays" — was Yeats's more fine-tuned physical awareness. Yearning for a Wagnerian total theatre of the poetic, he tried, like Wilde, to show the interconnection between the sensual and the spiritual. However, beyond seeing the dancer as symbol, it is open to question whether Yeats knew much about, or even liked, dance. Doody tells us how his daughter Anne mused to her, "I can't imagine father being interested in dance".

Photo courtesy Gate Theatre

Coralie Carmichael as Salomé, 1928, Gate Theatre

But he obssessed early in life with "the energy of the body", and did realise there was something there. He tried many different approaches to unleash this energy in his work. For a while, "influenced by the magical belief that the unconscious is tapped by keeping the body still, the mind awake and clear, so as to avoid any confusion between 'the images of the mind and the objects of sense'",[15] he made his actors rehearse in barrels. It was rather paradoxical that the author of *Four Plays for Dancers* and instigator of the Abbey School of Ballet with de Valois suggested that actors rehearsed in barrels in order to "forget gesture and have their minds free to think of speech for a while".[16]

Being a writer, Yeats's main focus naturally was on words. He developed his own system of declamation, comprising distinct styles: peasant dialect, iambic pentameter, impassioned lyric verse and pitched

> *On his own body-journey, at least, Yeats knew there was something to be reckoned with in the notion of the body, and did his best in his own misinformed, but earnest, way to do something about it.*

incantatory verse. Though his knowledge of movement was negligible by comparison to his knowledge of voice, he did progress from his initial limited view of actors as mere "reverent recitors of majestic words".[17] Yeats took physicality seriously. He experimented with different approaches, from the Eastern disciplines of Michio Ito (even if a little misunderstood in classic "orientalist" form) whom he met through Ezra Pound, to de Valois and their visionary initiative, the Abbey School of Ballet. On his own body-journey, at least, Yeats knew there was something to be reckoned with in the notion of the body, and did his best in his own misinformed, but earnest, way to do something about it.

By inviting Ninette de Valois to help develop his theatrical idiom, and putting himself truly at the vanguard of European theatre, Yeats also set in motion a movement awareness training for actors. It is a terrible lost legacy that de Valois left in 1933 to found the British Ballet, relegating physicality to take a back seat in Irish theatre once again.

Yeats's influence trickles down to Samuel Beckett's neologistic theatre work in the 1950s and 1960s, from *Endgame's* Nagg and Nell mired in bins — and subtly echoing Yeats's project of having his actors rehearse in barrels — to the stillness of the "prematurely aged" blather-free lady rocking backwards and forwards in *Rockabye*. Beckett's choreographic oeuvre was way beyond any narrow nationalist project and the fevered obsession with inventing an Irish identity. Director Walter Asmus, who worked closely with the playwright, offers us a glimpse of Beckett the choreographer, who apparently did not suffer the effects of any traditional Irish inferiority complex.

Meanwhile, growing out of the loamy soil back on home turf, Patrick Kavanagh's 1946 poem *The Great Hunger* captured the prevalent *malaise* perfectly. Ireland's new famine was not about potatoes, but about spiritual and sexual deprivation. "It is not about growing up and away but about growing down and in," says Seamus Heaney of Kavanagh's bleak poem. "Its symbol is the potato rather than the potato blossom."[18]

"The body was not to be mentioned in '30s, '40s and '50s Ireland," physical poet Tom Mac Intyre says of the Ireland he grew up in — the same Ireland of which Kavanagh writes. Appropriately, it was Mac Intyre who brought Kavanagh's insightful, heartbreaking poem to the Peacock stage in 1983. In so doing he, along with his collaborators Tom Hickey and Patrick Mason, created a new theatrical idiom. Theirs was a vision that was charged by sexual repression: "I'm sure my insistence, my pursuit of articulating the erotic, the sensual, the sexy in theatre has a great deal to do with the Hitler-censored world into which I was born and reared," Mac Intyre confirms, below.

Speaking of his body-centred theatrical oeuvre, which spans nearly thirty years now, in terms of a "spirit journey", Mac Intyre says that "to try to express the spirit magic through the magic of the body — that is one of the beautiful challenges". For this breakthrough Irish playwright "the magic, the mystery, the explosive colours of the sensual, the sexual, of love, are one of the great challenges in our lives". He relates below how "storytelling all the time is about that".

Mac Intyre's pioneering work prepared the way for an ebullient second generation of physical theatre with companies like clown-inspired Barabbas the Company, Corn Exchange and their Chicago-style *Commedia dell'Arte*, Olwen Fouere's work with Operating Theatre, Niall Henry's work with Blue Raincoat Theatre Company, and embodied play scripts like Brian Friel's Tony Award-winning 1991 play *Dancing at Lughnasa*, also directed by Patrick Mason.

In an explosion of *fin de siècle* physicality, the body began to be taken more seriously in theatre, as seen with choreographer David Bolger's collaborations with Conall Morrison on his adaptation of *Tarry Flynn*, and with Garry Hynes on plays by Martin McDonagh and J.B. Keane. Actor training picked up with the advent of both the Gaiety School of Acting and TCD's acting course at the Samuel Beckett Centre. Catching up with our literary alter-ego, Leopold Bloom, these developments are all symptomatic — we hope — of a society that is becoming more at home in its body.

> *The 1990s were an eventful decade for Irish bodies. That classic Irish inferiority complex must have exited stage left as the nation reconfigured itself in movement, in the form of* Riverdance.

The 1990s were an eventful decade for Irish bodies. That classic Irish inferiority complex must have exited stage left as the nation reconfigured itself in movement, in the form of *Riverdance*. Like ferocious tigers that had escaped their cage after oh, about 64 years of captivity, the Irish Superman and Superwoman were unleashed onto Broadway in 1995. Heralding a new image of what it was to be Irish, interestingly, these über-Irish were part of the diaspora. All part of the journey, often transatlantic, of becoming what we are moving towards today — more comfortable with who we are in our increasingly globalised bodies. *Riverdance* re-introduced the foreign influences that were so dear to us before the advent of fanatic nationalism, and tacked on some arm movements, signalling that it was, in fact, okay to move the upper body. Far from being anti-traditional, this initiative arguably harked back to a more cosmopolitan, pre-Gaelic League era, when, as Irish dance historian John Cullinane asserts, the first Irish dancing masters were more than likely French.

Traditional Irish dancing has been on a rollercoaster of its own. Take Birmingham-born Colin Dunne's personal odyssey, growing up in a world where girls at Irish dancing competitions would literally sew the arms of their costumes on to the bodices to prevent their arms from flailing about involuntarily. Below, he recalls a pad being put on his left shoulder to balance out an apparent unevenness that emerged as a result of one piece of intricate footwork. This outside-in aesthetic dictated that all focus was on virtuoso feats of the feet, to the detriment of gnarled, neglected shoulders. A tense, rigid upper torso, disconnected from what was going on in the feet, was part and parcel of Irish dancing, according to Dunne. (It was also an eloquent metaphor for Ireland of the time). *Riverdance* started the unravelling of this tightly wound form, began reversing it out of the *cul de sac* it had driven itself into, and celebrated the result on a world platform.

Now where artists like Jean Butler, Breandán de Gallaí and Dunne take it is anyone's guess. And of course there is Michael Flatley, the more showy Lord of the Dance, who demands inclusion. Flatley certainly did bring Irishness to a whole new level of self-belief — and he is after all in the *Guinness Book of World Records* for having the most taps per minute. But what really does matter is that the art form is going somewhere, developing and growing. No longer "deadly", to use Peter Brook's terminology, in the hands of these practitioners, Irish dancing is a living work-in-progress, with a world-wide audience. When you train your political gaze on the more holistic dancing style someone like Dunne has developed today — loose, comfortable upper body, intricate footwork which is not just for show — you can't help feeling that Irish dancing is on its way somewhere to finally being a metaphor for a more grown-up, enlightened nation.

As Micheál Ó Súilleabháin intimates, below, maybe, just maybe, the green shoot is bursting through the tarmacadam that has been poured on it over the last hundred years. Because as Peter Brook put it, "when we say deadly, we never mean dead: we mean something depressingly active, but for this very reason capable of change".[19] Thanks mostly to the catalystic effect of *Riverdance*, traditional Irish dancing appears, Lazarus-like, to have snapped itself out of its hitherto comatose state.

Despite the unsavoury fact that until the 1990s one avant-garde dance movement after another was allowed to fizzle out and disappear into obscurity, re-invigoration has been afoot in the contemporary dance world too.

In the stop-start story of contemporary dance in Ireland, Joan Davis's pioneering struggle in the 1970s was all the more difficult, and uphill, for not knowing that Erina Brady had been there before her. (Even if Brady was rooted in German *Ausdruckstanz*, and Davis steeped in the techniques of the mother of American modern dance, Martha Graham.) Yet she persevered and won over bewildered audiences. "The highest form of praise you could get after a show was that somebody would come up to you and say 'you must be very fit'," attests Davis, below. "Then you knew you had touched them somehow or somewhere."

The ruthless and arbitrary (Pinteresque even) 1989 cuts in Arts Council funding are typical of the "against the odds" story of contemporary dance in Ireland. Valiant efforts kept getting doused out, washed away by the tide, leaving no trace. Healthy developed audiences for dance were repeatedly abandoned. Robert Connor and Loretta Yurick give their visceral first-hand rendition of the unheralded 1989 cuts in funding, which, remarkably, they overcame. Phoenix-like, today's main companies emerged from those flames: Dance Theatre of Ireland, Irish Modern Dance Theatre, CoisCéim, and later, Rex Levitates. As much as stories of dance in

> *As much as stories of dance in Ireland, theirs are exemplary, inspirational creative life journeys. Below, they divulge what kept them going when there was so much pitted against them.*

Ireland, theirs are exemplary, inspirational creative life journeys. Below, they divulge what kept them going when there was so much pitted against them. Even apart from the artistic idiom they have developed, their steadfastness and unflagging tenacity to their artistc vision is quite a phenomenon on its own.

Then there are our dancing wild geese. Marguerite Donlon, from Longford, landed via the English National Ballet as soloist in the Deutsche Oper in Berlin, before taking up residency as Ballet Director of the Saarlandisches Staatstheater Saarbrücken in 2002. Noted for her "black Irish sense of humour", and incorporating Irish dancing-inspired movement into a classically based movement vocabulary, she is today stamping out her own idiosyncratic movement signature with Donlon Dance Company.

Finola Cronin returned to Dublin in the mid-1990s after almost twenty years performing in cutting-edge dance theatre on major stages internationally. Her odyssey through German Dance Theatre culminated in being a key performer with Pina Bausch's legendary Wuppertal Dance Theatre for a decade. Most recently she has taken up a position as Dance Specialist on the Arts Council, feeding her breadth of experience back into Ireland.

Dubliner Michael Keegan Dolan, whose early choreographic work was nurtured by Mary Brady at Cork's Institute of Contemporary Dance in the Firkin Crane in the late 1990s, built an international career with the likes of Sir Peter Hall and the English Opera. More recently he has been garlanded with accolades and nominated for an Olivier award for his 2003 Dublin Theatre Festival-produced rural Irish anti-fairytale *Giselle*, and was the subject of great controversy in 2005 for his risqué version of ancient Irish epic The Táin in *The Story of the Bull*. He elaborates on his uncompromising ethos, in which choreography has the potential to be the most subversive of art forms, below.

Subversive or not, audience figures from the Second International Dance Festival Ireland (2004) indicated that the dance scene here is flourishing. Up 10 per cent from 2002, audiences are at an all-time high. All around the country dance is thriving, from Cathy O'Kennedy's Fluxus Dance in Wexford, to Daghdha Dance Company and its innovative work with Austrian choreographer Michael Klien's social choreography, and before him New York/Japanese Yoshiko Chuma in Limerick; the nurturing Institute of Contemporary

> *Subversive or not, audience figures from the Second International Dance Festival Ireland (2004) indicated that the dance scene here is flourishing. Up 10 per cent from 2002, audiences are at an all-time high.*

Dance in Cork (whose Arts Council funding was unfortunately cut in January 2006), as well as Half/Angel's experimental work with Jools Gilson Ellis and Richard Povall; Julie Lockett and Ella Clarke's intense work on the principles of Deborah Hay. Then there are body-based projects like theatre director Selina Cartmell's collaboration with dancer Ella Clarke in *Shutter* and, bordering on performance art, her work with Operating Theatre's performer Olwen Fouere in *La Musica*, *Passades* and *Here Lies* (a live installation on Artaud in Ireland) — plenty to constitute an *Irish Moves 2*.

Dance is being endorsed in academia as well with the 1999 advent of Ireland's first ever MA in Dance Performance at the University of Limerick, and with dance featuring on the drama syllabus at University College Dublin. The circle is getting wider, as if they had all been listening to Seamus Heaney's whispers:

> When they make the circle wide, it's time to swim
>
> Out on your own and fill the element
> With signatures on your own frequency,
> Echo soundings, searches, probes, allurements,
>
> Elver-gleams in the dark of the whole sea.[20]

Our national body-journey has brought us to a place where we are free to throw anarchic, abstract shapes as in John Scott's work with Irish Modern Dance Theatre.

Scott has been working recently with survivors of torture to produce such important expressions of where we are as a society as *Fall and Recover*. David Bolger is experimenting with unconventional performance spaces like the city hotel room where *Chamber Made* takes place; Dance Theatre of Ireland's adventures in motion-capture found Robert Connor and Loretta Yurick exploring how new technologies can be factored into their choreographies; while Liz Roche's work with her company, Rex Levitates, has been interacting with civilians (in *Proximity*, for the 2005 St. Patrick's Day Festival in Dublin). Irish step-dance has reached a place in which the foot-impulse is carried right through the body and out into the stratosphere, as with Colin Dunne. We can learn Jean Butler's more holistic notion of what Irish dance can be from her new DVD. Contemporary and traditional dance practice are meeting in the laboratory atmosphere of University of Limerick. That's how unproblematic this "Irish Body" has become. A national style?[21] Contemporary dance is international by nature, often sidestepping nationality (though some choreographers do have that unshakeable Irish tendency towards the anecdotal) — not unlike Beckett, our greatest master of the body on stage.

Photo courtesy Gate Theatre

Olwen Fouere as Salomé, 1988, Gate Theatre

So, in an effort to put right a massive historical, cultural and social blind spot, from Ninette de Valois to Jean Butler and Tom Hickey, what follows showcases — and in some cases salvages — the stories of Ireland's unsung movers: actors, dancers, choreographers, playwrights, directors and the few academics who dare to go where no words have gone before. Focusing on people who value what's in between the words as much as the words themselves, it presents stories of the creative journeys taken by people who have devoted their lives to physical expression — despite the fact that their medium was ignored, or even erased from memory.

But be not afraid, lending an ear to the oft-quoted "Come, dance with me in Ireland"[22] resonating down through the centuries does not necessarily mean you will fall foul to the same fate as Herod who made the foolhardy promise:

> If you dance for me you may ask of me what you will and I will give it you, even unto the half of my kingdom.

No, not necessarily.

Notes

[1] Elias, Norbert, *The Civilising Process*, Oxford: Blackwell Publishers, 1994 (first published 1939), p. xiv.

[2] MacIntyre, Tom, *I Bailed Out at Ardee*, Dublin: The Dedalus Press, 1987, p. 66.

[3] Brennan, Helen, *The Story of Irish Dance*, Dingle: Brandon Press, 1999, pp. 29-30.

[4] Kiberd, Declan, *Inventing Ireland*, London: Vintage, 1996, p. 1.

[5] O'Connor, Barbara, this book, p. 40.

[6] O'Connor, Barbara, below, p. 39.

[7] Whelan, Frank, *The Complete Guide to Irish Dance*, Belfast: Appletree Press, 2001, p. 17.

[8] *Inventing Ireland,* p. 117.

[9] O'Brien, Kate, *The Last of Summer* (1943), London: Virago, 1990, p. 96. Set in 1941, in County Limerick.

[10] "Ballet in the Bog", *Guardian*, 23 February 2005.

[11] Patrick O'Farrell, NY, 1971, p. 14, quoted in *Inventing Ireland*, p. 116.

[12] Extract from an unpublished manuscript by Jacqueline Robinson, quoted in full below.

[13] Whelan, Frank, op. cit, p. 9. See also Dáithí Ó hÓgáin, p. 33, below.

[14] Michael Seaver in *Everything Irish* (Dublin: Mercier Press, 2004, p. 97) starts with seventeenth-century "performance dance" in the Theatre Royal, Smock Alley theatre — yet another area for excavation.

[15] J.W. Flannery, *Yeats and the Idea of a Theatre*, New Haven and London: Yale University Press, 1976, p. 205.

[16] Quoted from Yeats's "Explorations" by J.W. Flannery in *Yeats and the Idea of a Theatre*.

[17] Flannery, J.W., op. cit, p. 206.

[18] Quoted by Vincent Hurley in "The Great Hunger: A Reading", *The Great Hunger, Poem into Play*, Dublin: Lilliput Press, 1988, p. 73.

[19] Brook, Peter, *The Empty Space*, London: Penguin, 1968, p. 45.

[20] From *Station Island*, by Seamus Heaney.

[21] Dancer and co-founder of Rex Levitates, Jenny Roche, is currently exploring issues around this question in her Ph.D: "Meta-morphologies: multiplicity embodying difference, the Irish contemporary dancer's moving identity".

[22] Fourteenth century — see Ó hÓgáin, below, p. 35.

Chapter 1

Chapter 1

The Origins of Dance in Ireland –
Did We Dance?

I n the absence of pictorial or written records all we can do is speculate on whether there was dance in ancient Ireland and, if so, in what kind of regard it was held. This is a worldwide conundrum, as dance scholar Alexandra Carter points out: "the low social status of dance, the equation of its sensual nature with its sexual potential and the difficulties of studying such a transient event have all contributed to the lack of a substantial or seriously considered scholarly heritage."[1] So I thought it wise to leave the speculation to people best positioned to know, namely widely published Associate Professor of Folklore at UCD, Dáithí Ó hÓgáin, and ethnochoreologist and step dancer Catherine Foley of the University of Limerick's World Academy of Music and Dance. So – did we or didn't we? And if so, how?

Among other fascinating theories, Ó hÓgáin postulates that ritual movement in ancient Ireland was powerful, and had a range of magical functions, from casting spells to making people fall in love with you (as Dearg Corra allegedly did by leaping back and forth over a hearth while food was being cooked). Foley continues, informing us that the 250-year-old written history of step dance begins at the end of the 18th century with the advent of agriculturalists/travel-writers like Arthur Young who mention dancing masters.

On a downwards spiral from the foundation of the restrictive Gaelic League, we skip on with social historian Barbara O'Connor to the 1920s and 1930s invention of asexual Irish bodies, a somewhat insidious nation-building project. We refresh our memories of the 1935 Dance Halls Act, born as it was out of de Valera's notion of an "ideal Ireland". Finally, glancing from the general to the particular, Seosaimhín ní Bheaglaíoch, Kerry Gaeltacht woman and renowned *sean nós* singer, shares the curious case of her father's fish-salting factory turned dance hall, which, in the true spirit of the times, was condemned from the pulpit by *an sagart paróiste* with fire, brimstone and *bastairdai* ("illegal offspring").

Dáithí Ó hÓgáin
Department of Folklore, UCD

From County Limerick, Dáithí Ó hÓgáin is Ireland's leading folklorist. He has written over twenty books including The Celts: A History; The Sacred Isle: Pre-Christian Religions in Ireland; Irish Superstitions; Historic Ireland: 5000 years of Ireland's Heritage; Ireland: People and Places; Celtic Warriors, *and* The Hero in Irish Folk History. *Associate Professor of Folklore at University College Dublin, here he helps us to imagine the significance of movement in ancient Ireland.*

Dance or No Dance in Early Ireland?

A reasonable empirical definition of dance would be "deliberate posturing in rhythmic fashion, using either feet or hands, or both together". Such a definition would entail various body movements performed in regular or measured manner such as stepping, gesturing, jumping, hopping, swaying, tiptoeing or stamping. It is self-evident that physical exertion as a means of attracting attention or acclaim comes naturally to individuals of healthy constitution, and one could postulate that activity such as dance is an inevitable development within social groupings. Such a point would indeed gain support from the fact that dancing of one kind or another is found in cultures of widely different circumstances and epochs. The Irish tradition has been recorded better than most for many centuries, and scholars are puzzled by the fact that evidence for dancing is slight, or perhaps even non-existent, down to the late mediaeval period. The question has often indeed been asked: was there in fact any dancing in early Ireland?[2]

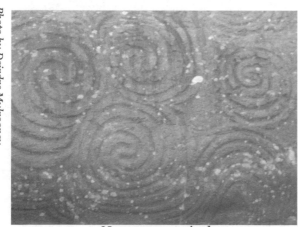

Photo by Deirdre Mulrooney

Newgrange spirals

Archaeologists are reluctant to comment on such immediate issues that concern human activities of a perishable nature and which do not leave definite material evidence. There may, however, be indications of such things. In his fine study of the great mound at Knowth in County Meath, Professor George Eogan considers the type of seasonal rite which would have been performed there in the late Stone Age – the orientations of the two passage tombs in the mound suggesting an emphasis on

28

the spring and autumn equinoxes. "Part of the event might have involved an enact-
ment of ritual outside the tomb, for instance a procession around the mound, taking advantage of the decoration on the kerbstones – each one perhaps representing
a 'station' within a system." He goes on to state that one can picture "ceremonies
being performed by priests – indeed the leading figure may have been a priest-king
– before and around the entrances, using exotic objects (maces and conical 'idols')
and unusual stones".[3] One might speculate that some measured footwork was involved in these ceremonies. It should of course be borne in mind that dancing need
not always have an entertainment function, but that – and more specifically in ancient times – it could more appropriately be considered as a ritual activity.

The motif of circumambulation is long established in Irish tradition. It may have
been used to designate particular spaces as sacred at archaeological sites, such as
megalithic alignments of stones, the Bronze Age stone-circles and henges, and the
circular enclosures of the Iron Age. Similarly, pacing around areas would have been
intended at all stages to set such areas apart, whether for "secular" or "religious"
purposes – or, as is most likely, for both purposes at once. To judge by references
in Irish literature and folklore, such movement would take place "with the sun", i.e.
right-handwise while facing the east where the sun rises. Contrariwise, to move in
a left-handed circle was a way of inflicting a curse. Ritual directional movements of
this kind are attested by Irish literature from at least the eighth century onwards.[4]
Here the circumambulation was described as a ritual to claim possession of land
and, though this in itself is formal pacing rather than dance, it is performed within
specific time-limits. Such controlled measuring of steps is to be distinguished from
the legal ceremonies known as "marking the boundaries" in, for instance, mediaeval Dublin, when the mayor went on
parade to the limits of his jurisdiction.

Deliberately ordered steps of a posturing nature are more to the point, especially where such are carried out in
consort with another body part. For instance, there are several references in the
old literature to the dangerous power of
an individual with a blind left eye,[5] and in some cases this is connected with deliberate body or foot movement. Several early mediaeval literary texts describe a specific
ritual of this type, and in such differing contexts that it can be taken to reflect very old
tradition. This is the practice known as *corrghuineacht* (literally "heron-wounding"),
probably because the performer mimicked the image of that bird. It was a magical
ritual with the explicit purpose of weakening or damaging a foe.

Most dramatically, it is described as performed by the mythical hero Lugh, the
Irish version of the deity Lugus, who was venerated in much of Continental as well
as in insular Celtic Europe. The text, which dates to as early as the ninth century AD,

> *Here the circumambulation was de-*
> *scribed as a ritual to claim posses-*
> *sion of land and, though this in itself is*
> *formal pacing rather than dance, it is*
> *performed within specific time-limits.*

recounts the story of the great mythical battle fought between the two sets of deities, the Tuatha Dé Danann and the Fomhoire. Lugh had been designated leader of the Tuatha Dé, but he was kept under guard for his own protection by his army. He broke loose, and came to the place where the battle was being fought. The text states that "there Lugh sang a recitation, on one foot and one-eyed, around the men of Ireland". The recitation is in antique language, probably dating to some centuries earlier than the text, and it seeks for ritual effect "through the strong skills of druids". Lugh calls to his support the heavens and the earth, the sun and the moon, which four elements were often stressed in druidic oaths and which therefore underline the magical nature of the act he was performing.[6] His posturing was deliberate and purposeful, involving circular measured movement and with special use of the feet.

Versatility is a crucial element in another account of the ritual in mediaeval literature. Here the performance is by the mythical hero Cúchulainn during the Cattle Raid of Cooley, and the structured and skilful nature of the ritual is stressed. Cúchulainn is described as cutting a sapling of oak with a single stroke and, using but one arm, one leg and one eye, making a hoop of it and writing a message on it in the difficult *ogham* script. He fixes this on a stone pillar, and when the enemy approaches their leader interprets it to mean that the invading army should go no further until one of them can make a hoop in the same way. The result is that they circumvent the place.[7]

The ritual is referred to also in another text of the ninth century, which recounts some lore concerning the tragic death of the mythical Conaire Mór. That celebrated Tara king had broken ritual prohibitions, most specifically that he had left his royal seat before sunrise, with the result that his destruction was inevitable.[8] He took shelter from inclement weather in the house of Da Dearga ("the red god", a sombre designation of the sun-god), where he was surrounded by foes. In the eerie atmosphere before the final attack, and just after sunset, a strange figure enters. She is a hideous woman, described as a *banscál* ("female satirist") and she begins to revile the king. Conaire enquires for her name, and she recites a list of several mysterious designations, all with mythical connotations. The text states that "on one leg and one breath she sang all of that to them from the door of the house". This

> *What this amounts to is the expression of one's emotions ritually through body movements, and this is undoubtedly very ancient in Ireland. Poetry was rhythmical and was understood as the expression of great feeling, such as awe, anger, or sorrow . . .*

strange woman, called in the text Cailbh, is obviously the type of a druidess acting on behalf of divine destiny, and Conaire is slaughtered in the ensuing siege.[9] Although she is not described as doing rhythmical foot movements, the co-ordination of foot and breath is significant, for the breath of a poet was often thought to contain the essence of their artistic performance.[10]

What this amounts to is the expression of one's emotions ritually through body movements, and this is undoubtedly very ancient in Ireland. Poetry was rhythmical and was understood as the expression of great feeling, such as awe, anger, or sorrow,[11] and it must have been customary to express the same feelings through demonstrative and rhythmical actions. There does not appear to have been a rigidly set formula, each practitioner to a greater or lesser extent making their own of the rhythmic performance,[12] and as such there would have been no need for a definite and distinctive word for it. The manner, indeed, in which the Irish language describes such actions tends to be dependent on verbs or prepositions indicating to "do" or to "go". When one bears this in mind, it is easy to concur with John MacInnes who, in discussing the question of dance in mediaeval Gaelic Scotland, considers forms of traditional verse (such as that found in waulking songs) as strongly suggestive of not only hand but foot movement.[13] Dr MacInnes draws particular attention to the old Scottish custom of dancing at wakes, and indeed there is plenty of evidence for the same in Ireland. From the seventeenth century onwards there are accounts of merry dances at Irish wakes,[14] but in earlier times some at least of the dancing may have been mournful, as a bodily expression of grief corresponding to the verbal laments which were customary on such occasions.[15] The import of the "lamentation games" (*cluichí caointe*), mentioned frequently in early Irish literature in connection with funerals, may indeed have included dancing.[16]

There are references to ritual movements in war, stretching back through Irish culture to its Celtic antecedents. Thus, for example, the clashing of spears and the playing of trumpet music is mentioned in accounts of Irish warriors,[17] and a similar practice is found in sources on the Continental Celts of antiquity.[18] The rituals of the Fianna, the famous group of hunter-warriors led by Fionn Mac Cumhaill in Gaelic romance, reflect some early hunting-lore, and though dancing is not mentioned among their feats, other related practices concern rhythmic chanting (their celebrated mouth-music called the *dord Fiann*), and feats of unusual bodily dexterity and footwork (such as picking a thorn from the foot while at full speed, or running under a low cross-post without slackening pace). In particular, we may mention the strange description of one of Fionn's men, called Dearg Corra, in an eighth century text. We read that, while food was being cooked this character used to leap to and fro over the hearth, and that this caused a young woman to fall in love with him. He engaged in other notable postures also. While in the forest, he gave food to the deer, and "he used to go about on shanks of deer, he was so light". Dearg Corra has the features of a god of the hunt, and this account would seem to be detritus from ancient hunting-lore which involved mime dancing.

> *We read that, while food was being cooked this character used to leap to and fro over the hearth, and that this caused a young woman to fall in love with him.*

Other references in early Irish literature entail similar ritual elements. What, for instance, can be made of the mysterious image of the Ulster goddess (originally the Mór-Ríoghain but who came to be known as Macha) racing against horses in a scene of great dramatic intensity? A separate reference has Meadhbh (originally the goddess of Tara) racing against horses, and the conclusion can hardly be avoided that the rituals of kingship involved the idea that a king's reign was paced out by the land-goddess in the mythic realm.[19] Social time is thus determined and symbolised by the movement of feet. In Middle Eastern terms this "race of life" was parallelled by the "dance of life", a fact echoed in Platonic terms by St Basil in the fourth century AD when he referred to how the souls of the departed do a "heavenly dance" just as "they performed a spiritual dance of life here on earth".[20] Given the sophistication of thought in early societies – which we are only just beginning to realise through recent scholarship – it would be plausible to consider that similar parallels existed in Irish ritual lore. Indeed, an Irish monk of the seventh century may have been aware of such an analogy when he referred to the angels rejoicing "in holy dances" (*tropodis sanctis*).[21]

Here we may consider the widespread folk beliefs in Ireland and other western European countries concerning the performance of dance in the otherworld. Often in folk tradition, indeed, otherworld activities are a reflection of the material world. The folklore of recent centuries is adamant that stone formations, and particularly the circular formations found frequently throughout the landscape, are "fairy circles" at which the *sí* people dance at night.[22] The supposed activities of these otherworld beings are in many cases reflections of things done by real people in the past, and it is possible that the stone circles – which date mostly from the Bronze Age – were indeed once sites for such ceremonies. Attention may be drawn to a striking description in a text written in the seventh century AD concerning St Samson of Dol, who lived a century earlier. According to this, on his mission in south-west Britain, the saint encountered people who were engaged in a pagan *bacchantum ritu* – which can only have meant a kind of dance – around a stone idol.[23]

> *It would indeed be strange that the early Irish, who placed great store by gaming and horse-racing, ball-games, music, acrobatics and buffoonery, would not also have rhythmic footwork among their accomplishments.*

It would indeed be strange that the early Irish, who placed great store by gaming and horse-racing, ball-games, music, acrobatics and buffoonery, would not also have rhythmic footwork among their accomplishments. Such is indeed suggested by a fourteenth century account of the above-mentioned Lugh, who was portrayed as the master of all arts and skills. In this account, his skills include prodigious swimming, carrying a vat on his elbows, and "leaping on a bubble without bursting it".[24] When one recalls that in folklore otherworld hurling is sometimes represented as taking place on lakes or sea,[25] this posturing on water begins to look like a reflection of a popular pastime. Acrobatics, one would say, but it is well to remember that individual dancing performances in post-mediaeval Ireland included "acrobatic" postures, such as in *rince an ghadraigh* ("the withy dance") and *damhsa na scuaibe* (the brush dance").

Clear evidence for dancing as a pastime is not forthcoming from western European literatures until after the mediaeval period, and it is even difficult to identify native words in Norse, Celtic or even English for the activity.[26] The Irish words *damhsa* and *rince* are borrowings – both apparently having come into Irish from Old French ("dance" and "renc") via Middle English ("daunce" and "rink").[27] Not only is the English word "dance" itself borrowed from the French, but the words used in several other western European languages are similarly borrowed. Much attention has been paid to the eleventh century religious text in Irish, based on St Jerome's Vulgate, which describes the dancing of Salomé before Herod but seems to have difficulty in finding an exact word for the activity.[28] The word Jerome used in his Latin was *saltare* (indicating the movement of limbs to a measure or tune), but the Irish translator used the terms *léimneach* ("jumping"), *cleasaigheacht* ("acrobatics") and *opaireacht*, a variant of *obaireacht* ("antics").[29]

None of these three terms satisfactorily describe dancing, but as noted above the Irish language stressed the specific aspects of the activity rather than its formal designation. We are left, however, with the question as to what terms in common usage most approximated to the generic description of "dancing". One such word may in fact have been *macnas* (with an original meaning such as "youthful energy"), referring to any kind of playful activity, particularly that of a wanton or exuberant nature. One mediaeval text gives the combination *ceol agus cuideachta, meadhair agus macnas* – "music and company, mirth and *macnas*".[30] In this context we could easily read "dancing" for the latter word. When – either ritually or as a pastime – dancing was being described, it seems to have been customary to refer to it as movement which is "deft" (*deas* or such) with feet or hands.

That dancing existed in early Ireland as a social pursuit, as a pastime, or as a "courtship ritual" is suggested by several factors. In calendar custom, for instance, the basic seasonal division of the year in Celtic culture from time immemorial was between the dark season (winter) and the bright season (summer). In Ireland this imagery gave rise to traditions of a figure called Donn contending with a figure called Fionn at both May and Halloween. Not only do we find this contention in Irish heroic saga and in legends of Irish fairies, but it was also part of entertainment lore at these festivals.[31] Hurling matches were played between teams representing winter and summer, and significantly in our context dances were also held with similar imagery. The May dances, celebrating the greenery and featuring dancers referred to as the king and queen of winter and summer, are evidenced from the sixteenth century onwards, but their practice as well as their imagery must date from a much earlier time. It was a longstanding custom for young people, especially girls, to go tripping through the fields and houses "bringing in" the summer.[32]

It is well recognised that, in the later Middle Ages, singing traditions in the Irish language were greatly influenced, indeed largely transformed, by the fashionable love-songs which had come into English through French. What actually happened to Irish dancing traditions would appear to have paralleled this,[33] but with even greater effect, i.e. older dances were gradually displaced by English varieties. By this time, ritual dances would of course have greatly declined anyway, and the new type of entertainment or "courtship" dances proved much more attractive to young people – perhaps because of their more regular figure movements. Inevitably, of course, the older Irish dances left their mark on the new ones. Thus, one of the most popular dances in sixteenth and seventeenth century Ireland was called by English writers the "Trenchmore". Accounts show it to have been a longways dance without any limit to the number of dancers, and the posture seems to have been stamping over a large area with hands on hips.[34] The term "Trenchmore" in fact seems to have been a corruption of *rince mór*

Photo: National Library of Ireland

May pole dance, Co Waterford, c. 1910

("great dance"), which was well-attested in the Irish language.[35] Though the word *rince* itself was a mediaeval borrowing, this actual dance must have had native origins, which are reflected also in the May dancing described above. The more usual term *rince fada* ("long dance"), which seems to have become known even in England in the seventeenth century, is likely to have been of similar import.[36]

In conclusion, it can be said that all prerequisites for dancing are evidenced from pre-mediaeval Irish literature. One could, of course, argue that mention of everything else, but no clear mention of dance, suggests that dancing did not exist at all, but that would hardly be a plausible explanation. It is much more likely that types of dancing, more in the nature of ritual or acrobatic posturing, were well-known in early Ireland, but that dancing as a courtship activity was much enhanced by the introduction of new figure-formations under Norman and English influence.

Thus, the much-quoted Middle English quatrain on "come ant daunce wyt me in Ir-launde"[37] (written in the early fourteenth century) would probably refer to English settlers or their influence in the country, as would the reference to convivial dancing among the companies of the Mayor of Waterford and the O'Driscoll chieftain in the year 1413.[38] The fine figure-dances mentioned in sixteenth and seventeenth century sources,[39] such as "the Hay", would be of similar derivation, as indeed were the sets of more recent centuries. The special poise and gusto of Irish traditional dance, as we know it, must however owe something to the original native element, which could also be traced in the spirit of Irish traditional music.

Catherine Foley
Ethnochoreologist and Irish Step Dancer

Catherine Foley's Cork upbringing was steeped in Irish traditional music and dance. Her PhD thesis on Irish traditional step dance in North Kerry at the Laban Centre for Movement and Dance, London, was the first ever on the topic. Director of Tráth na gCos, an annual festival of traditional dance in Limerick, Catherine has worked as a collector of Irish traditional music and step dances, and is herself an Irish step dancer. Course Director of the MA in Ethnochoreology and the MA in Irish Traditional Dance Performance at University of Limerick's Irish World Academy of Music and Dance, Catherine has published internationally on Irish dancing. Here she speculates on the importance of dance in Ireland, despite the lack of written records.

We don't know how the early inhabitants of Ireland danced. As there is no written documentation on it, the information we have is based on speculation.

However the fact that there are no written references doesn't mean that there weren't dances. Though the words "dancer" or "dance" did not yet exist, we can presume that there were dances associated with ritual and fertility.

In early Irish literature, the terms "clesaigecht" or "lemenda" were used to describe Salomé's dance before Herod. But these words might also be associated with acrobatics, jumping, trickery and leaping. In the Middle Ages across Europe dancers were mostly looked upon as acrobats or jugglers. They weren't very privileged, which is probably why there is no terminology referring specifically to dance in Ireland in early and middle Irish texts.

However, just because the words *rince* and *damhsa* are relatively modern terms borrowed from the English word *rink* and the French word *danse* respectively, doesn't mean that the early Irish inhabitants didn't dance. On the contrary, dance was so integral to their ritualistic and social activities that there was no need for them to talk about it as a separate activity. While today everything is specialised – we go to dance classes, music classes, singing classes, riding classes and swimming classes – centuries ago these activities were part and parcel of a wider ritualistic or social context.

The earliest written reference to dance comes from the fifteenth century. But from the seventeenth century onwards there are more numerous references to long dances, round dances, the *rince fada*, the Trenchmore and the Hay. Some of these come from travellers – predominantly English and French gentlemen – who journeyed around Ireland. People like the English agriculturalist Arthur Young or the Halls wrote about the Irish people and referred at times to their dance. However, beyond a few scant references here and there, there is very little on dance.

As he travelled around Ireland between 1776 and 1779, Young was the first to mention the existence of dancing masters, who were responsible for the beginning of Irish step dance. So we say the history of step dance begins at the end of the eighteenth century.

In the nineteenth century music, dance, song and storytelling were integral to the rambling house in rural Ireland. Step dance would have taken place together with set dancing and miscellaneous couple dances. It became more specialised with the dancing masters, who perfected the craft, honing step dance into a disciplined physical activity. The Gaelic League appropriated step dance in the early decades of the twentieth century and developed it further.

Looking at it within a broader context of the mind/body split, dance generally suffered. The word was prioritised while the body, the instrument of dance, was subverted. Dance knowledge was transmitted by word of mouth and by imitation. While collections of traditional music and song started as far back as the eighteenth century, Irish traditional dance had to wait another hundred years before any attempt was made to document it.

> *Looking at it within a broader context of the mind/body split, dance generally suffered. The word was prioritised while the body, the instrument of dance, was subverted.*

The first written documentation of some long and round dances in Ireland is found in O'Keeffe and O'Brien's 1902 book, *A Handbook of Irish Dances*. Unfortunately for posterity, in their book, O'Keeffe and O'Brien write that the step dances were so familiar, that any description was superfluous. However, these dances were going to change, and it would have been interesting had they documented this change. Thankfully, with our dance documentation skills today, dance need no longer be devoid of written or technological representations.

We live through mind–body connections. Dance as a physical and thinking activity assists us in feeling moments in life intensely. In his 1983 book, *Frames of Mind: The Theory of Multiple Intelligences*, Howard Gardner states that kinaesthetic intelligence is one form of intelligence and dance is generally now perceived as an intelligence. From that point of view it is extremely important that we take dance and dance scholarship seriously.

People are beginning to realise that dance and the body are important, and studies thereof should no longer be neglected. People need to invest time to understand what is going on when dancers dance. Why do people dance in a particular manner? Why do some cultures have sitting dances? Why do dancers in other cultures use their upper body sparingly? Why do dancers use their legs alone? Do some cultures differentiate according to gender, age, race, economic background or religion in their dances? Is there a political or economic agenda within particular dance practices? How does the dance relate to culture?

In this context, the two Masters programmes in dance at the Irish World Academy of Music and Dance, University of Limerick, are timely and extremely important.

The MA in Ethnochoreology allows us to look at dance within the context of wider cultural issues, such as history, politics or religion. While validating the study of dance academically, it allows us to look at ourselves and others through dance.

The MA in Irish Traditional Dance Performance has performance practice at its core. I grew up as an Irish step dancer, and completed my PhD at the Laban Centre for Movement and Dance in London in 1988, so I wanted to incorporate the best of Irish step dance practice within the framework of a broader knowledge of dance practice and history.

Growing up, I remember teachers who had such regard for what they were doing that they would say, "there should be a degree in Irish step dance". And now at last, after 250 years, it is a degree. To date the University of Limerick is the only university in the world that validates Irish step dance at both undergraduate and postgraduate degree levels.

Step dancers need to remember that we have this 250-year history of dance training in Ireland, but we can always improve on it. Currently, there are dancing teachers teaching, promoting and developing this art, and doing great work. But the MA programme is situated within an academic context, so it allows Irish step dancers to excel at performance through master dance classes, body awareness classes, and technique classes, while interacting academically as well.

There is so much happening in dance practice and dance scholarship at present, hopefully it will continue on an upward spiral.

Barbara O'Connor
Lecturer in Communications, DCU

*B*arbara O'Connor has a background in sociology and social anthropology, and lectures in the School of Communications, Dublin City University on aspects of popular culture and communications including dance. She has published widely on dance in Ireland, including "Riverdance, Encounters with Modern Ireland" (Irish Sociological Profiles); "Safe Sets: Women, Dance and 'Communitas'" (Dance in the City), and "Ruin and Romance: heterosexual discourses on Irish popular dance, 1920–1960" (Irish Journal of Sociology). Currently researching the social and cultural role of recreational dance in Ireland from 1900, here Barbara shines some light on the most peculiar Irish body politics that were at play in 1920s and 1930s Ireland.

Body Politics: Shaping Social Dance from the 1920s

Social dancing in post-independence Ireland was marked by a concerted effort to shape and control it in line with a particular vision of an ideal Irish dancing body. The Irish body was to be "pure" both in terms of its being "authentically Irish", i.e. untrammelled by any outside influences, as well as in terms of sexual modesty and constraint. Culturally nationalist groups such as the Gaelic League consolidated this vision at the end of the nineteenth century.

By the 1920s the Catholic Church, and later the State, became involved in public debates on dance. They sought to impose their views through public pronouncements and legislation respectively. The dominant attitudes of these institutions towards the dancing body can be traced back to the increasing dominance of cultural nationalism at the end of the nineteenth century. Cultural leaders sought to

Photo: National Library of Ireland

Girls at gym class at the Ursuline Convent School, Waterford, 1908

establish what they perceived to be an "authentic" Irish culture free from "foreign", particularly English, influence.

This applied to dance as well as to other aspects of popular culture. The Gaelic League, which was the main promoter of dance at this time, set about creating a canon of social dance in the form of *céilí* dancing. The Catholic Church had long had a Puritan attitude towards dance and the body. This attitude was to intensify in the post-famine era due to changes in land inheritance and the consequent need to control population growth, and therefore sexuality. Since dance was seen to be "an occasion of sin", the increasing power of the institutional Church was concerned with policing it.

After its foundation in 1922, the State was also concerned with building a "pure" and "authentically Irish" national culture as witnessed in the move to censor books and films towards the end of the decade. It was seen as necessary therefore to mould individual bodies to reflect the body politic of the new state. The State's interest in dance can also be seen as part of a broader concern with the moral state of the nation and with the conduct of its youth in particular. So the combined anxieties resulted in public social dancing becoming an object of scrutiny and a site of struggle over identity politics.

The concerted efforts to shape dancing bodies was as true of social dance as it was of step dance. *Céilí* dance was lauded as being superior to other forms. In the words of one contemporary commentator, it was "triumphant proof that a Gaelic entertainment is one of the most potent factors we have for the fostering amongst us of the traditional Irish kindly spirit".[40] It was also praised for the fact that there was very little contact between the sexes. As another writer on the subject remarked: "It is a fundamental characteristic of Irish danc-ing that the nearest ap-proach to contiguity is the joining of partly outstretched hands."[41] For elite cultural nationalists, then, the ideal Irish dancing body was an asexual body.

Photo by Jim Horgan

Dancing at the crossroads, Youghal, Co. Cork, 1910

In the 1920s "Irish dance" was at least partially defined in relation to its opposite, "foreign dance". The latter was largely defined in terms of contemporary popular social dances in Britain and the US – dances that were becoming increasingly popular in Ireland throughout the decade. It was during this time that social and recreational dance became a symbolic border to be vigilantly patrolled. The mid-twenties saw the initiation of a vociferous anti-jazz movement, which included members of the Catholic clergy, members of culturally nationalist organisations, in particular the Gaelic League, and indeed politicians at local and national level. Spokesmen for the movement railed against the multitudinous evils of jazz music and dance.

Photo courtesy of Irish Examiner

Outdoor dancing, 1920s/30s, Cork

The clergy made frequent reference to the sinful qualities of jazz in pastoral letters and ecclesiastical publications that were widely reported in the national press of the time. They regarded it as indecent, immoral, degenerate and totally unsuited to the Irish dancing public who were exhorted not to attend such dances. The clergy who objected to jazz may not have been clear about the actual dances involved. Newspaper reports indicate that there was confusion about the definition of "jazz" in public discussion amongst those taking part in the debate. The term was frequently used as an umbrella term to cover all contemporary and popular non-traditional dance.

So what were the main objections to it? They were various. One clerical objector believed it to be part of a Communist plot and for others it was tainted with the degeneracy associated with cosmopolitan living. More importantly, though, it was seen to bear the marks of its origins in African culture and was associated in particular with African musical rhythm, which in turn had connotations of an unrestrained and dangerous sexuality.

> *So what were the main objections to [jazz]? They were various. One clerical objector believed it to be part of a Communist plot and for others it was tainted with the degeneracy associated with cosmopolitan living.*

This was seen to manifest itself in the defining "swing" musical style, which elicited relatively more "wild" and "unrestrained" dance movements than those of the pre-jazz era. Jazz dances would typically have been faster, have more body movement including torso and hip movements and would have involved close bodily contact between partners. The physical proximity and contact between dance partners was one major basis of objection. Because female fashion had also changed, with the advent of short skirts and so on, dancing women were now exposing more of their bodies than previously. This was considered to be vulgar, at best, and at worst grievously sinful.

However, it is only fair to point out that fear of the sexualised and racialised dancing body was not confined to Ireland. There were also very active anti-jazz movements in Britain, the US and mainland Europe. But what appears to be unique to Ireland was the decision by the government of the day to row in behind the movement in the early 1930s. This led to legislation being introduced on the conduct of public social dancing in 1935.

The alliance of State, Church and voluntary groups referred to above led finally to the introduction of the Dance Halls Act in 1935 to "make provision for the licensing, control and supervision of places used for public dancing and related matters". This legislation signalled the relative success of those groups who wished to control and monitor public dancing. In order to hold a dance one had to apply to the District Court for a licence. The granting of the licence was at the discretion of the District Justice. This meant that only "reputable" people would be granted a licence under certain conditions. The hours of dancing were also controlled, as were the kind of premises in which the dance was held. It is widely believed that the new legislation was at least partially to blame for the demise of house dances, which until then had been the cornerstone of the rural dancing tradition.

Prior to the legislation, all-night dances were popular but ceased to be licensed after the introduction of the new legislation. Members of the clergy had objected on the basis of the belief that late Saturday night dancing was a deterrent to attendance at Mass on the following morning. In addition to a concern for the moral welfare of parishioners, there may have been some element of self-interest insofar as the clergy were also involved in the construction and management of parish halls so that dance profits could either accrue to them personally (for instance, to pay for improvements/repairs to the priest's house) or to some parish service under their management, like the local primary school. It also meant that they were well situated to monitor access to the parish halls and to supervise dancing activity. While the State was supportive of the Church's effort

> *In addition to a concern for the moral welfare of parishioners, there may have been some element of self-interest insofar as the clergy were also involved in the construction and management of parish halls . . .*

to morally police public dancing, legislation was not totally concerned with sexual issues. Evidence indicates that the State was also concerned with public health and safety issues such as fire hazards, condition of buildings, sanitation facilities and so on, which were the responsibility of the government of the day.

Throughout the 1920s and 1930s dance as a leisure activity was being increasingly commercialised, and a number of dance venues were established. In addition to the building of parish halls a number of privately owned/commercial dance halls were built. The original "Ballroom of Romance", called The Rainbow, was established in Glenfarne, Co. Leitrim in 1934. Other well-known ballrooms such as the National opened in Dublin in 1945 and Seapoint in Salthill, Galway in 1949.

Many of these venues were relatively more "modern" and luxurious, and could boast superior facilities in terms of the quality of the floor, lighting, décor and music, than the parish hall venues. Some, such as the National, had wall mirrors, a crystal ball rotating from the ceiling and velvet-covered seats. The bands who played these venues – some even had a resident orchestra – were attractively and formally dressed in dark suits or uniforms and bow ties. The music they played tended to be romantic. The dance-goers also dressed up for the occasion. Much of the dancing was closed-couple dancing such as the waltz, foxtrot and quickstep. All of these factors helped to establish the dance hall as a romantic space where people expected not just to get a dance partner but, equally importantly for most, to meet someone for courtship and marriage.

Photo courtesy Fáilte Ireland Photographic Department

Crystal Ballroom, Dublin, 1954

Ballrooms were established not only in cities but also in provincial towns and rural areas. Increased geographical mobility – many young people now had bicycles and a small minority had motorcars – enabled dance-goers to travel further afield to dances. Halls had a better chance of success since they could now attract customers from a wider geographical area. Increased mobility was welcomed by dancers, too, as it gave them the chance to meet people from outside their local area, lending a further sense of excitement and anticipation.

However, this development was also frowned upon by the Church as it meant that young men and women were in each other's company unchaperoned, giving rise to fears of sexual licentiousness. The dangers of mixing in the company of strangers or "unsuitables from a distance" were expressed in the mythic stories of the "devil in the dancehall", which became popular with the development of commercial/private dance halls.

There are variations on the theme but it basically revolves around a young girl who is dancing with a very handsome, tall, dark stranger to whom she is very attracted. It is usually only at the end of the dance when she has accepted his invitation to accompany her home that she looks down at his feet and notices cloven hooves! The moral of the story, not too difficult to discern, is that young girls should beware of handsome strangers. Some "devil appearances" were motivated by more pragmatic concerns and were allegedly used as a ploy by dance hall owners to attract business to their own hall and take it from their competitor. The public response to these stories might be seen as a useful gauge of the relative decline in the power of the Church over social dance practice. "Sightings" continued into the 1960s, but dance goers were increasingly sceptical about their veracity and tended to ignore the clerical warnings given.

CoisCéim Theatre's Toupées and Snare Drums, *which was set in the showband era*

There were other indications that the cultural climate was changing and the 1960s witnessed the beginnings of an openness to cultural influences from abroad which paralleled and reflected changes in the economy at this time. By the early 1960s Irish showbands had burst onto the musical scene and were to become a phenomenal success over the next decade. They travelled all over Ireland to play the latest chart hits from Britain and the US to large crowds in towns and cities. Based on rock and roll rhythms, the dances of this era were generally faster, more informal and less restricted than heretofore.

While couple dancing was still popular, for example in jive and waltz, free-style individual dancing was now very much a part of the dance scene and allowed for more individual expression. Significantly, the new dances allowed for extensive body movements with special emphasis on hip movements. The thrusting rhythms, which had so scandalised the cultural leaders of the 1920s, were now *de rigueur*. Social dance of the 1960s therefore emphasised the body as freer, and more sexualised, than before. So the opposition between "traditional" and "non-traditional" dance which had been so diligently pursued from the 1920s on was in decline. The shape of the Irish dancing body as pure, authentic and graceful was now impossible to maintain amongst the dance-going public who wanted to jive and do "The Twist" and "The Hucklebuck".

> *The thrusting rhythms, which had so scandalised the cultural leaders of the 1920s, were now de rigueur.*

Further Readings

Breathnach, B. (1983) *Dancing in Ireland*, Dal gCais Publications, Milltown Malbay, Co. Clare, Ireland.

Brennan, H. (1994) "Reinventing Tradition: The boundaries of Irish dance", *History Ireland*, Summer, pp. 22–4.

Brennan, H. (1999) *The Story of Irish Dance*, Brandon, Dingle, Co. Kerry.

Foley, C. (2001) "Perceptions of Irish Stepdance: National, Global and Local", *Dance Research Journal,* Vol. 33, No. 1, pp. 34–45.

Lynch, L. (1989) *Set Dances of Ireland: Tradition and Evolution*, Séadna Books in collaboration with Dal gCais Publications, San Francisco and Milltown Malby.

O'Connor, B. (2003) "Ruin and romance: Heterosexual discourses on Irish popular dance, 1920–1960, *Irish Journal of Sociology*, Vol. 12, No. 2, pp. 50–67.

O'Connor, N. (1991) "The Jig of Life" in *Bringing it All Back Home: The Influence of Irish Music*, London: British Broadcasting Corporation.

O'Toole, F. (1997) "'Unsuitables from a Distance': The Politics of *Riverdance*" in *The Ex-Isle of Erin: Images of a Global Ireland*. Dublin: New Island Books.

Smyth, J. (1993) "Dancing, Depravity and all that Jazz" in *History Ireland*, Summer. pp. 51–54.

Tubridy, M. (1994) "The set dancing revival", *Ceol na hÉireann*, Píobairí Uilleann, pp. 23–34.

> *From Eamon de Valera's St Patrick's Day speech, 1943:*
>
> *"The ideal Ireland that we would have, the Ireland that we dreamed of, would be the home of a people who valued material wealth only as a basis for right living. Of a people who, satisfied with frugal comfort, devoted their leisure to the things of the spirit. Whose fields and villages would be joyous with the sounds of industry, with the romping of sturdy children, the contest of athletic youths, and the laughter of happy maidens . . ."*
>
> *(First Transmission: 17 March 1943. From RTÉ Radio Archives.)*

Seosaimhín ní Bheaglaoich
Traditional Singer and Broadcaster

*I*rish singer and broadcaster Seosaimhín ní Bheaglaoich is from a well-known *traditional Irish music family deep in the West Kerry gaeltacht. Here she recounts an interesting story about how her entrepreneurial grandfather's fish-salting factory turned into a notorious dance hall.*

My father Breandán Ó Beaglaoich and his brothers Micheál and Séamus had a dance hall in the West Kerry Gaeltacht of Corca Dhuibhne in the 1950s and '60s. It was always referred to in our family as "an Shed". The Gaeilgeoirí knew it as Halla na Muirí.

"An bhfuil tú ag dul siar go dtí an Shed anocht?" you'd ask your friends. If a fella you fancied asked were you going to the Shed a particular night, your "cóta bán" was déanta – you were over the moon.

My grandfather Micheál, or Seana-Bheaglaoich as he was known, was something of an enterprising individual. He was a brick layer by trade, which he learned in New York it seems. He went back and forth to the States in the 1930s. This was unusual enough as most people who emigrated just stayed there. I remember my father mentioning that he ran "a speakeasy" somewhere on First Avenue during prohibition; a brave man! I'm sorry now I did not ask for more details of that venture.

When he returned home he set up a fish-curing and fish-salting business in this shed of his. The fish were transported by horse and cart to Dingle – a journey of about seven miles – and from there exported. He must have decided at one stage that there was more money to be made from dancing than salting herring and mackerel, and so made the transition from fish to humans in the 1940s.

Being full of the joys of life in spite of lean times and clerical attempts at domination, the people of the West Kerry Gaeltacht took to the Shed and to the dancing. This meant that a whole new means of earning lolly fell into my grandfather's lap. Needless to say, this turn of events did not go unnoticed by the local clergy,who had their own parish hall.

> *Being full of the joys of life in spite of lean times and clerical attempts at domination, the people of the west Kerry Gaeltacht took to the Shed and to the dancing. This meant that a whole new means of earning lolly fell into my grandfather's lap.*

An sagart paróiste, the parish priest at the time, who was known as "Father Tom", was an extraordinary character. He was loved and feared in equal measure. I remember him in the '60s as a lovely old character who was quick witted and very funny. His sayings are quoted by older people in the Gaeltacht to this day. But in the '40s of course he would have been a much younger man and in keeping with the power of the clergy at the time, a man to be feared, whose word was or should have been law.

He condemned my grandfather and the Shed in Muirríoch from the altar of the church of Carraig. The Shed was a place of "unspeakable behaviour"; "Beidh an paróiste seo lán de bhastairdaí ag an áit seo" (this parish will produce any amount of illegal offspring because of this place).

My grandfather took no notice of him, and the Shed or Halla na Muirí flourished in spite of, or maybe because of, poor old Father Tom's pronouncements. Never having been colonised, Gaeltacht people are an independent type. So to this day the walls and rafters of An Shed ring with the music and dancing of Coláistí Samhraidh students who may be able to catch a whiff of salted mackerel as they take the floor for *Ionsaí na hInse . . .*

Endnotes

[1] Carter, Alexandra, ed. *The Routledge Dance Studies Reader*, London: Routledge, 1998, p. 2.

[2] Those inclined to believe that there was no dancing in Ireland include P.W. Joyce, *A Social History of Ancient Ireland* (London, 1903), 2, 445–6. According to Risteard Breathnach in *The Journal of the Cork Historical and Archaeological Society* 60 (1955), 89–94, no conclusion can be reached on the matter for lack of evidence. The contrary view – a firm belief in the antiquity of Irish dancing – was stated by Micheál Ó Sé in the same volume of the aforesaid journal, pp. 57–63, and the debate continued in volume 61 (1956), 58–70. Perhaps the most balanced statement of the situation is by Breandán Breathnach in *Dál gCais* 4 (1978), 103–7. It would, he states, be astonishing if dancing were unknown to the pre-mediaeval Irish, given that their frequently mentioned musical instruments must at least have created reflex movement among listeners.

[3] *Knowth and the Passage Tombs of Ireland* (London, 1986), 178–81.

[4] See many examples in Dáithí Ó hÓgáin, *The Hero in Irish Folk History* (Dublin, 1985), 41–6, 326; and *The Sacred Isle* (Cork, 1999), 211–4, 249.

[5] For example, *Revue Celtique* 3 (1877), 176; *Irische Texte* 3 (1897), 332, 415; Eleanor Knott, *Togail Bruidne Da Derga* (Dublin, 1936), 42; A.G. Van Hamel *Compert Con Culainn* (Dublin, (1933), 72. See also Georges Dumézil in Gerald J. Larson, ed., *Myth in Indo-European Antiquity* (Berkeley, 1974), 17–28.

[6] Elizabeth E. Gray, *Cath Maige Tuired* (Dublin, 1982), 58. See also Ó hÓgáin, *The Sacred Isle*, 74–5, 84–9, 137–46.

[7] Cecile O'Rahilly, *Táin Bó Cuailnge: Recension 1* (Dublin, 1976), 8–9 and *Recension 2* (Dublin, 1970), 13.

[8] For the symbolism of the Conaire stories, see Ó hÓgáin, *The Sacred Isle*, 159–63.

[9] Knott, op cit, 16–17.

[10] See Dáithí Ó hÓgáin, *An File* (Dublin, 1982), 73–6.

[11] Ó hÓgáin, *An File*, 93–102, 265–80.

[12] In this dancing would appear to have differed from mediaeval Irish poetry, which was more regularly structured.

[13] John McInnes, "Gaelic Song and Dance", *Transactions of the Gaelic Society of Inverness 60* (1997–8), 56–73.

[14] Seán Ó Súilleabháin, *Irish Wake Amusements* (Cork, 1967), 29–31, 147–9, 184.

[15] See MacInnes, op cit, 67–8. Cork folklore claims that the wife of the celebrated Scottish hero Alasdair Mac Colla Mac Dhòmhnaill, after he was killed at Knockanuss near Mallow in 1647, exclaimed "Mura ngolfad é rincfead é!" That is, instead of lamenting him, she determined to "dance him". This lady was a MacAllister from Scotland – see David Stevenson, Highland Warrior (Edinburgh, 1994), 220 – and thus would not have spoken the Munster dialect of the quote. This does not, however, preclude that she or somebody else paid respect to the dead hero in this way, nor indeed does it negate the saying as evidence for such a practice in more general terms.

[16] See "cluiche" under C (page 259) in *Contributions to a Dictionary of the Irish Language* [Royal Irish Academy]. Dancing was intimately associated with such athletic games in ancient Greece – see Walter Burkert, *Greek Religion* (Harvard, 1985), 485–6.

[17] Joyce, op. cit, Vol 1, 147–8, 583–91; Wolfgang Meid, *Táin Bó Fraích* (Dublin, 1967), 9–10; Dáithí Ó hÓgáin, *Fionn mac Cumhaill* (Dublin, 1988), 76.

[18] See Ó Sé, op. cit, 58–9; Dáithí Ó hÓgáin, *The Celts* (Cork, 2002), 19–20, 91.

[19] See Ó hÓgáin, *The Sacred Isle*, 175–8.

[20] E. Louis Backman, *Religious Dances* (London, 1952), 24. See Breandán Breathnach in *Dál gCais* 6 (1982), 61.

[21] J.H. Bernard and R. Atkinson, *The Irish Liber Hymnorum* (London, 1898), 80. See Aloys Fleischmann in *The Journal of the Cork Historical and Archaeological Society* 61 (1956), 58–9.

[22] See Ó Sé, op cit, 58; Seán Ó Súilleabháin, *A Handbook of Irish Folklore* (Dublin, 1942), 466.

[23] Arbois de Jubainville in *Revue Celtique* 27 (1906), 313–24. See Ó Sé, op cit, 57.

[24] Osborn Bergin, *Irish Bardic Poetry* (Dublin, 1970), 77, 246.

[25] See Dáithí Ó hÓgáin in Jim Larner, ed., *Killarney – a History* (Cork, 2005) ed., 45; Irish Folklore Collection Mss (as above) – 1747: 349–55.

[26] See Fleischmann, op. cit, 58; MacInnes, op. cit, 63; Curt Sachs, *World History of the Dance* (New York, 1937), 248–51.

[27] See Risteard Breathnach, op. cit, 93–4.

[28] Robert Atkinson, *The Passions and the Homilies from Leabhar Breac* (Dublin, 1887), 66.

[29] See Risteard Breathnach, op. cit, 88–9, 91–2.

[30] *Zeitschrift für celtische Philologie 4* (1903), 408. See "macnas" in *Contributions to a Dictionary of the Irish Language* [Royal Irish Academy] – under M (page 14).

[31] On this issue, see Ó hÓgáin, *The Sacred Isle*, 107–27, where such imagery in Welsh tradition is also discussed.

[32] For such May customs, see Kevin Danaher, *The Year in Ireland* (Cork, 1972), 86–109.

[33] See Seán Ó Tuama in Robert C. O'Driscoll, ed., *The Celtic Consciousness* (Toronto, 1981), 292–4.

[34] Breandán Breathnach in *Dál gCais* 4, 104–5.

[35] J.G. O'Keeffe and Art O'Brien, *Handbook of Irish Dances* (Dublin, 1912), 15–16.

[36] See Breandán Breathnach in *Dál gCais* 4, 104–5; Donal O'Sullivan, *Irish Folk Music, Song and Dance* (Cork, 1974), 45–6.

[37] Kenneth Sisam, *Fourteenth Century Verse and Prose* (Oxford, 1955), 166.

[38] See Breandán Breathnach in *Dál gCais* 4, 104.

[39] Ibid, 103–6.

[40] Quoted in the newspaper *The Leitrim Observer*, 7 April 1934.

[41] Joseph Anelius (1943) *National Action: A Plan for the National Recovery of Ireland* (second edition), Dublin: Gaelic Athletic Association.

Abbey Theatre

Lessees
Directors

- THE NATIONAL THEATRE SOCIETY, Ltd.
W. B. YEATS, LADY GREGORY, WALTER STARKIE, LENNOX ROBINSON

Chapter 2

PROGRAMME

———

Abbey Theatre School of Ballet

Sunday, 6th December, 1931, at 8.15 p.m.

CORRIGAN AND WILSON, LTD., DUBLIN.

Chapter 2

The Neglected Chapter:
Salvaging the Abbey School of Ballet

I n this chapter of archaeological salvage we'll look through a prism of perspectives at the remnants of the much-neglected Abbey School of Ballet (1927–1933). In an extract from her memoir, *Come Dance With Me*, Ninette de Valois shares her memories of the forgotten school she co-founded with Yeats, and of Dublin of the time.

Lecturer in English Noreen Doody gives us a literary perspective on Yeats's penchant for dance in his plays, and how this was influenced by the voluptuous, decadent work of Oscar Wilde, among others.

Victoria O'Brien, Daghdha Dance Company's Education Officer, who is completing her PhD at the University of Limerick's World Academy of Music and Dance on the history of classical and modern dance training in Ireland from 1925 to 1960, gives us a precise ballet perspective on the enterprise. Yeats's own vision for the school is outlined by himself on the programme note for the Abbey School of Ballet's 1931 performance of *The Dreaming of the Bones*.

Freda Freeman, a random paying student at the school, shares her memories of what it was like to attend the school, and of Ninette de Valois, mother of British ballet.

And finally, Doreen Cuthbert (who danced to Schubert's *Pastoral* in the first performance of the Abbey Theatre Ballets, in 1928), recalls the school from its first intake of breath to its last exhalation, from a pupil/performer/librarian's point of view. Doreen was one of three Abbey School of Ballet pupils who went on to open their own schools in Dublin, the others being Muriel Kelly (later Cuffe) and Cepta Cullen. It became a very competitve arena in which they vied for pupils. Eventually Muriel Kelly's sequel Abbey School of Ballet would supply dancers to the Rathmines and Rathgar Musical Society until the 1960s.

These are remnants, relics, designed to reclaim this lost gem of our national heritage, of which there are only two pictures left in existence, in the possession of Victoria O'Brien (given to her by Nesta Brooking, former Abbey School of Ballet dancer). She is keeping these pictures of the original Abbey School of Ballet dancers on the Abbey stage for her research, so do get in touch with her through Daghdha Dance Company if you would like to see them!

Ninette de Valois
Dancer and Founder of the Royal Ballet and Sadler's Wells

*B*orn in Blessington, County Wicklow in 1898, Edris Stannus grew up to become Dame Ninette de Valois, the internationally renowned mother of British ballet, and one of the greatest giants of twentieth-century dance. She was a leading dancer in London, and studied with Cecchetti, before joining Diaghilev's Ballets Russes in 1923 for two years, where her contemporaries included Anton Dolin (Patrick Helty-Kaye, whose father came from Kildare), and a very young Alicia Markova (Alice Marks, whose mother was from Cork).

She changed her rather unglamorous Victorian-sounding birth name legally to Ninette de Valois in 1921, adopting her professional name from an ancestor who had married into a French family. However she was more often referred to as "Madam" in the ballet world. In 1926 de Valois became choreographic director of both Dublin's Abbey Theatre (founding The Abbey School of Ballet at the invitation of W.B. Yeats) and the Old Vic Theatre (collaborating with Lilian Baylis), simultaneously founding the Academy of Choreographic Art. In 1931 she established the Vic-Wells Ballet, which later became known as the Sadler's Wells Ballet. This prestigious company, which she directed from 1931 to 1963, was granted the Royal charter in 1956, to become the Royal Ballet. De Valois also founded a sister company, which became the Birmingham Royal Ballet. Dame Ninette de Valois died at the age of 102 in 2001.

Before the extract from her memoir, here is a brief extract from an interview with Ninette de Valois, conducted by Frank Delaney for The Arts Show*, 8 May 1991, produced by Colin Morrison, RTÉ Radio One.*

Well he [W.B. Yeats] saw a production of mine at the Festival Theatre in Cambridge. In fact Gordon Bottomley, a very fine poet who I think is very neglected frankly, had a play put on there and I did some choreography in it. He was very pleased with it. He rang up Yeats in Dublin and said, "Come over and see this, I think it's what you're looking for." So W.B. came over and saw this. And he said, "I want you to come over to Ireland, and put on my *Plays for Dancers*."

While struggling with the other theatre in London – because there were no subsidies for anything in England – one of the amusing things was to go over to Ireland. I had heard about the Abbey Theatre, which according to my mother was on the wrong side of the river. They had the right and wrong side of the river in those days.

It was staggering to find this funny little old town, with a state-subsidised theatre. And a state-subsidised company that toured America every year as the Irish state theatre. Dotty!

Nothing happening anywhere else but in Ireland!

Below, in an extract from her 1956 memoir Come Dance With Me *(Dublin: The Lilliput Press, 1992; originally published by Hamish Hamilton, London, in 1957), Ninette de Valois reminisces on how the shortlived (1927–1933) Abbey School of Ballet came to be, and on her time in Dublin.*

In the summer of 1926 I opened a private school in a studio in Roland Gardens, Gloucester Road. I had left the Diaghilev Ballet about ten months previously, although I still appeared with them occasionally in London. That very summer I was with them at His Majesty's Theatre.

I was anxious to take up production work, and decided that the repertory theatre movement throughout the country would not only prove to be the best possible form of production experience for me, but might also be the only theatrical venture that would show any interest in the foundation of a repertory ballet company.

That autumn my cousin, Terence Gray, was to open the Festival Theatre at Cambridge, and he invited me to join the staff as choreographer. I had also managed to obtain an introduction to Lilian Baylis of the Old Vic.

The following years were to drive me to and fro over the Thames via Waterloo Bridge, and to and fro from London to Cambridge, sometimes stretched out in a third class carriage on the milk train after a first night, so as to get to my school early in the morning. By 1928 Dublin had joined in the fun, and I would find myself bobbing like a cork on the Liverpool night mailboat on my way to the Abbey Theatre.

How do I look back on those years? With affection and a very real nostalgia; one was young and full of energy and fired with an optimism that was sustained by as passionate a love of the theatre as the good clown has for the ring.

Cover for Come Dance with Me, *published by The Lilliput Press*

The furthest hills are greenest . . . and in retrospect some of the hills that I have climbed and left behind me are still the fairest and greenest of all, for their paths led as far as I dared my dreams to go ahead of me.

Sometimes I think that I planned everything. But does one ever really plan? It was no plan that taught a small girl an Irish jig on a cottage stone floor . . . it was some force at work – of which neither she nor others had any knowledge.

It was during that early summer of 1926, with its disturbing General Strike, its fair weather and my personal optimism, on one of those fine mornings that I donned the best of my summer wardrobe and, in a huge floppy hat, went to see Lilian Baylis.

Now time and events must wait awhile; for that fine morning when I first crossed Waterloo Bridge to visit the South side was the most important bit of bridge-crossing that I had ever undertaken, repercussions of which are to be felt to this day. I must therefore first recall Miss Lilian Baylis, who was to be known to me for the next eleven years as "The Lady".

> *Sometimes I think that I planned everything. But does one ever really plan? It was no plan that taught a small girl an Irish jig on a cottage stone floor . . . it was some force at work – of which neither she nor others had any knowledge.*

Strange is the weaving of the pattern, for Lilian Baylis was a pupil of a Wordsworth head teacher. One of Miss Baylis' early missions was to preach a little of the gospel of "fancy dancing" on the Road. Her history has been brilliantly recorded by far more skilful pens than mine. There is only left for me, as a member of her staff, to tell of the impact of her personality.

I arrived at the Old Vic on a Saturday – I suppose it must have been late in May. There was a matinée performance, I think, of *The Taming of the Shrew*, and it was the season when Dame Edith Evans was sweeping all before her. Evelyn Williams, The Lady's private secretary, was also present; I was nervous, yet determined to stand my ground and get as good a hearing as possible for my plans: the formation of a British Ballet through the good offices of the Old Vic. Looking back on it today, I cannot conceive why I struck The Lady as anything more than a slightly fanatical young woman.

At the end of my peroration concerning the possibilities of a British Ballet, she informed me that she liked my face; she then added that she thought I was practical and appeared to have had a great deal of professional experience. She next went on to tell me that she had no money and no second theatre as yet; there were no rehearsal rooms and there was nothing to be done.

My heart sank so low that only dimly did I hear the sequel; a sequel that showed that the pill had a thin coating of sugar.

She was looking, so the voice informed my dizzy senses, for someone to teach the drama students how to move. She said that they all had dreadful hands, and that most actors and actresses had dreadful hands, and as they did not know what to do with their hands, they appeared in the end to be even more dreadful; she added that she preferred beautiful hands to beautiful faces.

Having disposed of all hands belonging to the dramatic profession, she then fingered some letters on her desk and told me they were from people after the job that she was going to offer me; she was offering it to me because she was now convinced that I knew more than all the other applicants – although one was even recommended by Sybil Thorndike, but dear Sybil had a way sometimes of recommending people just out of the kindness of her heart . . .

She then came back to the sugared pill; she was looking for someone to arrange any little dance required in the Shakespearian productions; she wanted someone to give a look to her office workers, who obliged by appearing in a voluntary capacity in the opera ballets; she would like a short (expenses only) ballet performance put on at Christmas before *Hansel and Gretel* by some good ballet school, and a lot more angels from the same source for the Opera itself.

She thought that I had by far the highest qualifications to take on all this, but she did not expect all my work to be voluntary; I would receive £1 per week for teaching the dramatic students and £2 for arranging any choreography required in a Shakespeare production.

In addition I would lead a host of "expenses only" dancers in the Christmas Ballet production and supervise the voluntary Opera Ballet office workers, and guarantee student angels galore for *Hansel and Gretel*.

> *She thought that I had by far the highest qualifications to take on all this, but she did not expect all my work to be voluntary; I would receive £1 per week for teaching the dramatic students and £2 for arranging any choreography required in a Shakespeare production.*

I then visited her voluntary Opera *corps de ballet*. One girl had a wooden hand, but Miss Baylis informed me that an excellent kid glove was preserved for her special use. I decided there and then that this particular work should be given to a senior student from my school, who must, in return, receive a small pittance for her labour. Young Rosalind Iden, at that time a student of mine, most gallantly carried out the work of the Opera Ballet.

Thus, briefly, did Lilian Baylis contract me to the services of the Old Vic for four years, ever dangling in front of my eyes the rebuilding of Sadler's Wells in the dim future. I earned, on the average, about £40 per annum . . .

I am back now in 1926 and it is the autumn of my first season as a staff member of the Vic-Wells organisation, to which I have belonged – without a break – until this day . . .

My private school continued, and my students danced at the Old Vic or were carted up to Cambridge once or twice a term to take part in a Greek chorus or give a week of short ballet performances. Sometimes two or three of them would go to

Dublin with me to perform in a week of dancing at the Abbey Theatre when two little ballets might be given with one of Yeats's *Plays for Dancers*.

Cambridge in the spring and autumn; this charming theatre situated just outside the main part of the town on the Newmarket Road . . . it remains one of my green hills that has not faded with time and change: the Greek plays, the Restoration comedies, and Dekker's Shoemaker's Holiday, with Boris Ord at the harpsichord . . . the enchanting poet Gordon Bottomley and his delight with the choreography that I arranged for Yeats's *On Baile's Strand*.

Meanwhile the Abbey Theatre suddenly twined in and out of the busy life I led, a life which, for five years, was two-thirds dedicated to the wants and wishes of poets, authors, producers, actors, and actresses . . .

It is the year 1927 and I am sitting in the dark vestibule of the Festival Theatre in Cambridge. I am listening to a rich Irish voice that seems to intone a request that I should come to Dublin and produce for the Abbey Theatre. The voice belongs to William Butler Yeats, who has just witnessed a verse play of Gordon Bottomley's and some dance creations of my own. . . . It would seem that if I should return to Ireland at his impressive bidding (made to me in a light so dim that the speaker's features were not clear) I would work among those people whose efforts to establish the Irish Theatre were in progress at the time that I struggled with an Irish jig in a farmhouse at the foot of the Wicklow Hills.

> *Meanwhile the Abbey Theatre suddenly twined in and out of the busy life I led, a life which, for five years, was two-thirds dedicated to the wants and wishes of poets, authors, producers, actors, and actresses . . .*

The mind of Yeats was made up; he would have a small school of Ballet at the Abbey and I would send over a teacher. I would visit Dublin every three months and produce his *Plays for Dancers* and perform in them myself; thus, he said, the poetic drama of Ireland would live again and take its rightful place in the Nation's own Theatre, and the oblivion imposed on it by the popularity of peasant drama would become a thing of the past.

"W.B." carried the day with his distinguished directors, Lady Gregory, Dr. Walter Starkie and Lennox Robinson. I found myself in Dublin with a dancer who had been a student of mine (Vivienne Bennett, the actress) and the small school was opened. I then decided on some small productions that we should be able to present six months later, as Miss Bennett was only able to stay for that length of time; her place was then taken by Sara Payne, the sister of Rosalind Iden.

The work at the Abbey had much of interest. A number of Yeats's *Plays for Dancers* were given, two or three new works in verse, and several short Irish ballets suitable for young dancers.

In 1916 Yeats had written the following notes on *At the Hawk's Well*:

. . . Perhaps I shall turn to something else now that our Japanese dancer, Mr. Itow, whose minute intensity of movement in the dance of the hawk so well suited our small room and private art, has been hired by a New York theatre, or perhaps I shall find another dancer . . .

In the late twenties, W.B. Yeats found another dancer for *At the Hawk's Well*, for I danced this role myself. I was the first to achieve this distinction after Mr. Itow – and I even succeeded in wearing his costume. Yeats re-wrote *The King of the Great Clock Tower* and *The Only Jealousy of Emer* so that the "Queen" in the former and the "Woman of the Sidhe" in the latter could be interpreted by me in dance mime, wearing masks for both roles.

The Abbey Theatre in the mid-twenties was at the height of its international fame and had the distinction of being the only national theatre in our midst. The first company of players (which included Sara and Maire O'Neill, Florence Farr, Arthur Sinclair and the Fay Brothers) had broken away from the Abbey and were scattered mainly between the theatres of London and New York. In my time the Abbey's production director was Lennox Robinson and the second company consisted of such distinguished Abbey-trained artists as Barry Fitzgerald, Maureen Delaney, Peter McCormack, Eileen Crowe, Sheila Richards, Arthur Shields and Michael Dolan. They shouldered brilliantly the tradition laid down by their predecessors.

Photo: Fergus Bourke

Bríd Ní Neachtáin and Maeliosa Stafford in the 1984 Abbey Theatre production of At the Hawk's Well

The Irish are natural actors. They have a great sense of timing and interplay. Their voices are rich in feeling and they stress with ease the music that is to be found in words of common speech . . .

The Irish are natural actors. They have a great sense of timing and interplay. Their voices are rich in feeling and they stress with ease the music that is to be found in words of common speech; they can all intone; with them the "keen" becomes a strange chant within the range of any group of Irish players.

By the nature of its economic structure, life in the Abbey Theatre was a pleasant, leisurely affair, wearing an air of semi-professionalism. Most of the male actors had a further means of livelihood, in fact the full-time company of players represented quite a small part of the whole. How well these players knew their repertoire! They wore it with the affection and familiarity of old and comfortable clothes, growing into many of their characters and seeming to live them in life – both in gesture and intonation.

The famous green room, hung with framed copies of Yeats's early poems, was furnished with comfortable chairs, a coal fire burnt when necessary and there would always be a pot of tea brewing. This room might so resemble the parlour scene just enacted on the stage that to join the players in the interval was to make one feel that we were all continuing with the play. Conversation was parlour conversation, but eyes would light up if anyone mentioned America. I have seen Maureen Delaney roll her eyes to the click of her knitting needles at the recollection of the blissful speakeasies, for some of the last tours were at the height of the prohibition.

The National Theatre lived through many stormy times; most of its directors were Protestant and I think that in the early and difficult years this may well have added to the misunderstanding and confusion – absurd in fact, for never were a body of people at heart more in sympathy with the Irish as a race and with Ireland as a country apart. But the attitude of these cultured people towards the national self-expression in the theatre was a hundred years in advance of either Catholic or Protestant in the Ireland of that day. Only isolated members of the Anglo-Irish showed any interest in the national theatre movement; even as late as 1928, I heard it said that the trouble with the Abbey was that it was built on the wrong side of the river. Thus, at the beginning, a group of tolerant and idealistic poets and writers were misunderstood all round. Their idealism was hampered by lack of money and a naturally amateur approach to practical problems; but the saddest aspect was the lethargy of the country-house dwellers and the antagonism of the priests and half their flock, not to mention the inflammable political situation. Eventually the money that they needed to give the venture the mildest form of security came from Miss Horniman, the woman who had already founded one famous repertory theatre – the Gaiety in Manchester.

> *. . . but the saddest aspect was the lethargy of the country-house dwellers and the antagonism of the priests and half their flock, not to mention the inflammable political situation.*

The Abbey was unique. I hate to think of the green room and the tiny row of dressing-rooms resembling narrow log cabins gone for ever. It was the unostentatious back street setting that lent this theatre its individuality. Horse Show week would bring flocks of American visitors searching out the home of the famed Irish Players who toured the States from coast to coast. The small entrance hall was decorated with playbills from foreign countries and woolly oil paintings by Jack Yeats of players and playwrights; in the theatre's auditorium, there was that little miscalculation on the part of the architect which resulted in the dress circle being most rakishly off-centre.

Many are the stories that I heard of the early days. Yeats was supposed to have engaged Lennox Robinson as manager in obedience to the promptings of his Celtic voices, for he announced one day the post must be offered to a young man sitting in front of him in the theatre, because of the shape of his head. Unless my memory is at fault, it was the poet himself who told me of his determination in this matter. Then there is another lively story from the same source. In the early days a certain distinguished player, perhaps bored with her own distinction, announced that she wanted to produce a play. This request is not unusual from those whose creative talents are non-existent. It goes with a frustration that is based on a wish to express authority; it is the authority associated with the work of the producer that is the real source of the ambition. The directors decided to let her have her way. On the day of the first rehearsal Yeats and Lennox Robinson sat in the stalls. The play started and the lady, seated at last in the middle of the stalls, in her position of solitary splendour, said nothing. Yeats, resolutely overflowing with the milk of human kindness, felt that she might indeed be nervous, and so he would slip away altogether for a short time, but Lennox would only seem to slip away; in reality the latter was to return immediately and seek obscurity at the back of the pit. After a lapse of time, Yeats crept back to join the other in the pit and to inquire after production progress. "She hasn't said anything, and the play is well on", said Lennox. Undaunted, Yeats announced that it was quite possible that she might still be feeling their presence, and so they would make quite a show of going out together; Lennox would then creep upstairs and peep at proceedings from the darkest corner in the circle. Some time later Yeats joined him again. The back of the static silent female form was still visible; it appeared to be disconcertingly unscathed by the agile progress of the play, which was travelling forward with the speed of a driverless ghost train. "Nothing has been said at all, and the play is near the end", said Lennox.

Time, at the Abbey, of course, stood still for the general convenience of everyone. Productions were carried through in an atmosphere of leisurely Celtic twilight. I can recall the flautist who so beautifully rehearsed with us for *At the Hawk's Well*. When the rehearsal was finished he remembered that the days chosen for the performances would be out of the question . . . they were too inconvenient . . . he had not understood. . . . Faintly was his announcement relayed through the dark empty theatre with more curiosity than consternation; like an echo was the statement handed on, everyone hoping that someone had broad enough shoulders to accept the final

> *Time, at the Abbey, of course, stood still for the general convenience of everyone. Productions were carried through in an atmosphere of leisurely Celtic twilight.*

impact. A gentle half-sigh eventually dismissed the matter and the waste of time was generously written off; it was not the kind of waste that would bother a hair of the head of anyone born in Dublin.

It is always the unexpected that the Irishman expects of life; yet when it happens to him at home the effect is often sterile, for many an Irishman on his native soil seems to start the business of dying the day he is born. If, however, the unexpected should hit him as an emigrant on foreign soil, he shows every ingenuity, turns it to good account and thrives on it. The average Irishman can do half a dozen things and he can do them well – provided that he can pick his fancy. I am reminded of Barney, the Abbey theatre cleaner of those days, a gentle, silent, beautiful old man who, with a sad sense of care, carried out his cleaning duties by day. How would it be to find an English theatre cleaner installed in the prompt corner? Yet, Barney would be prompter with a range of plays from Shaw to Yeats's *Plays for Dancers*.

> *It is always the unexpected that the Irishman expects of life; yet when it happens to him at home the effect is often sterile, for many an Irishman on his native soil seems to start the business of dying the day he is born.*

I would sometimes hear further stories of those hearty days when the theatre would incense its fiery audience to the point of giving them a pretext for a riot. Proudly Yeats informed me that O'Casey's *The Plough and the Stars* inspired three riots in various prominent parts of Dublin. Dr. Larchet, the musical director, would describe happenings inside the theatre. There was a performance of the play, he said, when they came over the footlights like waves; their indignation was such and their sense of propriety and politics so confused that, with the excitement of it all, they wrapped in a rug a theatrically consumptive girl attired in a theatrical nightdress before they thought it fit to bundle her off and out into the street with the rest of the cast!

My days were quiet; but even then there was a charming Dublin priest, who could not attend performances, and so was present at all full dress rehearsals . . . and the old members of the pit would still obligingly prompt an actor suffering from a sudden loss of a word. There was the old suspicion accorded to poetic drama – and a deadly resentful silence would settle on the theatre's old-timers like a sulky fog. One night, a Yeats's play containing a line to the effect that a man grows tired of his wife resulted in penetration of the sulky fog; a fog-horn of a human voice announced "that's bloody true!"

In the twenties when Dr Gogarty was walking down Grafton Street he was also holding his fortnightly salons. I can see his drawing-room filled with the Yeats family, the Walter Starkies, the Lennox Robinsons, the John McCormacks, James Stephens, "AE" (George Russell) and the rest of Dublin's intelligentsia. I only met AE once; yet I can still see that Celtic mystic reclining in an armchair with his hands outspread and the tips of his fingers meeting, forming an arch over his chest. Has anyone described him with greater sincerity of feeling than George Moore? "The reason why I have not included any personal description of AE is because he exists rather in one's imagination, dreams, sentiments, feelings, than in one's ordinary sight and hearing, and try as I will to catch the fleeting outlines they escape me; and all I remember are the long pantheistic eyes that have looked so often into my soul with such a kindly gaze . . ."

Dr Gogarty would tell his stories and there would sometimes be mild cracks at America, mainly by those who had been there on lecture tours and felt that something of the sort was expected of them. One evening John McCormack (a staunch supporter of the New World) considered that the jokes had gone too far; his burst of irritation was followed by a shy silence, dispersed by Gogarty, who told of an old lady that he once knew who would end all moments of embarrassment by questioning the world at large as to which they would rather be eaten by – an alligator or a crocodile . . .

With affection and esteem will I always see two figures – Lennox Robinson, a long quiet untidy-looking eagle, peering at us from the gloom of the Abbey stalls with his glasses reflecting shafts of light; occasionally his look would stray to the book held between the long tapering fingers. Close to him there would be Yeats with his pince-nez dangerously near the end of his nose. This pince-nez was tied to a long flowing black ribbon attaching itself to some obscure point in the volu-

> *He would appear to me as a heroic legendary figure – a Cuchulain fighting more than the waves; for Yeats fought prejudice with passion, ignorance with irony, criticism with humility.*

minous cape – a cape which seemed to hold the great figure loosely together, turning it into a vague monumental shape. He would appear to me as a heroic legendary figure – a Cuchulain fighting more than the waves; for Yeats fought prejudice with passion, ignorance with irony, criticism with humility. The fighter in him showed a man with a passionate sense of justice and a curious practical streak. He was, though, an aristocrat at heart; his reasons were not based on sentiment, they were essentially practical. He told me that artists could only give of their best if the world permitted them the patronage of a leisured aristocracy. He maintained that the common mass of humanity was too concerned with the business of living: they had not the time at their disposal to make those singular demands for perfection which should be asked of the artist.

It has been said that Yeats was vain, and that he lacked humour. It struck me that his moments of vanity belonged to the modest variety that all artists acquire; their capacity of self-valuation is sharpened, as a result of intense self-criticism; their appreciation of any praise bestowed on them springs from the feeling that they have achieved a positive expression of their creative ideas. His views on life were tempered with a sensitive approach to the human side of earthly existence; on occasions this brought his reactions, in their lively imaginings, near enough to something more expressive of humour than scholarly wit.

Conversation with Yeats could be likened to a verbal switchback: up and down it would go, and then a corner would be taken at full speed, a long slow climb, a breath-taking dive, only to find that the impetus had carried you once more to the heights. He told me that at the beginning of the Irish Literary Theatre movement his friends would ask him what he was going to do about keeping trained actors in Dublin; his answer was that he was not going to do anything as the Dublin accent would do it for him. Then again it would be all talk of dreams and visions and he would affirm to me that all the greatest excitements of his life had taken place in his head. He could start a conversation with the announcement that the previous night he had had a vision, in a tone of voice usually bestowed on the remembrance of a round of golf. His relaxation was the reading of detective stories. Mrs Yeats, discovered in a faintly harassed frame of mind in Grafton Street, informed me that Willie was leaving for Cork and she had to find him a detective story for the train journey. I remarked that it should be easy enough, but Mrs Yeats said that it was not so easy as the book must have a love interest.

> *Conversation with Yeats could be likened to a verbal switchback: up and down it would go, and then a corner would be taken at full speed, a long slow climb, a breath-taking dive, only to find that the impetus had carried you once more to the heights.*

Someone should write a book to commemorate the wives of poets and artists. With their feet firmly planted on the ground and their heads concentrated on showing every ounce of feminine adaptability to the clouds, they dexterously weave their way through a maze of poetic turmoil and contradiction; they are patient, solid and practical, arriving at the end of an argument long before anyone else present; I have often compared their private solutions to post office savings, not to be drawn out without due notice.

I can remember a certain turmoil between Yeats and Dulac and the shock it was to the decorum of the BBC; the eventual disentanglement was the result of months of a feminine underground movement on the part of two devoted wives, brightly aware of male childishness. Yeats had been once more trying to broadcast an example of Irish poetic drama set to music by Dulac . . . the poet was upset over the English rendering of the songs, Dulac elated. Yeats expounded how such a rendering would make it impossible for him to face his Dublin friends again, so ashamed he was at the let-down to them all. The musical but fiery Frenchman, with quite different views as to who must not be let down, informed Yeats that he must, if necessary, offend Dublin, as he happened to be for the moment in a civilised country. The dignified pale young men of the BBC went several shades paler and Yeats stalked out. The broadcast was highly successful; two wives worked in mutual accord for several months to heal the wound inflicted.

The digression is over; we are back in the darkened theatre with Lennox Robinson and Yeats. Catching himself up in every form of seat and arm-rest, Yeats moves towards Lennox, for he would ask his old friend if he had any idea what he meant when he wrote the line that the actor has just declared. Maybe the line was almost the age of Lennox himself. But no matter. That understanding creature would always know something, enough to quieten even further the already almost stillborn silence . . . and we would continue our mime and our speech in the tranquil Celtic twilight that was the spirit and the secret of the Abbey Theatre.

One afternoon the self-same twilight seemed to have turned itself into a thick mist, stiff with obscurities and the dreams of poets. Down had come the curtain with a smack of despondency on the last rehearsal of *The King of the Great Clock Tower*. The gloom of the theatre was cut off and also those two whispering figures. I arose from my throne and removed my mask, behind which I had sunk for an hour, lulled to peace by the voice of that great actor Peter McCormack. Within the folds of his costume of the heroic age, he looked

> *"Well may the spirit of Mr Yeats be with us tonight, and may it spread itself a bit and give a clue to the audience as to what it is that we be talkin' about," said Peter McCormack, who could not open his mouth but to give a clue to all the mysteries that constitute great acting.*

at me, sighed and shook himself like a dog. "Well may the spirit of Mr Yeats be with us tonight, and may it spread itself a bit and give a clue to the audience as to what it is that we be talkin' about," said Peter McCormack, who could not open his mouth but to give a clue to all the mysteries that constitute great acting.

It is a still, late afternoon and Dalkey Bay is in an early summer mind; the Big and Little Sugar Loaf Mountains are in shadow and a splendid blue glow is theirs against the evening sky. I am sitting in the garden of Villa Sorrento, the cliff cottage, and home of the Lennox Robinsons. My companions are Lennox and Yeats. The poet is declaiming certain of his poems. The rich voice rises and falls on the air, an air that is rarefied by the music of the voice in a garden hushed to a gentle static attention. Lennox is motionless, but the glasses once more reflect small shafts of light.

When Yeats died some years later, his old friend spoke of that magic hour and finished his letter to me with the words . . . "for we have seen Shelley plain". They were happy inspiring years; but for me the English scene eventually crowded them out.

Today the greater part of the Abbey awaits reconstruction after the fire of a few years ago. Many of my old friends are dead, or they have retired or emigrated. I last met Barry Fitzgerald and his brother Arthur Shields (who used to be the Abbey stage manager) in Hollywood at a reception given in honour of the Sadler's Wells Ballet in 1951.

Hollywood had left no mark on these two; the soft brogue remained and the leisured approach to life . . . even in a city dedicated to life in its most hurried form. I lunched with Barry the next day. We were soon back in a Dublin "of night and light and the half light" as our poet had sung; treading we were on our own dreams of that yesterday.

Noreen Doody
Yeats Scholar

*N*oreen Doody is a Yeats expert, who has published and spoken on Yeats's *Plays for Dancers in Japan, among other places. A lecturer in the English Department at St Patrick's College, Drumcondra, Noreen here shares her thoughts on Yeats's idea of dance.*

Dance appealed to Yeats more as an idea than as an act. The dancer was the central symbol of so much of his work and represented an entire way of thinking, a whole metaphysical system.

I remember asking his daughter, Anne Yeats, whether there was a lot of dancing in the house, and whether she went to ballet classes. "You know, your father being so interested in dance . . .", I said. She looked at me and smiled, "I can't imagine father being interested in dance." I think she agreed with me that for Yeats, dance was of interest only in so far as it represented ideas.

While Yeats may not have been totally interested in dance for dance's sake, he did want the dance done properly, professionally and gracefully. He did want it to be a thing of beauty within his own plays. So in 1927 he approached ballet dancer Ninette de Valois, who was working as a choreographer for the Festival Ballet in Cambridge. De Valois writes about this in her memoir. She talks about being seated in the auditorium of some dimly lit theatre, when she hears the rich voice of Yeats emanating from somewhere within the gloom and announcing, "You must come back to Ireland!" Yeats invited her to come back to Ireland to set up a school of ballet in the Abbey Theatre. He wanted her to train young dancers so that he could put on professional performances of his dance plays. She agreed to come back to Dublin and brought with her some of her own students. They not only danced in Yeats's plays but from time to time performed short ballet sequences at the Abbey Theatre alongside longer plays. De Valois herself danced in a number of Yeats's dance plays including *The King of the Great Clock Tower*. Yeats actually dedicated this play to Ninette de Valois. He said his only misgiving was having to ask her to wear a mask and so cover her beautiful features.

Yeats first used the dance to express his metaphysical ideas in his *Four Plays for Dancers*: *At the Hawk's Well, The Only Jealousy of Emer, The Dreaming of the Bones* and *Calvary.* In the *Four Plays for Dancers* dance is a powerful, central symbol.

Dance features in his early play, *The Land of Heart's Desire,* but it is of a very different kind. There were also intimations of the dance in other plays such as *Deirdre* and *On Baile's Strand.* Actually, Yeats first started thinking seriously about dance as a useful symbol for his own work after seeing Oscar Wilde's play, *Salomé,* in 1905 in London. Once he had seen that play he began to rewrite three plays which he had considered finished, *The Shadowy Waters, On Baile's Strand* and *Deirdre.* It is interesting to see how within those plays he starts to use language expressive of dance.

In *Deirdre* he used not only language but also movement in a very specific way to suggest the dance. When *Deirdre* was performed in the Abbey in 1906, Lady Gregory and Synge, who like Yeats were directors of the Abbey, disliked this play intensely. They thought there was far too much sensuality in it. Lady Gregory even called it "a degradation of our stage". The critic Joseph Holloway, writing at the time, describes how the movements of Florence Darragh, the actress who played Deirdre, expressed a sort of sensuousness which was very much out of place for the stage of the time. I believe that it was from Oscar Wilde's play *Salomé* that Yeats took this very sensual dramatic movement. Also, his Deirdre in the rewritten play takes on a new independence reminiscent of Salomé.

Yeats was tremendously influenced by Wilde in any case and

Photo: Fergus Bourke

Stanley Townsend, Sean Rocks and Mary McGuckian in the 1991 Abbey Theatre production of Deirdre

writes in his *Autobiographies* "my first meeting with Oscar Wilde was an astonishment". I think Wilde just blew Yeats's mind away. He talks about Wilde's "hard brilliance", and his great wit. At the time of his meeting with Wilde, Yeats was 23 and was looking for what he most lacked, which was poise, elegance and the eloquence to articulate his ideas in the public domain. Wilde had all of these and Yeats very much admired him. Indeed, he looked on him as something of a hero.

As Yeats grew and developed, he often talked about disliking Wilde's work but I think that he protested too much – there is so much of Wilde's ideas within Yeats's work that it is astounding. Yeats himself admitted that some of Wilde's ideas were amongst the most original and the most profound that he had ever come across. He talked about Wilde writing about the "fundamental" and the "profound", as distinct from the transitory and trivial. These are strong sentiments and Yeats professed them at a time when people would have considered Wilde as being a trivial, if very funny, playwright. Yeats's ideas on dance draw very much from Wilde's work.

Yeats first saw *Salomé* performed in 1905 by a private theatre company in London and again in 1906. Of course, *Salomé* did not appear on the public stage in England or Ireland until 1928 when Edwards and Mac Liammóir put it on for the Gate. They had actually rented the Peacock Theatre from the Abbey for the first performance of their theatre company and *Salomé* was one of the first plays produced.

In a letter to one of the Fay brothers in 1906, Yeats says that he is re-writing *Deirdre*, and that there are subtleties in his Deirdre character that owe a lot to Wilde's *Salomé*. One has just to look at that play and watch how dance develops from there into his *Four Plays for Dancers* on into *The King of the Great Clock Tower* and finally into *A Full Moon in March* to see how much Yeats's depiction of dance owes to the dance of Wilde's Salomé – that cold, destructive dance, which contains such passion and heat within it. Yeats was so enthralled by Salomé's dance, it represented for him the reconciliation of opposites and the exposition of the fulfilled and the perfect image.

Fiona O'Shaughnessy in the 2000 Gate Theatre Production of Oscar Wilde's Salomé

In Yeats's *Four Plays for Dancers* the dance is both sensual and spiritual, and yet contains something cold, something supernatural. In *At the Hawk's Well*, it is the woman of the Sidhe, or the fairy woman, who dances. Yeats talks about the coldness that runs through her veins. She dances a dance that is supposed to be seductive and alluring at the same time as having this distant quality. For Yeats, as for Wilde, the dance contains both a physical sensuality and a separate aloofness. Yeats talks about the dancer as uncommitted.

In the last two lines of his 1926 poem, "Among School Children", Yeats writes: "O body swayed to music, O brightening glance/ How can we know the dancer from the dance?" Within those two lines we have Yeats's whole philosophy of the dance. There is sensuality in the "body swayed to music", while the "brightening glance" suggests the sexual informed by the spiritual or "body, quick with soul". The final line of the poem, "How can we know the dancer from the dance?" indicates the synthesis within the dance between the finished work of art and the execution of the art. The ideal of perfection which Yeats seeks is expressed by him through the symbol of dance.

Yeats believes that it is impossible for human beings to realise this total perfection because there is always conflict in life. Life implies struggle and this struggle Yeats characterises by unappeasable desire. Yeats says the only way perfection can be achieved is through art and, more especially, through the symbol or the image. The dancer represents the symbol of perfection: "All dreams of the soul end in a beautiful man or woman's body"; "All thought becomes an image, and soul becomes a body."

Yeats was very visual. He had studied art as a young man and had once said of himself that he had "the concrete mind of the poet". In other words it was the image that entranced him. He said "we cannot know truth, we can only embody it". Yeats held that images or symbols carry truth and he believed it was the duty of the artist to search for truth and to present it to others.

In the *Four Plays for Dancers*, Yeats represents his metaphysics but he does not represent the final expression of the perfect image within those four plays because in them there is always conflict, and unappeasable desire. In the later dance play, *The King of the Great Clock Tower*, fulfilment of desire is achieved and from this follows unity of being, or perfection of being. This is symbolised within the dance. In *The King of the Great Clock Tower* the dancer dances before the head of her dead lover. She holds the head in her hands and dances. When she kisses the lips of the dead head, life meets death. Towards the end of the dance her body starts to quiver,

> *According to Yeats, conflict is now at an end so human life is no longer possible – therefore the dancer becomes a poetic image, the symbol of perfection of being and the embodiment of truth. That is the final importance for dance in Yeats's work.*

representing sexual consummation. All is replete; physical fulfilment and spiritual fulfilment have been achieved; soul and body become one. When the dance has ended the dancer stands between the curtains as though she were a framed image. According to Yeats, conflict is now at an end so human life is no longer possible – therefore the dancer becomes a poetic image, the symbol of perfection of being and the embodiment of truth. That is the final importance for dance in Yeats's work.

It is often argued that his *Four Plays for Dancers* are heavily influenced by the Japanese Noh drama. What Yeats loved about the Noh was its aristocratic form. Also, he felt that the Noh plays were tending in the same direction as his own plays – this idea of looking for something transcendent was also a feature of the Noh plays. It was Ezra Pound who introduced Yeats to the Japanese Noh drama. He also introduced him to the Japanese dancer, Michio Ito.

Ito was not a professional Noh dancer but he would have been familiar with the Noh style. He had been trained in Tokyo and in Europe and was very much influenced by the freestyle dancers of the time such as Isadora Duncan. Yeats was impressed by his dancing and asked him to dance for him in *At the Hawk's Well*. In this dance Michio Ito was asked by Yeats to imitate the spiralling movement of a hawk. Yeats brought Ito to London Zoo to look at hawks in their cages. Unfortunately, when they got there the hawk was asleep. So they took turns with Yeats's umbrella at prodding the poor hawk, but he didn't wake up. They had to do with imagining how a hawk would dance, and that was how Michio Ito danced in the play. Later, Ninette de Valois would dance this role in a performance of *At the Hawk's Well* at the Abbey Theatre. She was the first dancer to perform that part after Ito and wore the hawk costume designed for the Japanese dancer by Edmund Dulac.

Apart from simulating the actual bird, there was another reason why Yeats wanted the dance in *At the Hawk's Well* to emulate the movements of a hawk: besides using the dancer as an image of perfection Yeats uses the dance to inscribe spatial diagrams and patterns on the stage which represent how he sees the world, how he explains the meaning of existence.

In his philosophical work, *A Vision*, Yeats uses a gyre or a vortex – a whirling kind of spiral shape – to talk about how life behaves. In the stage directions for the dance, he has the dancer dance in a circular movement, very often moving upwards – for example in *The Dreaming of the Bones* the two lovers dance "from rock to rock" as they ascend the mountain. And then while the dance is performed below on the stage, Yeats supplies an imaginary, verbal image, such as the ger-eagle in *Calvary*, or the hawk in *At the Hawk's Well* and *The Only Jealousy of Emer* or

> So alongside the dancer as symbol of perfection in Yeats's dance plays we have the inscription of diagrams that represent his conception of the movement of civilisations and the progress of human life.

the clock in *The King of the Great Clock Tower*, to situate an invisible apex to his gyre-like diagram above the stage. So alongside the dancer as symbol of perfection in Yeats's dance plays we have the inscription of diagrams that represent his conception of the movement of civilisations and the progress of human life. Dance and dancer are extremely significant symbols in Yeats's work. Yeats's understanding of the truth of existence and fulfilment of human potential is embodied in the images he employs of dance and the dancer.

Further Reading:

Noreen Doody, "Dancing to Diagrams: patterns and symbols in Yeats's dance plays", *Yeats Studies*, ed. Hiroyuki Yamasaki, Osaka, 2004.

Noreen Doody, "'An Echo of Someone Else's Music': The influence of Oscar Wilde on W.B. Yeats", *The Importance of Reinventing Oscar,* eds. Uwe Boker, Richard Corballis and Julie A. Hibbard, Amsterdam, 2002.

Victoria O'Brien
Abbey School of Ballet Expert

Victoria O'Brien trained as a dancer at the Irish National College of Dance, from where she went on to study at the Northern School of Contemporary Dance, the Laban Centre, and was awarded her MA in Dance from the University of Limerick, where she is currently reading for her PhD on the history of classical and modern dance training in Ireland from 1925 to 1960. Victoria has worked in dance education for over ten years and is the Education Development Officer with Daghdha Dance Company. A specialist in the Abbey School of Ballet, here she shares a few of her insights on how the school functioned in its brief existence.

In its first incarnation, from 1927, the Abbey School of Ballet existed up until 1933. During that short six-year period it produced an influential generation of Irish choreographers, dancers and teachers.

There was a core group of sixteen students who attended, aged around eleven and twelve when the school opened. They took classes three times a week, and would have mainly studied ballet. The second subject was character dance, and the third was *mouvement plastique*, or "modern dance" as it would be called today.

Yeats had heard of Ninette de Valois, an Irish-born dancer who had worked with Diaghilev's *Ballets Russes*. She had left the Russian company in 1925 and was working in Cambridge at the Festival Theatre. Yeats heard that she had choreographed the movement for *On Baile's Strand* and went to meet with her. During this meeting, he invited de Valois to choreograph his *Plays for Dancers* and to open and direct a dance school at the National Theatre. The sequel to their meeting was quick. Within six months the Abbey School of Ballet had been established.

Yeats was fascinated by the dancer, and by dance. In 1913 Ezra Pound introduced him to Japanese Noh theatre. It was the key that unlocked this format for his dramatic works. This aristocratic and ritualistic art form provided Yeats with the framework he had long sought for his dramatic work. He used this Noh style as a template, adapting and developing certain elements for his own purposes. So his interest in having a dance school was two-fold. He wanted to bring about and produce indigenous dance in Ireland, but he also wanted the choreographers and dancers to produce and perform in his *Plays for Dancers*.

De Valois would cross the Irish Sea once every three months for a period of about ten days, to teach the students, and set new pieces of choreography for them. She would oversee rehearsals and also perform in Yeats's *Plays for Dancers* herself. Sara Payne, from her London school, also worked with the Abbey students.

The studio was located on the top floor of the then Peacock. In one corner of the studio de Valois had established a little library of dance books, covered in the same green colours as the Peacock. They held photographs of Diaghilev's *Ballet Russes*, Nijinska and so on. She was very much influenced by the French, Italian and Russian Schools. There was a piano on one side of the studio, which Julia Gray would play for the class.

They did use some Irish airs, encouraging young Irish musicians to compose, but not Irish dancing. From pictures of *The Faun* in 1928 we see the dancers are in bare feet. The style was very modern and sculptural.

The evenings could start with a play, followed by six or seven dance pieces. As there was an orchestra at the Abbey in that era, there would have been an interval with music, followed by another two dance pieces and perhaps another play.

The school had different areas of activities. One area would have been pure dance. Over the period of six years there were fourteen pure dance productions. These productions were incredibly specialised. They would have opened on a Tuesday evening and ran every night until Saturday, with a matinee on Saturday. They were very much part of the theatre itself.

There does not seem to have been a standard type of production. An example of a programme would have been an evening with up to fourteen different dance pieces. Generally, each work lasted three to four minutes. The repertoire was made up of anything from character dances to *Les Sylphides*, and also most of the choreography was by de Valois. Interestingly, though, de Valois staged a work by Leonide Massine.

> *Ireland had a critical theatre-going audience, who were open and interested in dance as well as in theatre. We can see from contemporary newspaper reviews that the little school was well received.*

Ireland had a critical theatre-going audience, who were open and interested in dance as well as in theatre. We can see from contemporary newspaper reviews that the little school was well received.

The Abbey School of Ballet was a dance school but it was something much more special as well – it was a semi-professional company. The young company trained three times a week in various techniques and performed regularly on a

Abbey School of Ballet dancers in the 1929 Abbey Theatre
première of Fighting the Waves

professional stage. To equate it to the Abbey School of Acting, they were producing professional experimental works at the Peacock Theatre.

As well as the specialised dance programmes, the school would have collaborated in plays staged at the Abbey. The Abbey dance teachers and students were used in these collaborations – for example, Molière's *The Would-be Gentleman*, in 1929, as well of course as Yeats's *Plays for Dancers*. The Abbey School of Ballet would have collaborated in two or three plays a year staged by the Abbey Company. And re-member, the Abbey Theatre at the time was a repertory company, so they were constantly rotating their plays. Some years these plays would be mounted three times a year.

The Abbey School of Ballet students were an integral part of the Dublin theatre scene at the time. Interestingly, the Abbey School of Ballet was established in 1927 at the Peacock Theatre, and the Gate was established in 1928, also at the Peacock Theatre originally. So Mac Liammóir and de Valois would have worked in the same premises. Obviously, they would have gotten to know each other. Within about two years from its foundation the Abbey students worked with Mac Liammóir on some of his productions, just as today certain productions call for movement sequenc-es. The Abbey students were also involved in Lennox Robinson's Dublin Drama League, and collaborated in those productions.

As de Valois trained and worked with Cecchetti, Nijinska, Balanchine and Mas-sine, she would have been very influenced by this whole movement of modern dance, character dance, or *mouvement plastique*. So we can imagine, and see from photographs, that though it was called the Abbey School of Ballet, it was much broader than that.

De Valois still had her work in London. She was establishing what was to become the Royal Ballet Company and School. Slowly, that work began to overshadow her work in Ireland. As well as that, by 1931 there was also a change of teachers. Sarah Payne left and was replaced by Nesta Brooking. The students were getting older and probably had other interests as well. De Valois's last production at the Abbey was one of Yeats's *Plays for Dancers*, *The King of the Great Clock Tower*, in 1934. Yeats dedicated it to her.

There was, however, a sequel to the school. In 1933 Cepta Cullen and Muriel Kelly, who had been students at the school since its establishment, began to take over the Abbey School. They would have only been aged about seventeen at the time. They continued to teach and produce a repertoire very much suggestive of de Valois's. The choreography they staged often had a dramatic Celtic mood. We know that the "new" Abbey school existed up until 1941, and indeed probably later.

In the late 1930s, Cepta Cullen left and established the Irish Ballet Club at the Peacock Theatre with F.R. Higgins, who was the manager of the Abbey at the time. This club promoted dance in Ireland. The Club was similar to ballet clubs that were springing up around England at the time to promote indigenous choreography, music and art – collaborations between the different art forms and dance. They had a wonderful *coup* when they invited Kurt Jooss, who was in Ireland performing *The Green Table* at the Gaiety, to come and give a lecture. Muriel Kelly, who took over the Abbey School, went on to become a respected Royal Academy of Dance teacher in Dublin. She also worked with Mac Liammóir at the Gate choreographing his productions.

We are lucky to have photos of de Valois at the time. She would have come over and performed works such as *Pride* in a Peacock costume and on *pointe*. The young dancers were quite versatile – doing classical, character-dancing, and *mouvement plastique*. So they had varied styles within their own repertoire.

There is a trickle-down effect from the Abbey School of Ballet. It is said that Beckett was very influenced by Yeats's *Plays for Dancers*. Also, the Royal Academy of Dancing, which is a syllabus of dance used throughout Ireland to this day to help raise and evaluate the standard of ballet, was first introduced to Ireland via the Abbey School of Dance. The teacher Nesta Brookings brought it over from London. It is still very much part of Ireland's dance landscape today.

Another example of the consequence or trickle-down effect of the school would be Joan Denise Moriarty's re-staging of Cepta Cullen's *Puck Hill*, and *An Coitin Dearg* for her opening season of the Irish National Ballet in Cork. So, she must have known about the Abbey School of Ballet, its choreography and personalities.

Freda Freeman
Abbey School of Ballet Pupil, 1932–1933
(and sequel school 1933–1936)

*B*orn in 1924, Freda Freeman here describes what it was like to be a young pupil at the Abbey School of Ballet during its final transition period (1932–1936).

It was 1932 – I was eight years old – when I joined the Abbey School of Ballet. I was there for about four years, until I was twelve. Then I went to boarding school. I was in Evelyn Burchall's first, when I was five.

My dad was in the film and theatre business. Maybe it was through that somebody told my mother about the Abbey School of Ballet. I was too young to have asked myself. There were a few other ballet schools around. I think it cost two guineas a term. There were boys and girls. Ninette de Valois interviewed you to see if you had any music in you, or any rhythm. In those days she was only starting.

She didn't seem to be very talkative. In a way she seemed quite strict. But then her only interest

> *She [de Valois] didn't seem to be very talkative. In a way she seemed quite strict. But then her only interest was in the ballet. All she wanted you to know was how to be a good ballet dancer, and to have the right positions. She was very keen on the classical end of everything being perfect.*

was in the ballet. All she wanted you to know was how to be a good ballet dancer, and to have the right positions. She was very keen on the classical end of everything being perfect. You had to do your barre-work, your legs had to be right – just as it would be if you went to learn music, where you would do scales and studies before you would actually play the piano. She made you do all the basic barre work before she taught you to dance in a ballet.

We wore little ordinary soft ballet shoes. She didn't put you up on blocks. There was resin-like stuff on the floor. Muriel Kelly used to come in and demonstrate the finished step. It was not until you were about eleven that you went up on pointes – because it could damage your toes. My last year there I was up on pointes for a short time – not a lot. You had to do an awful lot before you went up on pointes.

We wore round-neck purple long-waisted tunics, with a slit both sides, and knickers to match. That was it. I suppose she must have had somebody there who made them. I don't think that there was a shop my mother went to, to get a ballet frock.

Once or twice a week we went to ballet. There were about fourteen in the class. The studio was just a room upstairs in the old Abbey that burned down, with a pine floor, and ballet mirrors. It had barres all the way around. And a piano in one corner Julia Gray played. The mirrors reflected what you were doing. The bars would have been either side of the room. Ninette de Valois would go around with her little pointer to get your positions right. She'd get the pointer out to get your foot a bit more this way or that way.

The music would be similar to what they would use today – very melodic. There was nothing Celtic about it at all. It was classical ballet, and classical music, with a live accompaniment.

We did miming – "blow your nose"; "call somebody to you", or "go away" – because in classical ballet it's a story. How to convey a story was part of it. She didn't do choreography with my age group. But then I was young. One of her star pupils, a boy, ended up over in the Royal Ballet.

Ninette de Valois used to put on an annual display. For my age group there was a session that you would do something in. For the older ones she would probably take excerpts from the ballets.

She wasn't particularly warm, no. I think she was just finding her feet at that stage. She hadn't become the choreographer of the Royal Ballet. People weren't afraid of her, not really. You were supposed to go there to learn and to love ballet – and you did. I don't think I would have had any interest in ballet if I hadn't started at that stage.

She had a very nondescript accent. Not Irish, not English. She was quite timid. She didn't shout and yell. She said more with a prod than with her voice. She wore a longish skirt, and would fling her legs up to show you something. She wore her hair up, and was small and slim. She never danced for us – she was just our teacher.

When she got involved in London, she left Muriel Kelly in charge of everything that she wanted done. She would come in and expect that the work was done. Nothing was left up in the air. After the Abbey fire a lot of the archives went. But the purple books could have gone to London to the Royal Ballet.

I never took exams. I just went for fun.

Doreen Cuthbert
Abbey School of Ballet Dancer, 1927–1933

*B*orn in 1913, Doreen Cuthbert, whose mother made costumes for the Abbey *Theatre, was one of the first pupils of the Abbey School of Ballet at its outset. She soon started her own Doreen School of Dancing, and eventually would bring Royal Academy of Dancing exams to Nairobi where she moved with her family in the 1950s. Here she reminisces on what it was like during her time at the Abbey School of Ballet, working with living legends Ninette de Valois, W.B. Yeats and Lennox Robinson, and performing on the Abbey stages.*

In 1918, at five years of age, I started going to little fancy dancing classes where you'd probably bring a shilling with you for the class and learn nothing. From there I went to Madame Rock's School of Dancing on O'Connell Street opposite the Gresham. When I was 14, the lady in charge told my mother, who made costumes at the Abbey Theatre, that Ninette de Valois was opening a new school there. The fees at the Abbey School of Ballet seemed exorbitant after paying a shilling a lesson.

I remember Ninette de Valois gathering all the pupils and telling us what was going to happen, and when it was opening. I sat down on the floor. She said we would all need tights and soft shoes first, before progressing to block shoes. Our uniform was a little plum colour shift with a blue belt, and a blue band on your hair.

Ninette de Valois kept eyeing me – I had a mass of blonde ringlets, like a cloak, down to my hips. I didn't know what was wrong. The next day we were all in our uniforms, and were delighted. In we went and she told us to go to the barre, and to stand in first position – heels together, toes turned out. She then went down the whole row examining our limbs. Doing first position, with your feet flat on the floor, shows whether you are slightly bandy, or knock-kneed. I was alright physically. But she took a grip of my hair and said "this is all very nice but it's all got to come up in a band, in a bun". I was disgusted. The next day I brought a

> *Ninette de Valois was a woman, I'm telling you. Well we all eventually taught with sticks. It was more or less to save our voices. It was also to beat out the 1-2-3-4 rhythm. So you could beat it out with the stick at the same time as correcting faults . . .*

large packet of hairpins and all the others helped put the curls up, putting the hairpins in, and then putting the band on to hold it up. That was my introduction to Ninette de Valois: "This is all very beautiful, but it's got to come up."

Ninette de Valois was a woman, I'm telling you. Well we all eventually taught with sticks. It was more or less to save our voices. It was also to beat out the 1-2-3-4 rhythm. So you could beat it out with the stick at the same time as correcting faults – "Margaret, turn out your foot"; "Hilda, keep your back up" – while still keeping the beat up.

In the summer when the Abbey School of Ballet was closed I used to go over to Sadler's Wells to get classes. I was the only Irish girl in the class. They were all English. I remember a girl beside me did something wrong, and Ninette de Valois got the stick and she let fly. She threw it at her, and it landed right at her feet. I shivered absolutely, and said to her, "Aren't you going to pick it up and give it to her?" "I will not," the girl replied. "She threw it at me, let her go and get it." No respect whatsoever. Whereas I was absolutely terrified of Ninette de Valois. But she was a lovely person.

De Valois was very proud of being Irish. She loved coming over to Dublin. Every time she came she gave a recital, and the pupils would be the *corps de ballet*. Also, she loved to play with our water, because it got so soft and sudsy. She used to come in to our dressing room and play with the suds. Then she would turn around and say, "That's why you Irish have got such bad backs, no lime in the water."

We wouldn't have appeared in the first year of the school, in 1927, because we were all very immature and not good. It would have been no advertisemment. But as we got on in years the shows got more advanced. She used to put the programme

Doreen Cuthbert

of what she was going to do on the back of the ballet-room door. We would be dying to know "is the notice up yet?" to see who was going to be picked.

For the first performance of the Abbey Theatre Ballets, in January 1928, Cepta Cullen and I danced a piece to Schubert called *Pastoral*. Oh, it was a lovely little number, just the two of us, intertwining one with the other with arm movements to *Moments Musicales*. I had to come onstage first and do a little bit, and then Cepta would come in. It was very funny – it was dark in the back and the tabs were right around the stage. I remember I could hear the introduction from the back, but couldn't find the opening to come out. The performance went down very well though, because we were both quite young at the time. It was bare feet. The other pieces in the programme were performed by English girls that

Ninette de Valois brought over with her. It took the audiences a while to get used to it, because I think up until then they were mostly used to just Irish dancing. *The Eloquent Dempsey*, with F.J. McCormack and Barry Fitzgerald, was in the same programme.

I remember once Cepta Cullen and myself ran in when we heard the ballet notice was up, and read that Anton Dolin, Cepta and Doreen would dance *Nautical Nonsense*. Ninette de Valois confirmed it, saying, "Oh yes, you are going to dance with 'Pat'," as she called him. For days we were walking on air because we were going to dance with Anton Dolin. We got nearer to the show, and no Anton Dolin. We kept asking, "When is Anton Dolin coming?" She replied: "Oh he won't be here until the last minute, and you two are very quick, it won't take you long to pick up the number." Two days beforehand she told us Anton Dolin wasn't coming. He was appearing in *Roses for Me* in the States. We came down to the ground, the two of us, with a flop. That was the biggest disappointment.

We were paid the large amount of 30 shillings for a week's performances. At the age of 14 to get 30 shillings into your hand was huge.

Ninette de Valois's aim was for the Abbey Theatre Ballet to be a miniature Russian Ballet. We were to travel with the Abbey Players. Sometimes we were in plays. In 1927 I appeared in a play called *The Pipe in the Fields*,

> *I remember Lennox Robinson coming over to the ballet room, saying, "I am looking for a vision." He used to talk as if he was in a dream. He pointed to me saying, "You're the very girl."*

by T.C. Murray. F.J. McCormack was playing a recorder. Every time he played it, he was to see a vision. I remember Lennox Robinson coming over to the ballet room, saying, "I am looking for a vision." He used to talk as if he was in a dream. He pointed to me saying, "You're the very girl." I just came in when F.J. McCormack was playing the recorder, and did a whole dance that was arranged for me. Of course he was only miming, and it was played off-stage. When he finished playing I disappeared. Ninette de Valois and Lennox Robinson worked together all the time.

I was also in Moliere's *The Would-be Gentleman*, with Barry Fitzgerald. He was in satin knee-britches, white socks, patent leather shoes with a big buckle, and a little velvet jacket. Upstage there were three steps up. He would make his entrance and stand at the top of the three steps. Maureen Delaney was downstage. She was looking up, waiting for him to come in. We were supposed to be the pupils of his ballet teacher, and were down on the floor on our knees. With his brand new leather-soled shoes he went to come down the three steps, and went skating down onto the stage, landing with his two legs splayed apart wide open. He hooted. Maureen Delaney hooted. As he couldn't get up with the trousers and the shoes, Maureen Delaney, a fine hefty woman, helped him up onto his feet. We were able to laugh because we had our heads down. It was terribly funny – we were in knots.

> *There were no such things as stage-hands. The Abbey Players would run on and say their lines, then run off and start painting the scenery. Another one would come on and say his lines and then run up a ladder to fix the lights. That's how it worked.*

I was on the drums in the first production of Yeats's *The Dreaming of the Bones* in 1931. We were the accompaniment. Julia Gray the pianist played a zither. It was very Oriental. We wore all black, black kimonos, and typical Chinese black hats. All Yeats's plays, like all our plays, went down very well. There was always a buzz. And a smell – of white paint. The Abbey Players were constantly painting the flats. Maybe painting a pub on one. There were no such things as stage-hands. The Abbey Players would run on and say their lines, then run off and start painting the scenery. Another one would come on and say his lines and then run up a ladder to fix the lights. That's how it worked. And that was the smell – as well as the musty dusty smell, there was the constant smell of that paint.

Despite all the shows we were in together, the actors didn't get on with the dancers. The players were jealous of us. I don't ever remember them coming and having a conversation with us. That was one reason the school eventually closed, and the other was the fees, which were far too high.

> *And he [Yeats] shouts at him, "Fred, I told you to come down to the footlights to say that line, you bloody fool." Fred comes down stage and says, "You told me to stay up there and say my line and I'm no bloody fool." It was good fun.*

I remember Yeats well. When you did what he asked you to do you were alright. Once I had to apologise to him for being late for my rehearsal. Yeats was in the auditorium taking the rehearsal from the stage, and I sneaked around back up onto the stage. The Abbey Players, as I told you, weren't too keen on us. They were disgusted, and ordered me, "You'll go down now and apologise to him." I said I'd be afraid to. They insisted. So I went down and I remember looking up at him and saying, "Excuse me, excuse me . . . I'm sorry for being late." He was a huge man. A lovely man. "It's alright", he said, looking down at me, and he went on with his rehearsal. He had Fred Johnston up on the stage. And he shouts at him, "Fred, I told you to come down to the footlights to say that line, you bloody fool." Fred comes down stage and says, "You told me to stay up there and say my line and I'm no bloody fool." It was good fun.

Once the Abbey Players and some of the ballet were invited down to provide evening entertainment for the opening of Senator Gogarty's newly converted House Hotel in Renvyle, County Galway. He had invited a party of Americans over for the opening. I remember doing a solo in my bare feet. The ballroom floor was just new, and I picked up a splinter. Eventually I couldn't put weight on it, and was off classes. Ninette de Valois said, "Don't think because you're off classes, that you are going to miss your work. You'll sit at the back of the class and learn. You learn just as much sitting down as in a class."

The school was full-time – we had class every morning. There would have been about twenty of us, no boys in my time. But later when I started my own "Doreen School of Ballet" on Beresford Place in 1930 I had a men's ballet class. Victor Wynburne, Michael Scott the architect, and his architect partner Edwyn Williams were in it. One night a week we had double-work in which they would do *pas de deux*.

Our ballet class was in the ballet-room at the top of the Peacock. There was a communication door in the balcony between the old Abbey and the Peacock Theatre. My introduction to the old Abbey green room, which was lovely, was when word came over to the ballet studio that Lady Gregory was there. We wanted to see her, so we sneaked across. Because we weren't supposed to be there we all crouched on the floor peeping around the corner. She looked quite like Queen Victoria to me, sitting there in front of her barm-brack cake. There was some celebration, but we weren't asked to it.

We did performances about once every four months. We would have gone to the States with the Abbey Players had it gone on. It was exciting to be in the shows. We used to love to hear that Ninette de Valois was coming over. It was classical and character dance. The numbers we did called for bare feet.

She was lovely, and very friendly. Until she started to teach . . . when she became a different person altogether. De Valois wasn't there teaching all the time though. Nesta Brooking was a resident teacher, and did a tour of about six months at a time. Then she would go back to London, and Freda Bamford would come over and take us for six months, and then she'd go back. When we were training for our exam, we had Edith Carlyne who did nothing else but trained us for the Royal Academy of Dancing examinations. I did elementary and intermediate Royal Academy of Dancing exams, all with honours, and then advanced, which I failed. I cried my eyes out because I failed by one mark. I thought that was very hard.

Ninette de Valois made it known that we should know the history of ballerinas that had gone before. There were pictures on the walls of famous ballerinas. De Valois also said that "the ballet must see an Abbey play each week", and she got us the passes for every Saturday matinee. She thought it was part of our education. You'd have to be an all-rounder. She was a terrific person.

As I became a senior girl there I was appointed librarian. I had to keep note of who had taken out what book. When the school was closing down I went to Ninette de Valois and inquired what was going to happen about the library. There was one book in it, written by Cecchetti, Pavlova's teacher, that I had my eye on. He had a whole lot of *enchainements* – a collection of steps linked together to form a little dance. I was dying to get that. All the books were to do with ballet and the history of ballet. They were covered in

He looked through the lens and Ninette de Valois said, "We're ready." But the photographer said, "You're too sausage-y." Well now, to say that to Ninette de Valois!

blue like oil-cloth, like the walls of the classroom. So in the end de Valois said, "Let the girls take a book in seniority." I was the first one and got the one I wanted.

In those days when taking photographs they had a stick with a container on the top, into which they put powder. When the photographer was ready he would put a match to it. It would flare up with a flash like an explosion so he could take the photograph. I remember the photographer had a wax moustache. We were in our *Les Sylphides* costumes. I was in the front with Cepta Cullen and Ninette de Valois, and the others were grouped behind. He looked through the lens and Ninette de Valois said, "We're ready." But the photographer said, "You're too sausage-y." Well now, to say that to Ninette de Valois! He probably meant that the dresses were all too big.

And he said, "I can't see." So they got a few boards and put them over the seats in the auditorium, to make a platform for him to stand on with his tripod. Finally he said, "Ready!" the thing flashed, and there was a crash. One of the boards went, and he went. Everything went including one side of his moustache. . . . We had great old days. I'd love to know where those only photographs that were taken of the Abbey School of Ballet went to. When my husband and I moved to Africa a lot of things were lost.

> *Lennox Robinson and Ninette de Valois came over and announced that the school was to close in 1933. That's the only intimation we had. That was it, Ninette de Valois said goodbye and we all went our different ways. It was very sad.*

Lennox Robinson and Ninette de Valois came over and announced that the school was to close in 1933. That's the only intimation we had. That was it; Ninette de Valois said goodbye and we all went our different ways. It was very sad. We used to have good fun, we were a great bunch. Particularly Cepta and I were very friendly. There was Thelma Murphy as well, and Chris Sheen.

It certainly didn't go to waste – anything but. It was the foundation for me. It also taught me how to run a school. We had a marvellous pianist in Julia Gray. She worked for me afterwards, and also used to play for the silent movies in the Corinthian Theatre.

I had started my own school, the Doreen Academy. It was run the same way as the original only it was called after me. It went very well. I gradually got to be known, had quite a number of pupils, and moved to Beresford Place. I used to have my own shows in the Olympia Theatre, and I gave my own show in the Abbey Theatre. It consisted of different numbers, revue-style, like the Abbey School of Ballet programme.

Muriel Kelly started a different Abbey School of Ballet, in the Peacock Studio – but the original school was finished, over and done with.

Ninette de Valois did keep in touch. My mother, who made costumes at the Abbey, was very close to her. She brought the more intricate stuff home to her workroom. One day Lennox Robinson saw my mother in the Abbey Wardrobe department and said, "Mrs Cuthbert, you're not on a tread machine, surely". And she said, "Yes." He said, "I'll have that rectified immediately, you'll have an electric one tomorrow morning." Fair enough, the next morning she did have one, and was able to fly through the work. He was very nice and easy-going. His wife, Madame Dolly Travers-Smith, did the designs.

My school went on until I got married to Percy (Lovegrove), in 1946. We met when he came to me for private ballroom lessons. I had learned ballroom from Victor Sylvester in London. Percy got so good then that we used to do demonstrations together at dances. He had it in him. He hadn't two left feet. Our son David was born in 1947, and in Spring 1952 we went to Nairobi where Percy got a job with the transportation system as Administrative Assistant to the General Manager.

They covered the whole of East Africa, providing transport: railways, roads, lake steamers, ports, the whole lot. Percy went out first to learn Swahili, and to get a home, and then David and I followed six months later.

I joined an established school in Nairobi where they were teaching a very antiquated ballet syllabus. I wasn't happy with it, so I opened my own school, the Doreen Lovegrove Academy of Ballet, to teach the Royal Academy of Dancing syllabus. I brought out a teacher every year from London to examine my pupils.

Two of Doreen Cuthbert's pupils in Nairobi

Then the Mother Superior in the Valley Road Convent Loreto approached me, saying, "I believe you've got a flourishing school of ballet; would you be interested in taking the post here as ballet teacher?" I said, "I would be very interested." I used to start there at eight o'clock, and teach until five in the afternoon. Then she got me into the Goanese convent as well. It was all ex-pats, and very international. I used to give ballet shows in the National Theatre in Nairobi in aid of the Valley Road School. Dancers from the Festival Ballet in London performed in it. It went great. In 1953 the *Coronation Ballet* ran and ran in the National Theatre in Nairobi.

I had one girl who went on to be a Bluebell girl. I often wonder what happened to her. I love this photograph of my two pupils here – they are perfect in it, the pair of them. The girl in front, Pauline Holman went to the Vic Wells from my class. I don't know what Beverly, the other girl, did . . .

I also taught beginners ballet – they were only little tiny tots – in "Karen", which is where Karen Blixen lived. It was a suburb of Nairobi, named after her. I taught there in a little private school out in the Bundu. Then I used to go to Nakuru, which was like driving from Dublin to Belfast, through Mau Mau country. I would drive with my Danish assistant teacher Sonja, up across the Rift valley, one day a week for a hundred miles. I taught there for a number of years. It sure was a far cry from the Abbey School of Ballet! When it became dangerous, Percy put a stop to it.

I did a weekly radio show there on the history of ballet – about its origins – and another one called "Ballets I Have Seen" on the Forces Radio Station in East Africa. Percy did the script for me. We would intersperse the story with music from the ballet.

I WROTE this and other dance plays for performance in private houses before very small audiences. It is essential that there should be no scenery, no lighting effects; the players suggest scenery, light and darkness by their movements and their words. To increase the power of suggestion I have followed Japanese examples and substituted a dance for the actual climax of more naturalistic drama, and, where it suited the story, ritual for naturalistic action. A movement round the stage to the accompaniment of drum and flute represents a mountain climbed, a movement from one side of the stage to the other a shorter climb. There was a time when I wanted every word sung to be as audible and intelligible as the spoken dialogue; but now I let the musician write as the theme moves him; I think of my words as a half secret between myself and the singer. I do not print the words in the programme because I do not want my audience to divide their attention between the stage and the programme; they can find them afterwards in my book, " Plays and Controversies."
W.B.Y.

Music by DR. J. F. LARCHET.   Play Produced by U. WRIGHT.

INTERVAL—TEN MINTES.

FEDELMA

A MIME BALLET IN ONE SCENE.   Music by WILLIAM ALWYN.
Costumes designed by D. TRAVERS-SMITH.

ARGUMENT :
(From " The King of the Land of Mist ")
" . . . Then the King of Ireland's son came to the seventh gate. And before it was seated a Hag surrounded by doves, and ravens flew down and tried to take them away. When the Hag saw the King's son she ran towards him, but with a sweep of his sword he cut the long poisoned nails from her hands . . . and the raven who went to pick them up fell dead. Then the Hag opened the gates and showed the conqueror Fedelma asleep. As he bent over her she awoke and danced to him, and he took her away . . .
And the Hag went her way into the mist, followed by two ravens.
Only the doves were left to mourn the loss of Fedelma and the son of the King of Ireland."

Fedelma	...	DOREEN CUTHBERT
The Son of the King of Ireland		VICTOR B. WYNBURNE
The Hag	...	NESTA BROOKING
Doves		MOLLY FURLEY, MURIEL KELLY,
		EILEEN KANE, AUDREY SMITH.
Ravens		N. CURTIN, R. FRANCIS, J. REYNOLDS.

Choreography for Dances and Ballets, unless otherwise stated, by NINETTE DE VALOIS.

THE ORCHESTRA, under the direction of DR. J. F. LARCHET, will perform the following selection of Music :—

Overture	" Ruy Blas "	*Mendelssohn* (1809-1847)
Ballet Suite	Scheherazade No. 1	*Rimsky-Korsakov* (1844-1908)

A page from the Abbey Theatre School of Ballet's programme, of 6 December 1931, for Yeats's The Dreaming of the Bones, *including Yeats's own programme note at the top of the page*

Chapter 3

Chapter 3

The Lost Chapter:
Modern Dance in 1940s Dublin

While the Second World War was raging throughout mainland Europe, modern dance was burgeoning in Dublin. Erina Brady, born in Germany to a County Cavan father, was one in a wave of bohemian refugees here fleeing mainland Europe's rise of Nazism. In her case she brought with her Mary Wigman's philosophies of modern dance. Part-Jewish Jacqueline Robinson was another who arrived as a pianist and left, after attending Brady's Irish School of Dance Art at 39 Harcourt Street, as a pioneer of modern dance. She went on to found France's first professional school of dance in Paris, *l'Atelier de la Danse*. Others in that bohemian "emergency" milieu who attended Brady's soirées of poetry recital, music and dance were Basil Rakoczi and the White Stag Art Group, physicist Erwin Schrödinger, poet John Betjeman, as well as other thespians Patrick Pye, Gordon Lambert, Mainie Jellett, Liam O'Laoghaire and David Hendrick. This was a cosmopolitan Dublin, the kind of place that would lead Carolyn Swift and Alan Simpson to believe there would be an audience for a cutting edge cultural enterprise like their (sadly doomed, 1953–1964) Pike Theatre.

Brady cut a dash on Grafton Street in the 1940s, with her ubiquitous black beret and leopard-skin coat. Flouting convention some more she used to sleep in the alcove of her studio, and go camping in Sneem, County Kerry. Yet she managed to get De Valera himself to open her 1945 *TB Ballet* at the Mansion House, and to send her pupil-teachers to teach her philosophy of movement and dance at Brigidine Convents in Castleknock, Kildare and Kilkenny. Nonetheless, "you had to keep very quiet about being a dancer", recalls Ireland's first modern dancer, the septuagenarian June Fryer. "Barefoot – can you imagine? It was considered almost indecent." These progressive women were unusual for their time, frequenting pubs where they discussed ideas and art with fellow bohemians.

Dublin in the 1940s and 1950s was a hot-bed of classical ballet from Madame Ducktoe (wife of the Russian Ambassador) on Ely Place to the Abbey School of Ballet splinter groups, headed by Muriel Kelly, Cepta Cullen and, until she went to

Kenya, Doreen Cuthbert. With the advent of Brady, championing Mary Wigman's barefoot "dance of expression" ideas, the same dramatic antipathies played out in Dublin between ballet and modern dance as everywhere else in Europe. Brady was sent up at balletomane dinner parties.

Ultimately, however, despite her Herculean efforts, in an atmosphere where anything vaguely bodily was taboo, Brady's avant-garde modern dance movement could not thrive. In 1947, before founding the shortlived 1948 Dublin Dance Theatre Club, Brady wrote, "I simply must get myself out of Dublin or I shall simply die of it . . . My last years without dance have not been life for me. By now I have learnt to hate Ireland . . ." And so Erina Brady quit the land of her ancestors for Switzerland in 1951, where she died ten years later, aged 70.

Adding to the myth, some had speculated as to whether Brady was, after all, a spy. Mysteriously, when the epic anti-war ballet *The Green Table* by exiled German choreographer Kurt Jooss came to the Gaiety Theatre in 1946, Brady disappeared. This was despite the fact that she championed Jooss's work, and had pictures of *The Green Table* adorning her studio's walls. Interestingly, before they disbanded in 1953, the Ballets Jooss's last performance ever, in Dublin's Olympia Theatre, would feature June Fryer's future husband, Walter Kuhn, as the everyman "young soldier" and one of the circumlocutory diplomats around the green table.

> *Adding to the myth, some had speculated as to whether Brady was, after all, a spy. Mysteriously, when the epic anti-war ballet* The Green Table *by exiled German choreographer Kurt Jooss came to the Gaiety Theatre in 1946, Brady disappeared.*

After Brady's departure, June Fryer returned to Dublin from Oxford Theatre School where she had become a member of the teaching faculty, and took up a position at Stella Campbell's dance studio on Fitzwilliam Place. One fateful day, Campbell sent June Fryer to the mail boat to fetch a former Ballets Jooss dancer, Walter Kuhn, who was coming to procure his teaching diploma. The Swiss 32-year-old walked into Fryer's studio to see himself in a group photograph on the wall. They soon married, had three children, and after a brief spell giving ballroom dancing classes in their living room, and of June choreographing solos in two of the long-running Follies series of revues for Carolyn Swift at the Pike Theatre,[1] they disappeared into civilian life. The rather extraordinary Walter Kuhn took up a job in June's father's electrical contracting company in Ballsbridge, occasionally helping Brendan Behan, "drunk as an owl", home from the adjacent Paddy Cullen's pub.

And that was the end of modern dance – bare feet, second positions plié and all that racy physicality – until Martha Graham's bodily philosophies found their way here from across the Atlantic in the 1970s.

Jacqueline Robinson

Modern Dancer, Founder of L'Atelier de la Danse, Paris (from her hitherto unpublished 1999 reminiscences, Modern Dance in Dublin in the 1940s)

Part Jewish on her father's side, Jacqueline Robinson was one of many bohemian refugees who fled to neutral Dublin from mainland Europe during the Second World War. She arrived in Dublin in 1941 an accomplished pianist, and left a modern dancer, after training at Erina Brady's Harcourt Street Irish School of Dance Art. Robinson became one of Brady's two star performers, appearing in productions at the Peacock Theatre, in collaborations with the likes of Austin Clarke's Lyric Theatre Company, and George Fitzmaurice, as well as at the Mansion House. She also obtained a degree in History of Art from Trinity College Dublin.

Upon her return to Paris, Robinson founded l'Atelier de la Danse, the first school in France to offer professional training in modern dance. She also authored many books on dance, including Modern Dance in France, 1920–1970. *Inspired no doubt by Brady's teaching, and her own subsequent studies with the inventor of "Ausdrückstanz" ("dance of expression"), Mary Wigman, she translated Wigman's seminal book* The Language of Dance *into French.*

Robinson also wrote poetry, and became a close friend of French poet and dramatist Jean Cocteau. She married French poet Octave Gélinier, and they had three children, one of whom, Sophie Gélinier, wrote her thesis on Irish traditional dancing for the Sorbonne in 1982.

I could hardly believe – indeed it was a shock to me – when I found out, in 1996, that it is generally assumed that modern dance became known and practised in Ireland only in the 1970s, whereas it was quite lively in Dublin in the 1940s. This is a not uncommon feature in history of whatever kind: something is born, lived, then forgotten or cast aside and later, reappears, is reborn, discovered in its utter novelty!

This gives me a good reason for delving into my memories of a particularly rich period of my life, and knowing now why I kept so many press cuttings, programmes, notes, and so on! Having played a truly modest part in this first forgotten chapter of the story of Irish modern dance, I should like to attempt – 50 years later – to relate some of the events, tell of the coeval context, and render homage to Erina Brady who introduced modern dance in Dublin in 1939.

I arrived in Dublin, coming in a roundabout way from Paris in March 1941, result of the hazards of the war, with my parents and my brother Michael. We lived in Upper Leeson Street. Michael went to St Columba's College and I took up once more my interrupted training as a pianist (my passion), at the Read School of Music, with the fine teacher Lily Huban.

Once returned to the keyboard, I felt the need to move my body to compensate, and was recommended Erina Brady's dance classes. I had danced as a child (folk dance and Dalcrozian), and had loved it, but never considered it as a possible path for myself.

And so I went to Harcourt Street, met Erina, and started taking a few evening classes, which I enjoyed very much. It so happened she needed a pianist, not for the school but for her personal choreographic performing work. So I very soon became her pianist, and had the privilege of discussing this and that, seeking for adequate music, taking a tiny part in the process of composition – which absolutely fascinated me – and performing with her. She was a truly fine dancer, an artist.

Photo: PC Dublin

Jacqueline Robinson in The Hooded Lover *(J.S. Bach), 1946*

Two years later, gradually more and more fascinated by this art of dance, and encouraged by Erina – who inferred I had the makings of a modern dancer – I gave up my professional piano training and started that of dance, which gradually became the centre of my life. A whole world had opened up to me, in which I could discover, express, communicate, build up, build with others. . . . It was a field of activity which combined freedom and responsibility. To say something personal, according to one's own ideas, but to say it well! Obstinate wonderful hard work!

And so for a few years I took part in Erina's activities and performances, along with other dancers, musicians and theatre folk. I was passionately immersed in Dublin cultural life, attended exhibitions, concerts and performances of all kinds. I had the privilege of knowing several very fine persons, artists and musicians. So much to learn and appreciate! Very exciting! And it is to her that I owe my having entered into the realm of dance, of her having urged me to devote most of my life to this calling. I would like to quote a message she gave me along with a little present: "May your living and your working ever be worthy of the Dance."

> *I would like to quote a message she gave me along with a little present: "May your living and your working ever be worthy of the Dance."*

After the war, having finished the professional training course at the Irish School of Dance Art, I left Dublin in 1946, to return to Paris, and began my independent career. Unfortunately, I did not return to Ireland for many years, although I did stay in touch with my dear friend June Fryer with whom I had shared those years of training and discovery and launching out on our own! I also stayed in touch with Erina Brady, but she left Dublin in 1951, and seems to have broken the contacts she had there. I am therefore little cognisant of the ulterior development of modern dance in Ireland, the second part of this story. But those who have played a part in it are well placed to tell their own tales!

All I can say is: Yes, fifty years ago there was modern dance in Dublin!

Portrait of Erina Brady, 1941

Erina Brady and the Irish School of Dance Art

Modern dance in Dublin in the 1940s could not have happened had not Erina Brady settled in Dublin in 1939.

Who was Erina Brady? A mysterious woman, to be sure. Tall, elegant (in her leopard-skin fur coat), with her finely chiselled face, her limpid eyes and sleek black hair, speaking several languages, she was highly cultured. On stage she could appear as an angel or a witch, and as it were, an epitome of womanhood! In the intimacy of her studio, we knew her as exacting and considerate, aloof and tender, cold and passionate, ever filled with the desire to go further, deeper, with no compromise, into the veracity of the art of dance to which she was devoted and to bring us along that same path. We looked at her dancing, and were taken into another world. We listened and tried to do what she asked for in the dance classes, conscious of the length and richness of that path. She encouraged us to learn about and enjoy other art forms, music, painting, architecture, as it were ever opening up new doors, revealing new landscapes. We were aware of the richness of her past experiences, although she told us little about it in detail. However those great people, Rudolf Laban and Mary Wigman, with whom she had worked, were present in her studio. There were photos on the walls and very frequent reference to their art and teaching.

> *On stage she could appear as an angel or a witch, and as it were, an epitome of womanhood!*

Erina (perhaps christened Erna), was born 29 May 1891 in Bad Homburg vor der Höhe, Germany. Her father, Terence Brady, came from Cavan. Her mother, Elisabeth Wendland, had an Irish grandfather, O'Reilly. The family settled in Switzerland. It seems that Erina as a child saw Isadora Duncan dance, and decided she would be a dancer. It is likely she studied classical ballet in Paris, with Madame de Consoli, and equally likely that she was not satisfied with this type of dance. She returned to Geneva and studied with Emile Jacques-Dalcroze. It seems she was at the time very concerned about the "troubles" in Ireland, and wrote articles in the Swiss press. Thence did she go perhaps to Frankfurt around 1929 to work with Rudolf von Laban. She may have performed with his group. It has proven to be quite a difficult task to ascertain different facts in her pre-Dublin life. Maybe she was known under another name? One cannot totally rely upon the odd press cutting such as the article "Barefoot dancer at Mansion House", and in "Leader Page Parade", in *The Irish Times*, December 1941, which mentions her links with Cavan, her work with Rudolf von Laban, with Wigman and so on.

Erina's teaching was very much influenced by the theories and practice of Laban – of Dalcroze also – as far as dance and music relationship are concerned, but principally by that of Mary Wigman. It is presumably in the early '30s that Erina went to Dresden to study with Wigman. Did she perform within her company? Although the name we know is not to be found among the list of "official" teachers at Wigman's school, there is, in a beautiful 1933 prospectus, a reference to classes being given by professional students chosen by Wigman. Maybe Erina was among these? Years later, Wigman did speak to me personally of the fact that Erina taught at her Dresden school.

Most certainly these were very important years for Erina. She referred so often to Mary, to other dancers who were with her at the time, to Hanns Hasting and Alaida Montijn, Wigman's musician partners (who both wrote music for Erina).

There were fascinating photos on the walls of the studio, and we would gaze and dream over all these fragments of a rich, moving, eloquent world . . .

There were fascinating photos on the walls of the studio, and we would gaze and dream over all these fragments of a rich, moving, eloquent world – a world of quest into the possibility of speaking through movement, of reaching towards greater dimensions of being and doing, which we wished to attain.

I would like to quote Wigman – words which tell of this quest:

The dance is speech, communication, language of the body in motion. The medium of expression is the body. It is the vessel from which we pour out our desires for expression. It is interpreter, herald and instrument . . . Dancing is motion, the conversion of inner, invisible animation into visible bodily movement. What inspires the body? An inner, indefinable, undeniable urge that desires a visible, definable expression . . . (Walter Sorrell, *The Mary Wigman Book*, Wesleyan University Press, 1984)

And that was where Erina wished to lead us.

When did Erina leave Dresden? And why? More unknown elements in this biographical sketch. It seems she worked as a dancer and maybe as a choreographer for the Theatre Mogador in Paris. This theatre staged mostly musical comedies, and toured through Europe. It is there that Erina took part in *Rosemarie*, in which she was to play again, in 1942, in Dublin!

Another question: what prompted Erina to settle in Dublin? A desire to return to her father's country, to which she had always been morally attached? To bring modern, creative dance there? It is certain that the political situation on the continent was growing increasingly tense, with the risen Nazi power, the threats such as Munich 1938, and Ireland could appear as a relative haven. Anyway, she came to Dublin probably in 1938, and opened her school in January 1939.

> *What prompted Erina to settle in Dublin? A desire to return to her father's country, to which she had always been morally attached? To bring modern, creative dance there?*

It was at 39 Harcourt Street that she founded the Irish School of Dance Art. At the time, in that same building, encompassing several studios, other artists worked. In the basement, there were craftworkers who made stained glass. Also Hugh Barden, who became a faithful friend of Erina's studio. On record are other names such as that of Adolphus Grauer and Irish School of Art.

The Irish School of Dance Art studio, at the end of a long passage, was very large, filled with light, with a grand piano, several open cupboards with beautiful small percussion instruments – drums, cymbals – a fair-sized alcove, where Erina had her bed, and her richly stocked book-shelves. And in the passageway, the dressing-rooms and so on. The studio was perfectly adequate not only for the actual dance classes, but for performances, concerts and so on, with a most lively and yet serious "ambience".

How did she present her work, trying to make her school known? She obviously referred frequently to Isadora Duncan – a legendary figure, no doubt, to the non-specialised public, the best known renovator of dance at the turn of the century. More so than to Laban or Wigman, probably for that very reason. One may suppose that at the beginning, those who attended the dance classes were mostly children and amateur adults. Here is the text accompanying the enrolment form for small pupils:

> Dance should be part of every child's education because it not only develops physical suppleness and balance but also encourages aesthetic sensibility and an attitude for spontaneous creation, thus being beneficial to mental as well as physical development. Erina Brady is not only a renowned dancer whose work had been enthusiastically acclaimed on the Continent, but has also achieved distinction in her teaching after graduating from the Academie de Danse, Paris, and the Mary Wigman School, Dresden.

A 1942 article referring to her recital in Waterford, "an interesting exhibition of Dance as an Art Form", and to a talk, indicates:

> In a short talk on Dance as an Art Form, Miss Brady began by explaining the importance of Dance in the life of primitive man. She traced the evolution of Dance to the present day, naming Isadora Duncan as one of the outstanding exponents in recent years of "Contemporary Dance". She stressed the difference between Dance as an Art Form and the Ballet, and concluded by pointing out the importance of the Dance as healthy exercise, saying she was of the opinion it should be taught in all schools.

The publicity announcement current in 1942 (at the back of programme sheets for instance), ran thus:

> Classes and private lessons for dancers, teachers, actors, students of dramatic art, amateurs, children. Complete training for students over sixteen years intending to become either dancers, choreographers or teachers of dance.

I confess I know very little of what happened at the Irish School of Dance Art before I went there in 1941. I have referred above to my meeting Erina and how I started working with her. First as an interested and happy amateur, dancing a couple of evenings per week, then as her pianist, and then as a professional student! (A very important trip for me!)

I presume that she had not given recitals before that, nor had she sufficiently trained student-dancers to build up performances. There were plenty of nice, enthusiastic people taking part in the classes, to be sure. But obviously, Erina had not actually appeared as a dancer in Dublin before the recital she gave at the Mansion House on 9 December 1941, with myself at the piano, and May Carey reading a paper about Contemporary Dance Art. It must have meant a great deal to her, after several years of, shall we call it silence, to plunge once more into the excitement, hard work, discipline, of composing several solo dances. And she was 50 years old! One could never have guessed it!

We had worked for months together, and I had the privilege of playing a certain part in the building up of this programme of dances, insofar as Erina would consult me on the choice of music and sometimes tell me of her inner dreams, what she wanted to express, give life to, in the dance. A fascinating, moving experience! The programme comprised twelve dances (we made them short in those years!), all very different: tragic, such as *The Prisoner*, to music by Gabriel Faure; daemonic, *The Storm Queen*, Beethoven; delicately lyrical, *In the Moonlight*, Prokofiev; exuberant vitality of the Bartok *Moods*.

> *. . . Erina would consult me on the choice of music and sometimes tell me of her inner dreams, what she wanted to express, give life to, in the dance.*

Equally fascinating is to read over the press notices referring to this event, for there one can, as it were, evaluate what the approach to dance as a theatre art was in Dublin at the time. For instance:

> *Evening Mail,* 10 December 1941: "Erina Brady's dance recital was in the nature of a milestone in the history of dancing in Ireland. To some, her style of barefoot dancing is not dancing at all. To others it is thrilling, powerful and dramatic, standing among the highest forms of creative art. The rejection of the stereotyped and the desire to break new ground are its ever present features . . ."

> Liam O'Laoghaire in *Leader*, December 1941: "There is only good and bad dance art. I am not intensely interested in the partisan violences of Balletomane or Modern. . . . But when we come to that simplification which is so often the accompaniment of greatness we are aware of a supreme test being applied. Consequently when Erina Brady appeared at the Mansion House recently in the first public recital she has given since her return to Ireland some years ago, one felt she was treading on very dangerous ground. Her first dance revealed a sureness of purpose with a finished technique that led one to believe that she is possibly the finest dancer that has appeared here in years. Her sense of the stage is remarkable, her feeling for music is sensitive. . . . One's impression . . . that of a flawless artistry. . . ."

> *Irish Times*, 10 December 1941: "Steak-and-kidney pie is a very pleasant dish, but an eight-course dinner in which every course consisted of steak-and-kidney pie would lead to monotony. That was the trouble with Miss Erina Brady's dance recital at the Mansion House last night. She is an excellent dancer, possessing a perfect sense of rhythm, a feeling for music most uncommon, she can express more with her arms than the average dancer can express with her whole body. Withal, there was a certain dullness . . . the dances all were similar, they could not well be otherwise, for she favours the free bare-foot technique, which combines simplicity with a certain lack of variety . . . which one feels to be just a little too easy."

Jacqueline Robinson in Polka *(Strauss)*

And from then on, in 1942, Erina gave several solo recitals in different cities including Cork and Waterford, later in Kilkenny. She was also asked to work for diverse theatrical events, some of which proved to be of great interest, both for herself and the Irish School of Dance Art, but also for the actual theatre and dance world, and the Dublin public, who would become gradually acquainted with this "bare-foot" dancing! Her dances were very much appreciated in Cork, as the following lines indicate:

> "Modern Ballet . . . a delightful recital. . . . Her interpretation of a range of characters was so vivid. . . . In the hands of so accomplished an artist each dance became more delightful than its predecessor, and it was to the great regret of the audience that the final curtain was rung down . . ."

I must here refer to my own path in dance, in Dublin! For it is during the year 1942 that I began to feel uncertain as to my future as a pianist, feeling increasingly attracted to dance through working with Erina, along, as it were, parallel ways: attending regularly the evening dance classes, feeling my body awakening, and the wonderful moments of rehearsing and playing for Erina. Among the young people who attended the evening classes was "Lyrical June Fryer, a lovely-eyed willowy girl", as she was later referred to in the *Irish Independent*. June, then 17 years old, was obviously gifted for dance. We decided, that summer, to embark upon the professional training that Erina could offer us. I tried to keep up playing the piano in the following years, giving several wee recitals on Radio Éireann, but obviously the two activities could not be combined.

> *Among the young people who attended the evening classes was "Lyrical June Fryer, a lovely-eyed willowy girl", as was written in the* Irish Independent *later.*

So in the autumn of 1942, Erina had at least two apprentice dancers she could call upon for stage purposes – there were to be more later! And in the next few years there were to be several events in which June and I took part, under Erina's direction: At the Abbey Theatre, February 1942, the ancient epic *Everyman*, in Irish *O Cách. Dráma Moralta den 15adh Aois;* sundry lectures/demonstrations in various venues, principally on "Dance as an Artform"; and a major event: the production of *Rose Marie* at the Gaiety Theatre in December 1942. This world-known "Romance of the Canadian Rockies" was directed by John Stephenson. Erina was responsible for the dances, and played the part of the squaw, Wanda. It was known that she had plenty of experience where this musical comedy was concerned! In the press:

> "Dublin Musical Society's production of *Rose Marie* at the Gaiety Theatre, Dublin, last night was a marked advance on anything they have previously done. A great spectacular show . . . a riot of colour and movement. . . . A very enjoyable show."

But what of the professional training course that Erina gave in her studio? It was, in fact, very much like that given by Mary Wigman in her schools in Germany.

June Fryer and Jacqueline Robinson reheasrsing The Green Snake *in the Irish School of Dance Art Studio, 1941*

There were, on average, five hours work in the studio per day, apart from our individual or group rehearsals. To begin the day, "limbering", which meant re-fined gymnastics, striving to make the body strong, supple, learning the ways and means through the study of anatomy also. One could concentrate on the torso, on the legs, the back, the feet, the shoulders, balance, speed, trying to learn the body and make it more intelligent and competent. Then came the "class lesson" in which were studied more specific types of moving: walking, running, leaping, falling, turning, etc. Or problems of space: forms, directions, floor patterns, rhythm etc., and combinations of all these, along the lines of the endlessly rich work of Laban. We also studied specific Laban theories: the icosahedron, dimensional and A scales, and so on. Then there was the more specifically creative work: improvisation, which could start off from all kinds of things: music, poetry, dramatic situations, personal imagination; and from there to dance composition – the actual building, making of a dance piece, taking into account all the data that was gradually approached and integrated.

There were also classes in music (which I gave), aiming at a sufficient knowledge which would allow the student to read a score, analyse a piece, and a minimum knowledge of the history of music; the same for history of art. That is how June and I followed Françoise Henry's course at Dublin University; and then there were those great discussions with Erina on history of dance and all kinds of cultural topics.

We were present at many of the children's and amateur adult classes and this gradually became teaching practice. I had kept a notebook, a sort of diary recording the contents of our daily classes. I cannot resist quoting:

Thursday October 4th 1944: Limb: legs at the bar; pliés, battements; ronds de jambe, stretching – Class lesson: study of dramatic possibilities of disharmonious swings. Improvisaton in dimensionals, dramatic and lyrical. – Mime: expressive walking in a circle (fat man, girl, boy etc). Senior class: shoulders, ribs, swings, loose arms. . . . History: Noverre's letters.

Tuesday: Limb: general loosening, floor work, very energetic spine work – Class: Turns with inward and outward leg-swings, in great detail. Seniors: Energetic limbering. Tidy foot-work, leg swings in progression, improvisation – Music: precision work on drums. Mozart Rondo, attention to form – (National: Sistine Chapel)

And so on . . . Many hours of good hard work, with very happy and, naturally, some less happy moments!

As more and more students attended the Irish School of Dance Art, its activities increased. There were occasional concerts and dance performances by the children, the amateur adults or the small group of professional students. Some of these young people who danced with such fervour under Erina's guidance included: the Becker sisters, Rosemary, Barbara, Margaret; the Blake Kelly sisters, Bán, Claire, Ruth; Margaret Brady; Elisabeth Carr; Betty Fitzgerald; Christine Matthews, Margot Moffett; Lavinia Reddin; Elisabeth Sheridan; Maureen Walsh; Eileen and Kathleen Wann; and June's younger sister, gifted Ann Fryer; and many others! Sadly, I lost contact with most of them when I left Ireland.

Erina herself wrote and produced plays performed in the studio: *The Stranger within the Gates*; *The Statue*, a "ballet"; *The Green Snake;* and *The Beautiful Lily*. There were two major solo parts, one in, *The Green Snake*, danced by June Fryer, and one in *The Harbinger of Death*, by myself. We were asked to dance excerpts on several occasions.

In December 1944, the Lyric Theatre Company presented at the Abbey Theatre a series of performances in a programme which included two plays by Austin Clarke: *The Plot is Ready* and *The Viscount of Blarney,* and a piece combining

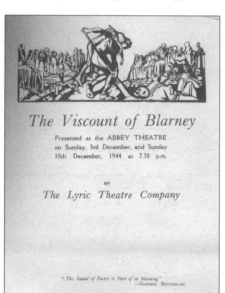

The Viscount of Blarney

Presented at the ABBEY THEATRE
on Sunday, 3rd December, and Sunday
10th December, 1944 at 7.30 p.m.

BY

The Lyric Theatre Company

"*The Sound of Poetry is Part of its Meaning*"
—GORDON BOTTOMLEY

Programme for The Viscount of Blarney *(Abbey Theatre, 1944)*

poetry and dance, *The Fairy Thorn*, by Samuel Ferguson, produced by Erina. "Interpreted by a dream-like dance-mime . . . on the plain of fairy-land . . . D.S." This piece was given again, later, in other venues.

In 1945, we all became much involved in the Irish Red Cross Society's project, the Tuberculosis Exhibition, insofar as Erina was asked to produce a "propaganda ballet against tuberculosis". And so for weeks we rehearsed what Erina called "a choric dance fantasy". The programme ran as follows:

> For this presentation we were very fortunate in securing the interest and co-operaton of Miss Erina Brady. Miss Brady is one of our foremost teachers of dancing and Modern Ballet.
>
> The story of the ballet is built around the community's struggle with Tuberculosis, and its ultimate victory over the disease. Music of Mozart and Strauss, and a mechanical "machine-rhythm" are blended with choric speech which features sonnets translated from the German of Rainer Maria Rilke . . .
>
> Jacqueline Robinson and June Fryer take the solo dances depicting "the Spirit of Youth", "the Harbinger of Disease", "the Spirit of Resignation". Both of these gifted dancers have been trained by Erina Brady, who is a Diplomée of the Academie de Danse of Paris and of the Mary Wigman School at Dresden.

And the synopsis:

> A warning voice tells of the Great Destroyer, Tuberculosis; but the masses will not listen. They do not appreciate the appeal of Youth, in its carefree dance; they repudiate the Spirit of Health, preferring the modern city life: crowds, hustle, excitement, machinery, noise.

Rehearsing for the TB *Ballet, 1945*

The Harbinger of Disease comes among them, but the masses try to ignore the presence by bringing themselves into night life and yet more excitement, by their own foolishness, falling victim to Tuberculosis. They make yet another mistake. Instead of fighting the disease, they become resigned to what they believe to be inevitable. Help comes in the form of Hope, Rest, Air, and Sunlight, restoring them to Health."

And so, after the official opening on 28 May by Eamon de Valera, we played for three whole weeks, which was both fun and an occasion to learn a lot, and for Erina's work and modern dance to be appreciated by a vast public.

During those weeks of work on the *TB Ballet*, we could but rejoice that the war in Europe was over. A stop to the horrors. This furthermore meant for us, in a neutral country, that doors would be opening up once more. We had felt isolated, for sure. A curtain was lifting, a promise of light.

In the autumn of 1945, June and I began our last year of training at the Irish School of Dance Art, before, we hoped, obtaining our diploma. We wore the label "master-year-students". We had the responsibility of teaching children's classes, putting on performances with them, both in the Harcourt Street studio and in other towns – Kilkenny, Abbeyleix, Castleknock . . .

I cannot resist telling of an anecdote concerning one of my first teaching jobs in a Brigidine Convent. For my first class I wore a long fluid skirt, which was a customary garment for dancing at the time. The class went very well, with one of the Sisters attending. Afterwards, I was summoned by the Mother Superior: "Miss Robinson, I hear that you lifted your skirt, revealing your legs, which furthermore, were in a wide stance." (We were doing second position *pliés*). *"No question of your doing that here!"*

What should I wear the following week? In order not to have to lift my skirt, I wore a short one, a tunic. Would this be considered decent? Before giving the class, I had to appear before an Areopagus of Sisters. They looked shocked and it was pronounced that there could be no exhibiting bare legs under any conditions. So what was I to do?

> *"Miss Robinson, I hear that you lifted your skirt, revealing your legs, which furthermore, were in a wide stance. No question of your doing that here!"*

"Give your class in your coat and skirt," said Mother Superior. Which I did, and for the whole term, at the end of which the Bishop declared that there were to be no more dancing classes of that type at the Convent. However, during those weeks, secretly, I did help a charming young Sister to stage a play on the life of St Patrick.

The spring of 1946 was quite exciting for us. Apart from working very hard for our Diploma, and that of History of Art at Dublin University, attending Francoise Henry's course, we were involved in several of Erina's projects. She was very intent on staging *The Voyage of Maeldune*, adapted from Tennyson. These poems obviously meant a lot to her and she shared many dreams with us, as she composed the choreography. This "dance-drama" featured George Green and Patrick Nolan, narrators; June and myself as soloists; and a group of dancers: Bán Blake Kelly, Christine Matthews, Margot Moffett and Maureen Walsh. The music included pieces by Chopin, Mussogorsky, Holst, Debussy, Paderewsky and Dukas. Erina also designed the costumes.

A first series of performances took place at the Peacock Theatre in April 1946. The programme also included a revival of *The Fairy Thorn* by Ferguson, with solos by June and myself. In the press we find:

> ". . . an unusual piece of work. The choreography by Miss Brady was original, and those taking part, as well as being graceful, showed feeling and understanding in their movements". (*Irish Times*, 2 April 1946)

> "Settings revealed imagination and dances originality in *The Voyage of Maeldune* . . . all the scenes had quality . . ." (*Evening Mail*, 2 April 1946)

> "Ballet without ballet shoes – such was the offering at the Peacock last night. Erina Brady was presenting half-a-dozen of her students in a programme in the so-termed natural style of dancing (bare feet and simple flowing costumes). The principal item was *The Voyage of Maeldune*, an interpretation of Tennyson's poem about the adventures of an Irish chieftain and the islands he saw . . . the dancers proceeded to suggest the mood of the various isles. In the result there was achieved much beauty of movement, and in June Fryer and Jacqueline Robinson were seen two accomplished dancers in this particular style. . . . The dance arrangements and costumes were by Erina Brady." (*Evening Herald*, 2 April 1946)

> "The dance-drama *The Voyage of Maeldune*, which is being presented at the Peacock Theatre by Erina Brady this week, is one of the most unusual artistic performances seen in Dublin for many years. The interpretations of the moods of the poem were dramatically and artistically effective. . . . When the dancers are as accomplished and experienced as Jacqueline Robinson and June Fryer, this art reaches great heights, because it has an irresistible suggestion of spontaneity. We feel that every movement is exactly right, and it is exactly the natural instinctive reaction to the mood of the dancer, the perfect physical expression of what she feels . . ." (D.S. *Independent*, 3 April 1946)

Needless to say, we were very pleased with this last write-up not only for the personal praise, but because at last a critic seemed to have really understood our approach, the fundamental approach to "modern" creative dance.

In June 1946, Erina was asked to participate in a programme at the Abbey Theatre produced by the Lyric Theatre Company, which included two short plays, *The Magic Glasses*, by George Fitzmaurice, produced by Evelyn MacNiece, and *The Second Kiss*, by Austin Clarke, produced by Cyril Cusack. Erina produced a tragic "poem for players", *Niobe*, by T. Sturge Moore, in which four of her dancers took part.

To end the season at the Irish School of Dance Art, called for the occasion "Erina Brady's School of Dance", June and I (this was no doubt to be considered as part of our Diploma exam), produced a fairy-tale, *The Princess of Cornucopia*, with the junior pupils. We worked in close partnership on the choreography to music by Grieg. Much hard work, but we were all quite happy. We went through all the phases of our exam, technique, choreography, music, history of dance, of art, etc. We did obtain the diploma which was largely based on the current teaching in Mary Wigman's school.

But there was to be yet another exciting event: the season in July at the Gaiety Theatre of the Ballet Jooss. This meant so much for us: at last the doors had opened, and we could really feel we were part of an artistic trend widely spread over the world. We could, with all due modesty, think: here come some of our family! For sure, there was a different approach in the work of Jooss from that of Erina – hers in the Wigman line, that is more "purist" with no use or reference whatever to the classical vocabulary. To quote John Martin, Jooss:

> employs much of the technique of the academic ballet, that part that . . . builds brilliance and control . . . and many of the principles of the modern expressional dance, that which concerns itself only with movement from emotional sources . . . in theory more convincing than in practice, for the two types of movement do not blend easily . . . a composer of great talent and individuality . . .[2]

(I had discovered John Martin's writings on dance on Erina's bookshelf. As she did, I admired his writings, and no doubt he fed my manner of thinking about dance. . . . I am ever recommending *The Modern Dance* published first in 1933,[3] which sets out in the clearest, briefest, most convincing way to define modern dance.)

So we attended several performances of the Ballets Jooss, watched classes, were deeply moved and impressed by *The Green Table*, *The Big City*, etc. For the company, we had the opportunity to talk with the dancers — such great people as Kurt Jooss, Sigurd Leeder, Hans Zullig, to discuss this and that, and it was a most inspiring experience. It was, for us young people, the first high-quality big dance works we saw. (Actually I had seen the Ballets Jooss in London the preceding summer, 1945, during my return to London after the war. I had experienced that shock, that wonder, of witnessing what I dreamed of.)

And that summer June and I spent our holidays in London, and attended a course given by Sigurd Leeder. It was interesting to approach dance problems in another manner!

On reading over various letters Erina wrote to me that summer, I see that she was going through a rather tense period. She had started writing a book. I do not remember whether she told me what it was to be about. Apparently, it never saw the light of day. She never ceased suffering from the lack of understanding of modern dance that was especially strong in England, and in Ireland. Referring to my future, she advised me to "go across the ocean [she meant to the USA] before tackling old-old Europe, and tackle Switzerland and France before confronting London. Prejudice once enshrined dies by a slow death, for those who have given hysterical applause at Sadler's Wells don't easily admit that they might have been mistaken. The ballet nevertheless is giving its last kicks and you will live to enjoy the triumphs of our work even there where it suffers persecution today . . ."

A long-living animosity!

Within six months, I was to leave Ireland, and can no longer consider I was a witness to the evolution, the place of modern dance in Ireland. I went to England, to Nottingham, then to Paris, where I worked in Mila Cirul's company, studied dramatic art at an avant-garde school, *Education par le Jeu Dramatique*. It was all very exciting and I persuaded June to join me in Paris. She had been more or less assistant for Erina after obtaining her diploma.

> *. . . she advised me to "go across the ocean [she meant to the USA] before tackling old-old Europe, and tackle Switzerland and France before confronting London. Prejudice once enshrined dies by a slow death . . .*

We gave a recital at the *Archives Internationales de la Danse*, in Paris, thrilled to dance in a venue of such high reputation! But post-war life was so difficult, and we positively starved! And finally we returned to our respective home countries. (France *was* partly mine!), June to Dublin, I to Nottingham where my parents had settled and where I began to teach and perform. June and I gave several recitals in Nottingham, much appreciated, if I may add!

During that year, we kept in touch with Erina of course. She continued teaching in Dublin, both children and amateur pupils, and pursuing the professional training of those students who had started after June and myself, among whom were Constance Brady (a young cousin of Erina's), Claire Blake Kelly and Margot Moffett. Erina was very attentive to what June and I were undertaking dance-wise. She naturally wished we would one day really "make it", and along the lines of what she believed in. She dreamed of leaving Ireland. She made no secret of her disappointment. Life had been for those last years a real struggle both financially and to obtain the recognition she hoped for – for herself no doubt, but also for dance as she conceived it, to which she devoted herself, with no compromise.

> *Life had been for those last years a real struggle both financially and to obtain the recognition she hoped for – for herself no doubt, but for dance as she conceived it, to which she devoted herself, with no compromise.*

She had returned briefly to Switzerland, for which she was deeply homesick, in the summer of 1947, with Constance Brady and Muriel Graham – the Irish School of Dance Art pianist, who was devoted to Erina – to look after her sick mother, who died shortly afterwards. She wrote in a pathetic manner:

> "Could I get permission to work in France? I simply must get myself out of Dublin or I shall die of it. . . . Dublin has hurt me so badly. . . . There are new dances budding up in me at the moment, and I may give up evening classes altogether, so as to be able to work regularly myself. I simply can't go on as I have been doing. . . . My last couple of years without dance have not been life for me. By now I have learnt to hate Ireland . . ."

Well . . . !

She dreamed of leaving her Dublin school to June, of settling elsewhere and forming the Erina Brady Dance Group, concentrating on performing and choreography. A first step in that direction came in April 1948 when she undertook the big job of producing an "Evening of Dance" in London, at the Rudolf Steiner Hall. The aim was double insofar as she wished to promote June and myself, "budding" soloists, and to show her own "modern dance" in England. For three nights June and I gave solos and two duets, and the second part of the programme was a second version of *The Voyage of Maeldune*. The group consisted of Claire Blake Kelly, Constance Brady, Margareta Fiddes, June and myself.

> "Tennyson's *Voyage of Maeldune*, expressed in dance, provided a most effective and imaginative performance, in which the mystic quality of the poem was freely interpreted in the choreography by Erina Brady. Exuberance and grace marked the performance of JF and JR . . ." (*The Stage*, April 1948)

This was the last time I was to see Erina for several years, because after a period of good hard work in Nottingham, I finally chose to settle in Paris. And I did work with Mary Wigman in the '50s, in Switzerland and in her school in Berlin! Wonderful!

Whilst preparing the London event, which did not quite reap what she had hoped for, in May 1948 Erina had started on a new venture in Dublin, founding the Dublin Dance Theatre Club. The President was District Justice Kenneth Reddin, the Hon. Treasurer Muriel Graham, and the Hon. Secretary Margot Moffett. "The aim of the club is the presentation, by local and visiting artists, of Dance Performances, Musical Recitals, and Lectures" ran the leaflet.

The *Sunday Independent* of 30 May put it this way:

> "Dublin Ballet Teacher Founded Club – 'I found it so difficult to get a stage in Dublin for performances of Modern Ballet and Musical Recitals that I thought the only way out of the difficulty would be to found a club' . . . Clubs of a similar type, Miss Brady said, are best known in America, where their rapid growth is due in no small measure to the fact that University students can now take Modern Ballet as an Art subject . . ."

The Voyage of Maeldune – The Island of Witches
(Choreography by Erina Brady)

In the Harcourt Street studio a raised auditorium and an equipped stage were built. The first programme included two group pieces by Erina: *John and the Magic Coffee Grinder* and *The Voyage of Maeldune*. Other concerts were announced and a joint recital with Michael O'Higgins, baritone, and June Fryer. It seems the Club had many members from the start.

I don't know how long it lasted or what happened there. I surmise that Erina's activities in Dublin diminished progressively. She suffered from ill health. She also probably regretted the absence of June, who went to work in England, then in Switzerland, married the Swiss dancer Walter Kuhn, and of myself, who could have collaborated with her. One could still find in 1954 the name of the Irish School of Dance Art at 39 Harcourt Street, alongside the Craftworkers, and a Burke Elocution School. But I visited Erina in her Swiss home in Brione, near Ascona, in the summer of 1952, and seem to remember that she had then definitely left Ireland. I recall Mary Wigman telling me of a visit to her there in 1954.

Muriel Graham went to live with Erina, as she had cancer and became increasingly sick. In fact, her last years were a desperate fight: frequent operations, long sojourns in clinics, in Montreux, and other cities, short stays in her beloved Casa Erina. She wrote to me: "It is heartbreaking that as a cancer victim my body has become stuck whilst my heart and my brain have remained intensely alive and mobile . . ."

And so it was, for months, years, attempting to rise, and falling again till she died in hospital in Vevey, 1 June 1961, at the age of 70. She died, as it were, in silence. There was no official announcement, nor private. Neither June nor I heard of it immediately or directly.

And so our mysterious Erina left the stage – a fairly long, no doubt very full life. But it does seem that the last years during which she struggled forward with so much energy and faith, she knew frustration and to conclude, physical and moral pain.

Erina had many friends in Dublin who appreciated her work, and several who collaborated with her. She was in a way close to artists, painters such as those of the White Stag Group, in particular Basil Rakoczi, sharing an "avant-garde" approach and reputation! Also Mainie Jellett, May Guinness, the architect Noel Moffett and others. The Reverend Roderick Coote, who was a fine musician, wrote music for some of her dances; Hugh Barden made décors. Other names come to my mind, good friends whom we saw in the studio: Liam O'Laoghaire, John Betjeman, Austin Clarke, and so many names I have forgotten!

What trace did Erina leave in Dublin, in Ireland? And for how long was there an echo of what she had brought about? Did the Irish School of Dance Art close when she left Dublin? Probably. Those dancers in her group in the last period also left Dublin, diversely to England, to Canada, to India. One could assume that there was no-one locally to continue what she had attempted to build. Or the time was simply not ripe. These ten years could be seen as a prelude – a forgotten prelude? It was in the '70s, practically 20 years later, that we find settled companies such as the Irish National Ballet – "classically inclined", Terez Nelson, in the Martha Graham line, and a few others. But that is another story! Leading up to all that is growing, blossoming, "modern-dance-wise" in Ireland today!

Dance in Ireland in 1939

This is just to indicate briefly the "professional context" extant in Dublin at the time modern dance breathed there its first breath, took its first steps. In order to see what changes were to be brought about, it is necessary to consider what was going on in the dance field in Ireland in the period. (I am aware that I shall be omitting many dance activities, considering the limited documentation presently available.)

Ireland echoed up to a point what was going on in England. How far had "modern dance", "free dance", "*Ausdrückstanz*", still considered "avant-garde" in the '30s, impregnated England? And Ireland? Classical ballet was still considered the essential, if not unique form of "serious" stage dance. There had been the novelties introduced since the blaze of the Russian Ballet, and in England, the undeniable achievement of, for instance, Marie Rambert, Ninette de Valois, Frederick Ashton, Robert Helpmann, with the Ballet Rambert, and the Sadler's Wells Ballet. There was, of course, all that belonged to the music-hall styles of dance. There was a trace of the influence of Isadora Duncan – often called "Greek dancing" – likewise "cen-

tral European dancing", of Dalcroze Rhythmics. There had been occasional performances, tours by foreign companies, and Kurt Jooss had settled in England, at
Dartington, in 1934, creating there a true centre for modern dance. However, one
must admit that it was quite a long way from what was going on in the USA and
Germany, for instance.

In Ireland, then, what was going on, locally? The ever vivid Irish dance, folk
or national dancing, of course, was practised and taught in several counties, cities,
festivals, and celebrations took place here and there. The Gaelic League approved the Irish Dancing Commission in 1931, seeking to protect and promote Irish dancing, and directed competitions – *Feise-anna Ceoil*– throughout the country. Thanks to Peggy Carty O'Brien, from Galway, I can quote a few names of people who were active in that field at the time: Brigid Hanley, Lily Simpson Daly, Ita Cadwell, Sean Stafford . . .

Photo by Derrick Michelson

The Silent Isle (Choreography by Erina Brady)

It does seem that there was a definite prejudice against theatrical dancing on
the part of the more conservative section of the community, and of several members of the Catholic Church. This is a very ancient phenomenon!

In Dublin, during that decade in which Erina Brady worked and tried to im-
plant modern dance, there were several groups, schools, companies working in different dance styles: the Irish Ballet Club, run by Cepta Cullen; the Abbey School of
Ballet, by Miss Kelly; the Merrion School of Dancing; the Doreen Cuthbert School
of Dancing, in the vaudeville line; the Royalettes, with Alice Delgano in a more
free theatrical style, it seems; *An Ceol Cumann*, with George Leonard, specialised
in Irish dance. And there were such larger groups as the Dublin Musical Society,
the Old Belvedere Musical and Dramatic Society, the Lyric Theatre Company, who
were interested in dance.

It is certain that none were in the line of what they called "modern ballet",
which I still like to call creative dance – *Ausdrückstanz*, expressive dance, sometimes called expressionist. Quite rightly, as it was born at the same time as the expressionist movement in painting, and has a definite "rapport" with that.

June Fryer
Ireland's First Modern Dancer

June Fryer is Ireland's first modern dancer. She trained from the age of 18 at German-born Erina Brady's Irish School of Dance Art on Harcourt Street, where modern dance was first introduced to Ireland. She soon became one of Brady's two star pupils, along with Jacqueline Robinson. Fryer performed in many productions at the Peacock, the Gaiety and the Mansion House, as well as giving modern dance classes in Brigidine Convents in Castleknock, Abbeyleix, and Kilkenny. June subsequently trained with Sigurd Leeder in London, and became a member of the teaching faculty at Oxford Theatre School for a few years.

Upon her return to Dublin from Oxford, June began to teach dance at Stella Campbell's Dance Studio on Fitzwilliam Square. There she met her future husband, former dancer with the Ballets Jooss, Walter Kuhn, whom she collected from the boat at Dun Laoghaire when he came from Switzerland to obtain his teaching diploma in ballroom dancing. Kuhn had been in Dublin once before with the Ballets Jooss, playing the part of the young soldier in Kurt Jooss's famous anti-war ballet The Green Table *at the Gaiety Theatre in 1953. June and Walter married, and went on to teach ballroom dancing in their Blackrock living room, before retreating from the world of modern dance to raise their three children in Dublin.*

We spoke to June, who was recovering from a serious illness, and Walter, in the living room where they once gave ballroom dancing lessons.

June Fryer:

I ended up training with Erina Brady's Irish School of Dance Art through the headmistress in my school, Park House, on Morehampton Road. She was very artistically inclined — at morning assembly we would have a "picture of the week", and there was art on the wall. At about 16 or 17 years old, I wanted dance classes so this headmistress suggested to my mother that I should go to Erina.

Erina was a very strong woman, very unusual, and very bright. She was tall, and very striking-looking with long dark hair, and a very strong profile – very exotic. She had quite a clipped voice — very definite. In some ways she terrified the life out of me.

That's Erina with the painter Benny (Basil) Rakoczi — part of the White Stag Group, and Brian Boydell. She used to wear a fur coat, and she always wore this black beret. She had very penetrating eyes. She was a most unusual person, and stood out a mile when she was walking down Grafton Street.

It was a very bohemian scene. Erina knew all the arty people: Mainie Jellett, Benny (Racoszi), John Betjeman and other artists. They all used to come to the studio.

Erina had worked with Mary Wigman, who in some ways was like a goddess to her. The whole idea, everything Erina did, the way she spoke and moved about, was Mary Wigman-inspired. There was a pen line drawing of Mary Wigman hanging in the studio.

Erina Brady and Basil Rakoczi, 1943

Erina was fairly tough, and strong on creative work. A lot of it was our own ideas and our own work. During holiday time we always had to compose. We were given the music and the idea, and had to come back with the composition finished.

Erina was very much against classical ballet. She had to push with tremendous drive with this idea of the modern dance. The only thing we had done in school was Greek dance. There were some touring companies. But there wasn't anything like modern dance.

Erina's father was Irish. I always took it that her mother was Swiss because she went back to Switzerland. But I never knew whether she was German or Swiss, because during the war the German connection probably wasn't so fashionable. There were questions asked to me, and so on. Perhaps it was a German connection, I don't know. But Erina did have Irish family. There was a cousin — Constance Brady — who lived in Dublin and came to classes. She came from down the country. That's the only one I can think of.

Erina Brady, after she had left Ireland, in Brione, Tecine, Switzerland

That is Erina there, when we went to visit her quite a long time after she left Ireland and went to live in Switzerland. She had a house in Brione in Tecine. Muriel Graham, Erina's Irish pianist, emigrated to Switzerland with her. She taught there in a finishing school, and examined for the Academy.

Dublin was a very conservative place at the time. She would have been seen as *very* unusual. In some ways you kept very quiet about being a dancer – barefoot . . . can you imagine?

Erina used to go camping in Kerry. I went on a camping holiday with her one summer in Sneem. I can remember the cows walking over the tent, tripping over the guy ropes!

Erina's school was in 39 Harcourt Street, above a Craftworker's Stained Glass nearly opposite Earlsfort Terrace. She had a beautiful big studio with a big glass skylight. Her bed was in the room's alcove. It's amazing when you think that she slept there, and lived in the studio. The grand piano was up the other end of the room. It was quite big. We very often picnicked there. Michael Mac Liammóir and Hilton Edwards lived just above the studio, and Liam O'Laoghaire, the filmmaker, lived downstairs.

I went to her Irish School of Dance Art for three years from 1943 to 1946, fulltime. It was a full day's class with Erina. We did barre work in the morning. I'm trying to think, I might mix some of it up with the work I did with Sigurd Leeder in England afterwards. It was barefoot. For Erina's classes we wore a tunic, I think it was brown, and we had a knitted crossover top. We had to design and produce the costumes ourselves. Luckily my mother was great at sewing. My sister, Ann, who was seven years younger than me and went to Trinity, also danced. My mother, who had an artistic flair, was the one who pushed me towards the dance. My father just about put up with me doing it.

Any of our solos were choreographed by ourselves. Not the ballets, but the solo dances were all our own. We wore Mary Wigman-type flowing dresses. Some were short. There were a lot of people in that ballet [the *TB Ballet*], including people who took classes. Jacqueline and I were the only two doing the professional course. We taught children's classes. I can't remember any boys being in the classes. She got quite a number of pupils, considering that it was modern dance, not classical ballet. In those days classical was the thing.

I remember going to Kilkenny to teach a class for Erina. They thought I was a new student in because I was so young. The girls there weren't allowed to go barefoot. They had to wear socks. The nun said "the night before dance class is mending night". Hence they could mend all the holes in their socks, so as not to disgrace themselves going to the class. We always remember that.

In Kilkenny, the students were not allowed to stand in second position. That was very difficult you know. You start a class, go through all the positions, but you can't go into second. First to third, can you imagine? I don't know how we managed that, but we smoothed over it some way. Times have changed so much.

Jacqueline Robinson was then staying with the concert pianist Mrs Boxwell on Hatch Street. She gave recitals in the RDS, where she was on the music committee. I was allowed to go and have my lunch over there while Jacqueline practised. They used to have a ten-minute recital on RTÉ in the morning, just before the news. The studio was at the top of Henry Street. Jacqueline would make me go with her to turn the pages.

June Fryer practising poses in her back garden

Jacqueline had a very strong personality — in a way the opposite to me. We got on very well. I was with her for the two years she was in Dublin. Then I was three or four months in Paris with her. We performed in some theatre — I can't remember where. We stayed in a hotel near Montmartre. There was a boxing studio across the way, which they let us use to rehearse every day.

Erina used the Peacock for the performances. It was Austin Clarke, and verse-speaking. The response was pretty good. Sometimes Austin Clarke would come to her Harcourt Street studio and recite poetry. There would be a programme. Michael O'Higgins sang. Then there would be a break and I would dance. Quite often pianists would play. It was always interspersed with dance. The artists were always musicians – cellists, violinists – it was very interesting.

Gordon Lambert [art collector], David Hendrick, Barbara Warren [painter], and the painter Patrick Pye were part of it. Patrick was a young fellow. His mother had some connection with it. But we all met once a week or a fortnight in a pub on Dawson Street. Between six and seven o'clock. It was lovely because we would all meet casually and have a chat. Then afterwards we met in Baggot Street. It was grand because you'd meet, you didn't have to arrange, and you didn't have to go if you didn't want to.

June Fryer rehearsing outdoors at Clogher Head, Co. Louth

In those days women wouldn't go into pubs. I remember going up to the bar in the Royal Marine. When they asked what I wanted to drink I said a gin and tonic. My mother was absolutely shocked, "How dare you!"

Walter [Kuhn, June's husband] wasn't with the company in 1946, the first time we invited *Ballets Jooss* to come over to Erina's studio. The evening after the performance, my mother had to entertain the dancers from the *Ballets Jooss*. They came up to Erina's studio, and had drinks and bits and pieces to eat. Erina disappeared. She didn't attend. We were always surprised about that.

Then my mother and I asked Sigurd Leeder, who was there, could I go and join his school in London. He said yes. I needed an invitation to go to London, which I got from Jane Winearls.

Walter:
When I first came to Dublin in 1953, in *The Green Table* with *Ballets Jooss*, we were invited by somebody called Morrissey in Bray.

June:
The 1946 performance took place in the Gaiety. When you [Walter] were in it, it was at the Olympia — because there is a double ramp in the Gaiety, which isn't nice for dancing. The Olympia has a single ramp, which was much nicer. The Olympia is bigger but the Gaiety is like a real theatre – it has more atmosphere.

Walter:

The Green Table was a tremendous piece of choreography. It took you by storm. The idea is that the big heads come to the green table – like a negotiating table — to decide for peace or war, and they decide for war. The ballet showed the beginning of the war with the flag, the soldiers, all that happens during a war, the mothers, the children, the bar-scenes, the refugees. . . . Hans Zullig was the profiteer. And death was very strongly through it. You had all these different scenes, and then at the end, it was back to the green table. It had original music by Cohen. *The Green Table* came again later to the Abbey with Anna Jooss while I was working in Dublin. We could do with a green table now. When Erina Brady first came to Dublin, she had a photo in her studio of the *Ballets Jooss*, and I was in it.

Walter Kuhn (arms outstretched) in The Green Table

June:

Hanging up in the studio, can you believe it! Through Sigurd Leeder I eventually taught in the Oxford School of Theatre on the full-time course for professional students. I became a member of staff and stayed for two years in the late 1940s. I could have stayed, but there were pulls to bring me home. I didn't particularly want to leave. Eventually Stella Campbell was thinking of expanding her school in Dublin to have ballroom and modern ballet, and asked me would I join. I decided yes, and came home. It went down very well actually. I went back to teach in Park House, where I had gone to school, and in the Holy Child Convent in Killiney. I was teaching most of the time — not choreographing or performing. The nuns in Killiney were wonderful. Actually Walter came and taught a couple of classes after we got married in 1956. I remember once I had to bring my newborn child to the Mother Superior. She said, "You can leave her in my room in the carry-cot while you are teaching the class." Then she said, "I hope someone doesn't come in and think it's mine." She was so nice, really. She went from there to France I think.

Walter:

I remember when you were teaching ballroom in this very room in the late 1950s. We had a barre here along the wall. I would teach the girls. How was it? "Back, side . . ."

June:

"*To* the side", you say – but you said "backside"! And I always used to say, "you mustn't say back, side! You have to say *to* the side!" Of course, he always forgot!

Walter:

I caught some girls giggling in the mirror.

June:

Erina's work was very modern. When she left Dublin there was nothing. Just this big gap. Dance here was always a bit of an uphill battle. You were definitely a minority. Erina couldn't have gone on that much longer anyway. There was always a time when it was going to be finished. Jacqueline left. I left. Then going to Leeder and doing the Jooss method, in a way I started a complete new career. It was completely different from Wigman in style — probably more balletic. Jacqueline never came back to Dublin after we went to Paris. She went to Nottingham, and then to Paris, where she opened *L'Atelier de la Danse*, and met her husband, the poet Octave Gélinier. When I saw Martha Graham dancing, it was a complete shock to me. I thought she would be more like Wigman. But in some ways she was stronger, with a slightly harder style of dance. I only ever saw Wigman teaching. I didn't really miss performing. My main aim was teaching. I went in with the idea of teaching.

Walter:

I never missed it either.

June:

It's strange, isn't it? But between the *Folkwangschule* in Essen with Jooss and the different opera houses you had worn yourself out, dancing so much.

Walter:

I started in the electrical contracting business here in Dublin. But occasionally when June couldn't take her classes, I stood in for her, and then we did some classes together.

June:

When my daughter Monica was born I eventually was just teaching, giving holiday courses and so on. It was much later, through Fitzwilliam Square, that I met and worked with Carolyn Swift and Alan Simpson — before they started at the Pike Theatre. I did the movement there.

Walter:

I saw that. I had just arrived in Dublin from Switzerland.

June:

I remember being at a party in Carolyn's in Leeson Street and Brendan Behan came in, drunk as an owl. Oh, you had to bring him home one day!

Walter:

He was up in Paddy Cullen's in Ballsbridge. He lived up on Anglesea Road. He was staggering. I had the car outside. He fell into the car. I drove him home.

Notes

[1] "Further Follies", January 1955, and "Folly it Up", August 1955. See Swift, Carolyn, *Stage by Stage*, Dublin: Poolbeg Press, 1985.

[2] John Martin, *Introduction to the Dance*, New York: Dance Horizons, 1939.

[3] John Martin, *The Modern Dance*, New York: Dance Horizons, 1933.

Chapter 4

Chapter 4

The Evolution of Ireland's Contemporary Dance Landscape

The history of contemporary dance in Ireland has evolved as a discontinuous series of interruptions. When American dancer Terez Nelson (who returned to the US in 1981) choreographed two short pieces for Dublin City Ballet at the Pavillion, Dun Laoghaire in 1979 she was described on the programme as "the pioneer of contemporary dance in Ireland", as if Erina Brady had never existed. It might have been a little easier for Terez Nelson and Joan Davis had they known about the ground Erina Brady had broken in the 1940s with her Irish School of Dance Art, and collaborations at the Peacock Theatre. But they didn't, and that didn't stop them.

Dubliner Joan Davis had studied ballroom, tap and folkdance with Evelyn Burchill, and after the birth of her third child took up contemporary dance with Terez Nelson. In 1977 she founded the Dublin Contemproary Dance Studio, in conjunction with Karen Callaghan. Two years later, they founded Dublin Contemporary Dance Theatre. Davis taught in the Studio, as well as dancing and choreographing for the company. Her choreography often used spoken verse or story-telling, but was perhaps at its best (according to Carolyn Swift, who saw it), "in exploring her Jewish roots in pieces such as *Ishmael*, from the Book of Genesis, with music composed and played by Jolyon Jackson and Sean Devitt". Finola Cronin was briefly part of the company, before Americans Robert Connor and Loretta Yurick joined in 1980. Later that year Mary Nunan became part of the company. In 1986 Paul Johnson[1] joined this influential company. In the meantime, John Scott (another dancer/choreographer who went on to found his own dance company), presented an evening of dance at UCD DramSoc, entitled "Exit Glympse", and occasionally hung posters for Dublin Contemporary Dance Theatre.

When the Arts Council withdrew funding from all dance companies in 1988/89, the dance community galvanised, and out of the embers of these cuts the current contemporary dance landscape was born. Robert Connor and Loretta Yurick incorporated Dance Theatre of Ireland in 1989 with *La Beauté des Fleurs*. The initiation of The New Music/New Dance Festival in 1989 (which ran until 1994) was instrumental in the development and nurturing of new talent, like John Scott, who in 1991 founded Irish Modern Dance Theatre; David Bolger, who founded CoisCéim Dance Theatre in 1995; and the younger Liz Roche who, fostered by them all, founded Rex Levitates in 1999. The festival enterprise continued until 1996 in the form of Dance Fest (1995–1996), after which there was a hiatus until the advent of the International Dance Festival Ireland in 2002 with Catherine Nunes at the helm. The developmental Institute of Choreography and Dance (ICD) in Cork (founded in 1995; Arts Council funding withdrawn in 2006) nurtured the work of Michael Keegan Dolan who would go on to found his own Fabulous Beast Dance Theatre in 1997.

Meanwhile, in the academic realm, the development of the Contemporary Stream of the Masters degree programme in Dance Performance, under the direction of Mary Nunan at University of Limerick's Irish World Academy of Music and Dance, is another watershed in the validation of contemporary dance as an art form in Ireland.

In this chapter these key movers tell their own stories of how (against all odds, usually), their companies, and the International Dance Festival Ireland, came to be.

Some Key Contemporary Dance Dates[2]

1979–1989:   Dublin Contemporary Dance Theatre

1983–1996:   Dance Council of Ireland

1985:   Peter Brinson Report ("The Dancer and the Dance")
for the Arts Council

1988:   Daghdha Dance Company

1989–1994:   New Music/New Dance Festival

1989:   Dance Theatre of Ireland

1989:   The Association of Professional Dancers in Ireland
(www.prodanceireland.com) (renamed "Dance Ireland" in 2006)

1991:   Irish Modern Dance Theatre

1995–1996:   Dance Fest

1995:   Institute of Contemporary Dance, Cork (www.instchordance.com)
(Arts Council funding cut in January 2006)

1995:   CoisCéim Dance Theatre

1997:   Fabulous Beast Dance Theatre

1999:   Rex Levitates Dance Theatre

1999:   MA in Dance Performance at University of Limerick

2002:   International Dance Festival Ireland (biennial; annual from 2008)

Joan Davis
Founder, Dublin Contemporary Dance Theatre

*J*oan Davis, founder of what has long been thought to be Ireland's first modern
dance company, Dublin Contemporary Dance Theatre (1979–89) is widely
known among her colleagues as the woman who, along with Terez Nelson, was
responsible for introducing modern dance to Ireland. This is of course after Erina
Brady's Irish School of Dance Art disappeared without a trace in the 1950s. While
Brady had imported the German aesthetic of Mary Wigman's Ausdrückstanz,
Joan Davis began by championing the American modern dance movements of
Martha Graham.

Dublin Contemporary Dance Theatre performed original work created by
company members and international choreographers (commissioned), touring nationally and internationally. The company also performed in schools, and
taught classes for the public from its studio (first in Harold's Cross and later at
the Dance Centre, Digges Lane). Classes were taught by company members as
well as guest teachers (open to the public). Originally set up as Dublin Contemporary Dance Studio, Inc. by Joan Davis and Karen Callaghan, Callaghan left for
New York within a year. The company operated as a collective from 1982 to 1989.
Here, Joan Davis explains how it all came about.

When I started in the early 1970s, basically there was no contemporary dance in
Ireland. It had not been seen at all.

I was born in 1945, and from a very early age I went to tap dancing class with
Christine Kane and Evelyn Burchall in their school on Harcourt Street. There was
no trace of Erina Brady. As far as I knew, and from the responses people were giving
us, they had never seen anything like this before.

The first time I saw contemporary dance was when Jean Erdman's dance production of Joyce's *Finnegan's Wake* came to the Gate Theatre. I was totally mes-
merised by it. Then I started dancing with Terez Nelson, who had trained with Martha Graham in the States. She had moved to Dublin and started teaching in a basement studio in Monkstown. I went to those classes, just totally fell in love with it,
and worked with her for about two years. First, in about 1974–75, we put on some
shows in Saint Mark's Hall in Pearse Street. Then we went into Project.

I remember the first performances we did in Saint Mark's Hall. People were
just astounded, and those who came loved it. They really were intrigued, the movements were so unusual. Then in Project, Terez choreographed the whole show. We
did *Barnarda Alba*, and she had a lot of pieces that she revived herself.

I remember Project being full. But they were more literal pieces, so people could follow the story. As I went on into choreography I wasn't so interested in that kind of dance. So initially people were intrigued, but when they couldn't quite get it, or it got more abstract, it was just an alien art form.

They would have been equally confused and bemused by Pina Bausch's work. We are so used to narrative, literal, and cognitive-type things. But it is very rare that the aesthetic of the body moving through space is appreciated in itself. unless it is a particular kind of body, doing particular kinds of things.

Eventually Terez and I parted ways. I had already started to teach a little bit for her, and to go and see what was happening in the London School of Contemporary Dance. I really believed in contemporary dance and wanted to bring it and share it with others here. So that's what I did.

For about two years I rented studios here and there. I would go over every second week to London and do a day of classes, then come back the next day and teach what I had learned in the classes.

What was most exciting to me was that I started to see some dancers who had very good technique but when left to their own devices without choreography were very lost. Other dancers didn't necessarily have good technique, but when they were left to their own devices to move in their own way, were exciting dancers to watch.

I wanted to cultivate the essence of the dancer, and the notion that everybody could be a dancer, really, if they had the passion for it. That came from the fact that I was 29 when I started to dance, and my body was very stiff. So technically I was very limited. But I knew I was a dancer, and still am to this day. It was something about really tapping into that for everybody. You didn't have to be ballet-based to be a dancer.

> I wanted to cultivate the essence of the dancer, and the notion that everybody could be a dancer, really, if they had the passion for it.

I got the studio in Harold's Cross in 1976, and started to teach from there. The classes were very popular. I couldn't cope with the demand. I was still going to London, where I met other dancers who were finishing their training, so I invited them over to take on the teaching. Ruth Way came and it took off from there even more.

People heard about it and started to come. So we started to choreograph, and we did some shows, at Project Arts Centre, and at the Eblana Theatre, and then it started to spread. We went into schools, and then around the country touring. It was very innovative and exciting – genuinely pioneering. Dublin Contemporary Dance Theatre was formed in 1976–77. Those first few years were challenging, but exciting.

It happened organically. Initially Ruth Way came from London. Judy Cole, an English woman who had been living in West Cork for a while, showed up at the door. She was a dancer from England but she wasn't using her dance skills here.

Then Robert Connor and Loretta Yurick read about us in a review. They had come to visit Ireland, and were down in Tralee. They came up and joined.

Prior to that, I had started out with Karen Callaghan, and we as a duet were going into schools and trying to choreograph pieces to show. I remember doing a duet with Finola Cronin to Eric Satie's piano pieces in the Project Arts Centre. Then Finola went to Germany and joined up with Pina Bausch. Paul Johnson came to the studio and started his dance work. He went away to train, and then came back and was part of the company for a while. Then of course Mary Nunan joined. So for a

Photo: Fergus Bourke

Mary Nunan, Loretta Yurick, Robert Connor, Joan Davis and Paul Johnson in Single Line Traffic *(1986)*

long time we were four or five, and then we went back to four for a number of years and toured around. It was Mary Nunan, Robert Connor, Loretta Yurick and myself. John Scott used to put up our posters, on his bicycle. We were always delighted to offer him the work.

The audience really couldn't relate to the work very well. They came initially out of curiosity, but it was very abstract for them. The highest form of praise you could get after a show was that somebody would come up to you and say, "you must be very fit". Then you knew you had touched them somehow or somewhere.

But for dance as an art form, to be really appreciated . . . well, I think it is still on that journey. It is very difficult for a country of people who are not body-based, and not used to seeing movement, let alone abstract movement. It is extremely hard to relate to it. Music, yes; drama and theatre, yes; but dance? That's still a challenge to get audiences in, and have it even moderately appreciated, aside from having it understood at all.

But for dance as an art form, to be really appreciated . . . well, I think it is still on that journey.

Dublin Contemporary Dance Theatre finished in 1989 when all the funding was withdrawn from dance. It was very abrupt. We were in rehearsal when we got the news that our funding was not being renewed. The main ballet company, run by

Joan Denise Moriarty, was struck off completely. I'll never forget that she sent us a cheque for £50 when she heard the news. I was very moved by that. That was a woman who really understood what it was like to try to keep a vision going.

Prior to that we had been getting quite good funding. We had been very highly recommended in the Brinson report. Peter Brinson had come to Dublin and strongly recommended what we were doing as deserving of funding. But even before his visit, we were getting about £80,000 per year, which was pretty good in 1987/88. It's never enough funding, but you could certainly do a lot with that amount – which we did.

So of course when you've stepped up to that level of operating and planning and then the funding gets cut, you can't do anything at all. But up to that the Arts Council had supported

Photo: Fergus Bourke

Loretta Yurick, Joan Davis, Robert Connor, Joan Smith and Randy Glynn in Modern Daze

us as best they could, given that there was no history of contemporary dance to be supported. It was all about ballet. I remember going in and almost crying on Arthur Lappin's desk: "What will I do? How will we keep going?" He was lovely; he was always very reassuring and hopeful.

We did keep going. We had very renowned choreographers come over, like Sarah and Jerry Pearson, Richard Haisma, Mark Taylor and Yoshiko Chuma. We also choreographed our own work. It was a unique company in that way, because we were all very creative beings. Part of my ethos was that we should all have an opportunity to create as well.

I would choreograph some pieces, Robert and Loretta choreographed, Mary choreographed, and then we would have choreographers come over to choreograph us. Then Robert, Loretta and I joined forces on artistic direction. We were co-artistic directors after a certain point.

I've actually stopped going to theatre and dance, and am now working from a different perspective in dance. So I'm personally not as interested in seeing set choreography as I used to be. But certainly the dancers generally are highly trained now. The training methods have improved no end. You could not get into a company now unless you had a very high level of technique, in both ballet and contemporary. The dancer has to be very skilled.

Recently I have been exploring a certain approach to dance and movement that comes from a place very deep inside the body. It is not improvisation but it is a search for authenticity of movement. Where an impulse will arrive in the body, and it will come through in a form or a movement, or a sequence of movements, and then it will possibly die away again. It is like learning to listen to one's own movement impulses, at a very deep level. So there is no choreography, no set, themes, or anything. You simply go out, and wait, and it happens. Hopefully.

> *It is like learning to listen to one's own movement impulses, at a very deep level. So there is no choreography, no set, themes, or anything. You simply go out, and wait, and it happens. Hopefully.*

It is moving into a performance context. The work is called *Maya Lila* — "Maya" meaning "illusion" in Sanskrit, and "Lila" meaning "play". So it is developing its own form now as well. I am working with some of the younger dancers who are interested in that kind of approach where they don't necessarily have to learn steps or sequences, although they also work in that field. They are learning to "source" movement in a different way, and to express it in the moment. It's very immediate, and very scary too because you don't know what's going to come up or appear.

I have been researching and developing it over the last two years. This will be my third year developing it. There is still room for other people to come in and explore it with me. I reckon there are about another two years of research and development before it can be offered to the public. Because it is very new, cutting-edge work to be using this approach in a performance context. This research and development has been funded by the Arts Council, for which I am very grateful.

I've sold my studio in Harold's Cross and I'm working out in a wonderful place between Bray and Greystones. I like to work outdoors. *Maya Lila* takes place out in nature, as well as inside.

Terez Nelson faded out fairly soon after we worked together – I think she went to live in London. I met Karen Callaghan through her. Adrienne Browne, one of Ter-

Photo: Fergus Bourke

Loretta Yurick and Robert Connor in The Longest Night

ez's dancers, is still working away. She and I worked together. But when Adrienne went to London to study, I was the only one working in contemporary dance in Ireland. So I did pioneer it here. Whoever had any interest in dance, they would come through me.

It is very exciting to me to see how people like Finola Cronin went on to do such wonderful things with Pina Bausch, and is now back here lobbying for dance. Paul Johnson did brilliant work with his Mandance. He brought a huge thing to contemporary dance. He's also lobbying for dance. Robert Connor and Loretta Yurick are still doing it and putting it out through Dance Theatre of Ireland. Mary Nunan of course with her MA course in Limerick, and also being on the Arts Council, is lobbying for dance. That is just so gratifying to me because in my day when I started the word wasn't even known. What is contemporary dance? Nobody knew what it was. It still has a long way to go. There are still very fixed and limited views of what contemporary dance is, or even what dance is. The attitude was, "It's only ballet. Do an arabesque. Oh, that's dance." So it's still down at the bottom. But it's a hundred times better than it ever was. So it's all good.

Robert Connor and Loretta Yurick
Founders, Dance Theatre of Ireland

*B**oth from America, Robert Connor and Loretta Yurick's dance training began in Minneapolis where they studied abstract expressionism with Nancy Hauser and Hanya Holm. Robert and Loretta, who have BAs in Psychology and Urban Studies, respectively, came to Ireland in 1980, and found Joan Davis. Once they began to perform in and choreograph for her company, Dublin Contemporary Dance Theatre, they never looked back. Here, they describe their journey to founding their company, Dance Theatre of Ireland, and how they became integral to the Irish contemporary dance landscape.*

Loretta:
We came to Ireland from America in the early 1980s, and met up with Joan Davis, a founder of Dublin Contemporary Dance Theatre. We worked with her from 1980 until 1989 when the Arts Council cut funding to all dance companies.

In those days there was a very vibrant literary and theatre world, with maybe even more theatre companies than today. Therefore it was very open to dance. We could do a lunchtime performance or an evening performance and it would be packed. But while there were lots of classical dancers, with Dublin City Ballet and Irish National Ballet, there were very few professional contemporary dancers. Many of the classically trained dancers – like Muirne Bloomer and Aisling Doyle – went into contemporary dance.

*Muirne Bloomer, Jeffrey Fox, Antje Rose, James Smith and
Loretta Yurick in* La Beauté des Fleurs

Some people who were into classical dance began to get into contemporary dance. Contemporary dance was quite new. Because it was theatrical, it was not that different for Irish populations. If you had a contemporary dance class there would be six to eight people, whereas a ballet class would have 25 or 30.

The Project Arts Centre and Peacock Theatre were the main venues for dance. Gradually the dance community and the number of dancers was growing.

If you look at Project Arts Centre statistics I have no doubt that the overall numbers who see a dance show have remained relatively the same. You'd be amazed at how many people went to dance in 1986.

Robert:

Every year there were visiting dance companies at the Gaiety and Olympia, like Murray Lewis, Harlem Dance Theatre, Bremen Dance Theatre, Lar Lubovitch and Ballet Rambert. The 1989 Arts Council cuts had a knock-on effect of losing audiences for the international shows too. So people stopped bringing the international shows to Ireland.

When Irish National Ballet was cut, that was the end of dance on the stage of the National Theatre, severing dance from the national image. That had a negative impact of putting dance off to the side as a performing art. Not until the 2002 International Dance Festival was a contemporary dance company (Merce Cunningham) allowed on the stage of the National Theatre again.

Loretta:

While there was a thriving local company scene in the 1980s, they could bring in Harlem Dance Theatre, Lar Lubovitch, and Bremen Dance Theatre. Then when local manifestations of the art were cut, there was deterioration in the international interest. It became easy to say that there isn't an audience for dance. Later, people thought that maybe the way to build it is through a dance festival. However, like the Edinburgh Festival, which has dance, theatre and opera all within the same festival, the Dublin Theatre Festival used to bring in international dance companies. It was a pity that dance stopped being programmed into the Dublin Theatre Festival.

Robert:

People speak about dance here in the 1950s, or in the '40s. There has been an audience for dance. Maybe in the '40s and '50s it was primarily for visits from the Royal Ballet. Perhaps the palate of taste has changed and grown. But there is probably a core of 2,000 people in Dublin who are the dance audience.

Loretta:

I don't want to shatter the idea that there is a blossoming of dance lately but I think it is vitally important to go below the surface. Just because there is more and more of it doesn't mean that there are many more people going to it. Sometimes I think if too many shows hit at the same time audiences are smaller than one would be happy with. I am sure that the International Dance Festival showing people different work from all over the world is a great shot in the arm. You need to feel like you see a breadth of work. It's exciting and inspiring for everybody — artists working here and anybody who enjoys dance.

There are a lot of people who are prominent in the dance community today who were around during the dearth period in the late '80s. All dance companies got cut, and you just worked on a project-to-project basis. But that was the beginning of people getting together and applying for money to do a production. Many companies had their seeds in that period. It has gone from a few companies, to quite a few independent companies, and continues to grow, but there are no large companies like Dublin City Ballet.

Robert:

What was interesting about working with Joan Davis was that she was into trying lots of different things. We did many of our performances in the Peacock Theatre — so the facility of the National Theatre was open to contemporary dance in the '80s. Think of it! If that had continued, contemporary dance may have become more mainstream, and faster than it has. Performing in the Peacock made a difference.

Joan's husband, the late Gerald Davis, was a painter and we did a piece in a show where Gerald painted on material that we were wearing while we moved. Joan called it "Action Painting". That was quite experimental. She also made a lot of headway in terms of collaborating with musicians, and in live improvisation, with Brian Dunning, jazz flautist, Jolyon Jackson, another innovator in music, and Tommy Hafferty. So there would be this element of jazz improvisation and dance improvising.

> *Joan's husband, the late Gerald Davis, was a painter and we did a piece in a show where Gerald painted on material that we were wearing while we moved. Joan called it "Action Painting"… That was quite experimental.*

For example, we could have a set number of sequences, and we'd be wearing different colours. The audience could call out to us, "Red! Do sequence six!"; they would get a feel for a live composition that's directed by the audience.

We did a whole programme based on using language in a performance, called *Word Works*. We recognised the literary strength of theatre, and we were trying to make a bridge with that. At that stage we were working somewhat collectively. Mary Nunan, Loretta, myself and Joan each made a piece. That was one of the great laboratory aspects of working with Joan. It was a fertile ground for us to develop as creative as well as interpretive artists. Joan would also invite, and we would help choose, guest choreographers. In the '80s predominantly emerging choreographers from the States would come and be in residence for six weeks. They would teach us, which was great for our technical training, and then make work with us, which was great for our creative training. So when we weren't working with a guest artist we would be collaborating on our own ideas with each other.

Photo: Tony Higgins

Robert Connor and Loretta Yurick in Fuschia

Loretta:

All those names Robert just mentioned are still in the dance industry. Mary Nunan, who is on the Arts Council, went on to be director of Daghdha Dance company; Paul Johnson has been an independent choreographer, has had his own company, and is now working for the Arts Council. So there was a brightness there to begin with. There was a company, which remained a framework within which you could evolve and make work.

Now, many years later, I realise the necessary support that dance needs in an administrative structure. You must have a place to work, some level of administration, and a continuity of somebody who can plan the productions. It was really important that people could grow out of a company situation where they had interpretive as well as choreographic contributions to what was going on inside the company and could work continually. That's harder to come by these days.

Photo: Tony Higgins

Robert Connor and Loretta Yurick in
Body Travels Time

In 1989, unbeknownst to us – we weren't very politically aware at the time – there was a change in the Arts Council. Paul McGuinness, Michael Colgan and others came on to the Council. It was probably a directive from the government at the time; they changed what they wanted to fund. In February they voted dance out, and film in. And that was the end of dance. They just cut the companies.

There was nothing so progressive then as there has been in the last eight years under Patricia Quinn and Ciaran Benson's direction, with such a high level of consultation with artists on a publicly acknowledged and known plan for the arts, derived from the population. With Quinn, you saw the document, could give feedback on it, say what you thought of it, and what they should do. In the last ten years the Arts Council moved to that level of openness. Whether they agree with what you do or not, you can actually have some input into the development until they arrive at a place where they can say, "These are the objectives of the arts, this is what we want to see happen, and these are the kinds of things we will fund." In the earlier days you just put your grant application in and maybe you were in, and maybe you were out. You hoped for the best, and you didn't know how you were judged. If you got funded, you didn't know why; if you got cut, you didn't know why you got cut. You had no idea.

One day we came to work and we got a letter saying we no longer were in receipt of funding. We had all kinds of dancers assembled for the next show, and we had to let everybody go. Nigel Rolfe was doing the design, Rupert Murray the lighting. We had to just turn to everybody and say, "We don't have a company, we can't pay you." Then there was the entire legal process of winding up the company.

Robert:

We did a performance in Powerscourt Townhouse several lunchtimes, put up banners, and gathered petitions to try and put it on paper and show the Arts Council the number of voices who said, "Hey, we don't agree with this." But we were really stonewalled in terms of getting a reconsideration or finding out the reasons why we were cut.

Joan had taken a sabbatical before when she made up her mind, and this really clinched it, that she didn't want to keep on trying to work with the Arts Council, and make performances. She was more interested in healing using movement and voice. So Loretta and I asked a number of our board members would they help us set up another vehicle through which we could keep going. We had a project underway with some French choreographers, Isabelle Dubouloz and Pierre Douissant.

Loretta:

We had a project scheduled to happen. We never told them that it was cancelled and we didn't have a penny to make it. We had a meeting with somebody in the Arts Council, and said we wanted to go ahead and make this show. Martin Drury, Dance and Drama Officer at the time, said to put in an application. We did, and lo and behold, under a new name we got some funding to make the show.

Robert:

We had already proposed that project as Dublin Contemporary Dance Theatre, and the same project under a different setup was funded.

Loretta:

That took us years to figure out. Years later we discovered it had nothing to do with what we were doing. In fact there were loads of people who supported what was going on in contemporary dance. But they had to be seen at Council level to have levelled everything. Not only the ballet company, which was in six digits at the time, and we may have been at about £80,000. They had to throw out everything. We thought it was really personal, that they didn't like what we were doing.

So we got enough money to make that project, *La Beauté des Fleurs*, and we incorporated Dance Theatre of Ireland, simply as a way to make work. You had to have an entity to receive funding. We were not finished making work. That project was with Dubouloz and Douissant. Having seen their performance in Florence, we really liked their work, so invited them to make this piece for which they had won Bagnolet. It was nominated for a *Sunday Tribune*/Dublin Theatre Festival Award. A very beautiful show, it was a blend of Butoh and dance. They had studied for years with Kazuo Ohno. I remember several of the Arts Council members coming backstage saying, "I know this might seem backhanded but that was the best thing I've ever seen. And I'm so glad you carried on." Again, you are so naïve, you don't really understand the significance of it at the time. We didn't know them or what role they might have played. We were just doing what we do.

That was our first production as DTI. I think the definition of an artist is that you are going to do what you want to do whether anybody wants it or not. You are going to find the way. That's a real hard lesson to learn. Maybe people think they are entitled. You are not really entitled. You have to make it happen each time.

> *I think the definition of an artist is that you are going to do what you want to do whether anybody wants it or not. You are going to find the way. That's a real hard lesson to learn.*

Robert:

We got our notice of being cut in February and we fought around it for a couple of months. Then we founded Dance Theatre of Ireland in June. It was incorporated in September. We put a show on in the Dublin Theatre Festival that year. The Festival programmed a lot of dance in those days.

We were able financially to do one production a year between '91 and '95. When we set up Dance Theatre of Ireland we wanted to keep up the outreach aspect, which was very central to Dublin Contemporary Dance Theatre. With Dublin Contemporary we would do daylight performances in school halls and then do workshops. With DTI we wanted to get the young people to come to the theatre (a) so they'd step across the threshold of theatre-going, and (b) so they would see a performance with the lighting and enhanced sound to get the full experience. We set that programme up by applying to the Ireland Funds.

At that time [1989] the professional dance community coalesced to create what later became the Association of Professional Dancers and Choreographers [and became Dance Ireland in 2006]. Loretta and I were part of setting that up as a way that dancers could continue to train when they weren't actually working on something. We were chairman and secretary for ten years.

Photo: Tony Higgins

Muirne Bloomer, J.J. Formento and Ella Clarke in
Like Water Flowing East

The Dance Council of Ireland, an earlier organisation which was around for about 10 years, from 1983, set up a number of workshops for composers and choreographers together, which developed into a showcase called the New Music/New Dance Festival (1989–1994). We'd do one production of our own and then do a shorter production that we could showcase in the New Music/New Dance Festival, giving us two performing opportunities for the year.

Loretta:

When I think about it now – after 1989 we were never paid well, and never paid through the year. It would be for a very limited period of time. We had other jobs to support ourselves. We were unemployed a lot between '89 and the mid-'90s when the Arts Council began to reinstate dance. There was a whole period when we would be employed by the company for maybe four months of the year. We would be unemployed for the rest of the year, or working other jobs plus working on the company setting up for the next show.

Robert:

I think our heels were too well dug in to leave. We were determined that dance wouldn't be snuffed out. Throughout the '90s the mission was to keep making work and keep dance on the map. Through our own work, through the Dance Council, through the APDI, there was a huge lobbying and politicising effort that needed to be done. For years all that writing, meeting and lobbying took a lot of our time. But that's not the art.

Loretta:

If you are a dancer you know what struggle is. Being a dancer *is* a struggle. You have to train so long. You do it because you love it. But it is a discipline, and does involve a bit of pain. You grow up on that. You don't stop doing what you do because it's painful, or because it's hard. The training of a dancer is really life-skill training. Because you try to be insurmountable, better than you were yesterday, and make a work that's better than the last one you made. That ethos of continual life-long learning and putting yourself in a situation where you are challenged and have to come up with the goods is a big part of what dancers do. That's why I have an enormous respect for dancers. They can grow into being good choreographers, lobbyists, passionate speakers, because they have the passion and they have developed the discipline and skill. So you don't just throw in the towel when something bad happens.

> *If you are a dancer you know what struggle is. Being a dancer is a struggle. You have to train so long. You do it because you love it.*

Robert:

Another decision we made when we set up DTI was to make work in a European format – full-length work – partly because of what we were seeing in Europe. Pina Bausch is the first one that comes to mind. In Dublin Contemporary Dance Theatre we had tended to work on performances or shows made up of a number of pieces. That model – a programme of three or four pieces – is an American model.

The first full-length piece we did, *Freedom's Gait*, in 1990, dealt with the essential concept of confinement and freedom. Not about being in jail but more about if you are in a relationship or a job you don't like, being trapped by your self, your own feelings. We looked at this concept of freedom in many different ways, brainstorming around associations, themes — personal and political. We used white helium balloons, swinging chairs, blinds, and a set designed by the performance/visual artist Nigel Rolfe.

Freedom's Gait coincided with the release of Brian Keenan. We were about to start rehearsals when we heard Brian Keenan on the radio giving his press conference from the castle. We contacted Brian to see if we could use any of that transcript in the piece because it was so much about the moment of release from confinement. He did give us permission, but we didn't use any of it in the end. We stayed in touch with him and he came and saw a studio performance just before we were going to premiere. He was very moved, saying he couldn't understand how we had managed in movement to convey so much about his experience.

> *He [Brian Keenan] was very moved, saying he couldn't understand how we had managed in movement to convey so much about his experience.*

Robert Connor, Sam Usher, Antje Rose and Loretta Yurick in Freedom's Gait

Photo: Tony Higgins

Loretta:

I had made this duet based on the loss of my sister, who was electrocuted in Alaska. It was actually a duet about she and I, but because I made it on two male dancers [Connor himself and Ming Yam Low, a Malaysian Dancer] it was coming from a similar realm of loss, pain and opening of great compassion. No matter how many premieres you have done – you are absolutely nervous, never feel good enough, and never ready. But that was probably the only premiere where I was very confident about touching the bone because Brian had seen it and he had wept. Watching the duet, Brian Keenan recognised the positions that he had been in. He wrote some beautiful things to us about the work. If you can move someone like that to tears you really

Photo: Tony Higgins

Rachel Lambert, Karim Karim, Loretta Yurick and Robert Connor in Dances in Dreams

know you have hit a chord. The wonderful thing about the power of dance is that it goes beyond language. That would be one of our objectives.

Our early '80s work would have been very experimental and very improvisational. There were a couple of years where we did improvisation as a performance. That really honed our skills as dancers, to be able to improvise on stage. It makes you a terribly creative dancer, and is a good skill for becoming a choreographer. Then we moved into a lot of post-modern work, with text and post-modern movement, like *Modern Daze*, with Nina Martin and Yoshiko Chuma, both from New York.

In the '90s we began to do more dance-theatre work which would have had thematic content like *Freedom's Gait* or a full-length programme called *Dances in Dreams*, very influenced by the Hopi Indians and tribal cultures. All these works used objects, sets and images.

Robert:

We commissioned *Touching the Moon* from Janet Smith, a British choreographer. In 1995 we made *Bonefire*, inspired by the ceasefire.

Loretta:

By the end of the '90s and increasingly now we have been working more abstractly. We pulled back a little bit from thematic content into just working with movement. That has led us to working with new technology. Technology gives you options of how to view the movement, putting it in three-dimensional form on screen, and giving different perspectives.

Robert:

In some of the shows we made a composite of what is moving on the screen with the dancers moving on stage. So compositionally we are working with both the projected elements and the live elements. It brought me closer to working from a stronger visual orientation, rather than emotive.

Loretta:

The concept was almost that of an installation. So if we got a review saying, "This wasn't dance, this wasn't theatre, this is more like installation", we would go "Yes!"

People are working in different idioms now. The profession has expanded and there are more approaches to dance. Dance is now happening across the country. That's exciting. In Wexford, Galway, Limerick and Donegal there are people working in dance, certainly more so than in the '80s and '90s.

Mary Nunan
Founder, Daghdha Dance Company

After attaining her B.Ed in physical education from Limerick's Thomond College of Education in 1976, Mary Nunan's considerable journey in dance began in New York when she studied Hawkins and Limon techniques from 1977 to 1980. Here she recounts how she began to dance professionally with Dublin Contemporary Dance Theatre in 1981, eventually leaving to found Limerick's Daghdha Dance Company in 1988, which she guided as artistic director until 1999. Since then she has choreographed and performed for other companies, and is director of the Contemporary Dance Stream of the MA in Contemporary Dance at University of Limerick's Irish World Academy of Music and Dance. Mary is also a member of the Arts Council.

I worked with Dublin Contemporary Dance Theatre from 1981 to 1986. Though it was a repertory company in which we created our own choreographies in addition to the work of guest choreographers, I felt that I needed to branch out on my own. So I left Dublin Contemporary Dance Theatre to spend more time exploring my own work as a choreographer.

In 1986 Teresa Leahy invited me to be dancer-in-residence in what was then Thomond College of Education, now University of Limerick. The residency was funded by the Arts Council, Thomond College and Mary Immaculate College.

Teresa had a real dedication and commitment to working with dance, so that was a fertile environment for me to come into. At the time I was working with the

Physical Education students who had quite a lot of dance programmed into their curriculum. They were great to experiment with ideas, because they were very physical and very open. I found it quite nice to work for a while with movement outside the demands of a professional company.

However, after two years in Limerick as a dancer-in-residence I began to feel isolated. I wanted to have more dance practitioners around. I thought the way to do that was to get more money from the Arts Council to start a company.

In 1989, Arts Council funding to Dublin Contemporary Dance Theatre and Irish National Ballet was cut. Apparently one of the reasons given was, "We have no infrastructure for dance in Ireland and we need to have an education company."

I had an education background, and an under-graduate degree in Physical Education, with a capac-ity to teach, and a comfort with that area. So when I approached the Council for support in 1988 they were very interested in sup-porting the company as an educational company. However, I had problems with a company being just an educational company. I mean "just" not in any way to diminish it, but I felt that

Megan Buchanan, Claire O'Dea and Paris Payne in Territorial Claims

unless I was going forward with a renewal of what was intriguing me about the form I could not enrich the work, either as a choreographic practice or as an element of dance education in schools. I felt it needed to have both aspects.

I was committed to engaging with the art form in the broadest possible sense of the word. Part of Daghdha's brief was to undertake dance-in-education, touring a programme to schools all over Ireland. We did that, eight weeks at a go, maybe five schools a week, and 8,000 children in eight weeks. Though it was great, and very welcomed by the schools, it was a gruelling schedule. We would drive to a school, get in, do the performance, teach the workshops in the afternoon, drive to the next place, get into a bed and breakfast, and so on. So Daghdha would appear in Mayo on a foggy or frosty February morning, out of the clouds! Many of the pupils would never have seen anything like "contemporary dance" before or afterwards. However, I felt it needed an awful lot more contextualising. People did get a lot out of it, but that's hardly what you'd call an education in dance.

As an education company we couldn't cover for the fact that there was little or no dance education happening in the schools. In fairness to the PE teachers, they did as much as they could teaching and preparing for us to come. They would teach five weeks of dance as part of their Physical Education programme for the year. But that was all they could teach because they had to include basketball and other sports on their curriculum.

We'd arrive, and immediately set up to perform on hard, cold concrete floors. It was very hard on dancers. We tried to find all sorts of strategies to improve it. Instead of having the whole school (500 to 800) pupils coming to see the show, we would try and limit it to 200, and each one of those would have a workshop. We always went on to modify to see if we could have a better environment for the dancers and more intimate contact with the pupils. Giving as much as we could, while trying to protect the professional dancers. I couldn't risk injuries to them.

Claire O'Dea and Tania Tempest-Hay in Territorial Claims

I have a problem with packaging "education". I continuously worked towards a model in which all elements of the company's programme were inherently educational. This has been kept up by Yoshiko Chuma, and Daghdha's current artistic director, Michael Klien. The programmes are always shot through with an interesting educational aspect. I like the sense of education in that broader sense.

While there was very little understanding of what we were doing in Ireland, we did establish an international reputation for our work. For example, when *Territorial Claims* was made in 1994 it was slammed. But I knew it was a good piece and was determined to get it shown outside of Ireland. It was invited to the South Bank Centre in London as part of Bagnolet choreographic platform. The feedback was very positive and we were consequently invited to show it at the prestigious *Tanz im August* Festival in Berlin and the following year to Munich. This recognition was important. I felt the work was valued and understood – not necessarily as "good" or "bad" but as unique and distinctive. It had something to say. After this the Company received invitations to tour other works to international festivals. In 1997 we made a screen adaptation of *Territorial Claims* which was selected to be shown at the Dance for Camera Festival in the Lincoln Centre in New York.

For my own work as an artist to survive, it has been important to have links not only with the community of practitioners in Ireland, and the general public, but also with the international community. There are incredibly sophisticated artists *here in Ireland* making very interesting work *right now*. It

> There are incredibly sophisticated artists here in Ireland making very interesting work right now. It has the range that you would get in any country.

has the range that you would get in any country. But I feel that – though it is not unique to Ireland – for all kinds of political or historical reasons, there still is a very deep level of discomfort with regard to conceptual work in dance. Though the community has expanded because there are more people practising, and there is a much more informed body of practitioners and audiences, the art form is still very marginal. I feel contemporary dance here is still almost an underground activity.

Between Daghdha Dance Company, the MA in Dance Performance and White Space, there is a great buzz around the environment for dance practice here in Limerick now. This has been building systematically since 1986.

White Space, which provided a framework for artists from the Judson Church era to meet with the community of practitioners here, was set up by myself and Yoshiko Chuma in 2000. Pioneering artists like Steve Paxton,

Jean Hall, Gideon Reeve and Paul Johnson in Fictional

Yvonne Rainer and Lisa Nelson brought a huge amount of energy, enquiry, expertise and experience, contributing to the evolution of our practice. This commitment to deep questioning, and a supportive environment to explore and develop work, continues to evolve here.

The emphasis in the MA in Contemporary Dance programme, of which I am course director, is on performance and practice. The guest tutors are all professional performers and choreographers, so the focus is on how we make performance, and how we are as performers. It is quite a deep investigation of principles.

Rather than training people in Graham and Cunningham to go into a repertory company, the aim is to tell the students, "You are an artist, you are a performer; how do you apply principles to get what you want out of your body, in order to express what it is that you want to say?" When people come from the traditional Irish background into this programme, we engage directly with them as artists. They are not on the programme to learn another style of dance. They are reminded again and again, "You are learning about you". We are asking questions like, "What do you want when you get up there to perform?"

> . . . the aim is to tell the students, "You are an artist, you are a performer; how do you apply principles to get what you want out of your body, in order to express what it is that you want to say?"

"How can you do it clearly, coherently, experiment, and try and come at it from all different angles?" So by the time you leave you are more equipped to explore the question, "How do I inhabit my dancing body?", from many different perspectives.

John Scott
Founder, Irish Modern Dance Theatre

John Scott is a dancer, choreographer and the founder of Irish Modern Dance Theatre. Through his recent work with Dublin's Centre for the Care of Survivors of Torture in Fall and Recover, *John has also become involved in lobbying for asylum-seekers' rights in Ireland. John has absorbed many diverse international influences into his work, finding natural affinities with legendary artists like composer/choreographer Meredith Monk (John is also a highly regarded classical tenor). Here he recounts the aesthetic journey that led him to develop his own unique note on the landscape of Irish contemporary dance.*

I grew up going to the theatre. My father Leslie was the lighting designer in the Abbey. I saw everything there as a kid. I was saturated in theatre. My brother Michael is also a theatre director.

We had no background in dance in the family. When I was 12 I saw the expressionist masterpiece *The Green Table*, choreographed by Kurt Jooss, at the Abbey, and was completely blown away. The Tanzforum Cologne were performing in the Abbey as part of a summer season. I saw Joan Denise Moriarty's production of *Swan Lake* shortly after that, and that got me too. That was my first exposure to live dance. I'd always had a perception that dance was tiny girls in *pointe* shoes and tutus and men in tights stomping around the place. When I saw this it engaged me in an immediate way. I was already in love with theatre, and then dance took me over more.

I went to university to study English with a view to becoming a writer, and ended up being diverted into theatre, musicals and avant-garde theatre. The work of companies like The Living Theatre at the Dublin Theatre Festival introduced me to physical theatre. This type of non-linear, non-narrative work left many things open.

My first ever dance class was when I was 19. I thought, I'm too old to do this, I'll just do a few classes. A few classes led to a few more classes. I was almost 22 when I started to train. Dublin City Ballet was starting the Irish National College of Dance in Blackrock, and the ballet master Babil Gandara was out looking for male students. I went and did classes with them, with a view to strengthening my work in theatre.

I also spent some time in France studying the work of The Living Theatre, and the work of an American company called The Calck Hook Dance Theatre, which was working in the American Centre in Paris. It was run by a woman who had worked with Meredith Monk.

Photo: Chris Nash

Philip Connaughton and Justine Doswell in Rough Air

I had also read about the Judson dance movement in the '60s and '70s and was becoming more aware of who choreographers were. Theatre had to be very special to make me jump out of my seat, whereas dance seemed like something that was becoming much more part of who I was. So when I was offered the chance to study, I jumped at it. I didn't know how I would do as a dancer. I wanted to explore it to its absolute potential.

I became an apprentice to Dublin City Ballet. I went in every day, and did *tendues* and *pliés*. The whole aesthetic of that is that if you are a man you are studying to become the next Rudolph Nureyev or Mikhail Baryshnikov. You are improving your pirouettes, you are trying to do your lifts, and your jumps. If you are a girl you're trying to become the next Margot Fonteyn or Sylvie Guillem.

I stayed with Dublin City Ballet and performed with them as an apprentice in some of their works. They brought the choreographer Anna Sokolow, who was one of the founders of modern dance in America, to set her masterpiece *Dreams*. She also created some new work. She was quite old at that stage.

I was interested in choreography. I loved how Anna worked and what she did. Everything I had done in Dublin City Ballet until that point had been about learning steps. It was about technical proficiency. Anna was working with another source. She taught at the Julliard School in New York, where her pupils included people like Pina Bausch, the German choreographer. It's considered that Anna Sokolow's work influenced Pina Bausch, and many other people. She left a huge mark on the history of modern dance, and on me too.

Exposure to her new form of creativity opened me up in many ways. It changed for me the way a choreographer makes work. It's not just about making up steps, telling a story. It's about finding other things – about seeing things. In the studio she didn't necessarily give the movement, she would watch what was coming from the dancers. When dancing with her, when you finished what was assigned to you, and then continued to move, she would watch to see what was happening. Then when she didn't like it anymore, she would say "Stop". Or if she liked it she would say, "Good, now lean over a little more this way". She would put you in positions where it almost felt that you were at a dead end, where nothing more was coming, and then at that moment something quite extraordinary and fresh and new would happen.

> She would put you in positions where it almost felt that you were at a dead end, where nothing more was coming, and then at that moment something quite extraordinary and fresh and new would happen.

In my summer breaks from Dublin City Ballet I started going to France. Dance was starting to explode there in the '80s with the culture minister Jacques Lang increasing the budget. Dance was blossoming because there were very enlightened policies taken out by the French government in the 1970s towards forming a dance culture in France. It was a very exciting time in France – there were wonderful explosions of choreography. I did courses with choreographers and teachers there. I studied with an American choreographer Andy de Groat who had worked with Robert Wilson and choreographed *Einstein on the Beach*. He also had other very beautiful, innovative ways to making work. For me the world of the ballet company seemed to be one where you go in and you're taught how to lift your leg higher, or you work on jumping higher. These are all necessary, but there was no awareness of other things going on.

In 1985 I decided that I wasn't going to continue to be the next Nureyev or Baryshnikov. I left Dublin City Ballet, and started trying to make my own work.

I went to study for a summer with members of Meredith Monk's company "The House", including Pablo Vela, at the Theatre Academy in Denmark. There I met a totally different approach to anything that I had encountered in the world of dance in Ireland. It was about finding material, using improvisation, discussing things, and various ways of finding what a piece is: how it's made; what the good material is; what dance is; where its place is; what theatre is; what music is. Performance could be a combination of several elements. As well as opening my mind, this posed some problems. At this stage I started to make my own work. I made a very small piece in Dublin, using dancers from Dublin City Ballet whom I begged, blackmailed and bribed to come into cold studios with rickety floors. In exchange for some bars of chocolate and cappuccinos they would dance for me. We would try and tape it. Then I would make another little piece.

Then Thom McGinty, the Dice-man, was doing a cabaret in a night-club, and they were looking for some acts for it. I choreographed a little piece for this cabaret, and started to make various little pieces of work.

Then the "New Music/New Dance" Festival happened just as the Arts Council cut the Irish National Ballet, Dublin Contemporary Dance Theatre and Dublin City Ballet in 1989. It was a genocide of everything that had happened in dance until then, and left a couple of dancers floating around, disconnected. This set the foundations for what is now the structure of dance companies in Ireland.

In this festival, started by the Dance Council of Ireland, several choreographers and composers would make maybe a 15- or 20-minute piece. It could be anything – a group piece, a duet or a solo. My company ultimately started from here. So in 1989–90, on a wing and a prayer, I made pieces which were quite successful in "New Music/New Dance". I supported myself by whatever means I could.

Photo: Chris Nash

Philip Connaughton and Joanna Banks in Left and Right

I travelled whenever I could, thanks to travel grants and bursaries. The Goethe Institute brought me to Germany where I could see much more dance and theatre production: Heiner Muller and Robert Wilson were a source of great inspiration.

Choreography became my biggest obsession. I started to work with theatre directors. Joe O'Byrne of Co-motion Theatre company asked me to collaborate with him on *The Sinking of the Titanic*, which I choreographed. The critic of the *Sunday Tribune* selected it as one of the best artistic achievements of the year. At that point I felt it was time that I founded a dance company. I wanted a structure where

I could create my own work, research and experiment. I could bring dancers in to show them other ways of working, and what's happening outside of Ireland where people were improvising and creating. I had travelled all over the world, slept on train station floors, sat in wet or overheated carriages going through Italy and Germany to do workshops, take classes and see performances. I wanted to attract the people I had met on my travels to Ireland, and create a place where those things could happen here, and start to develop.

I could do two things. I could invite other choreographers and dancers to come and work in this entity that I would create. I could also evolve myself as a choreographer, and develop my choreographies. So in 1991 I established Irish Modern Dance Theatre. I applied to the Arts Council for a small grant, and got it. I suddenly could say, "Yes, this is it, here we go." I could start to make work using the company name.

I was working mostly with dancers who had worked in Dublin City Ballet originally. It expanded to some exciting new dancers like Liz Roche who had been studying in The Place in London. Liz came back to Dublin and had her first professional job with me. Jenny Roche, Aisling Doyle and Laura Macken were all around. David Bolger worked with me. I was able to help David when he started to make his own choreographies, before he went on to form CoisCéim. It was a very exciting time when a lot of things were starting in Ireland.

We also started to tour this new work nationally. But we were making new work with new music, taking it places, and starting to develop audiences for modern dance. When I did my first full-length evening in Project Arts Centre in 1992, people were saying, "Dance is not going to sell, it's finished, you're not going to get any audiences, I don't even know why the Arts Council continue funding dance." But we sold out. We came back and we sold out again. And again.

> . . . people were saying, "Dance is not going to sell, it's finished, you're not going to get any audiences, I don't even know why the Arts Council continue funding dance." But we sold out. We came back and we sold out again. And again.

The first show was *Rough Notes and Dance Points*, which we subsequently toured around Ireland. We then received more money from the Arts Council, enabling us to make more work, to take more risks, and to pay ourselves. We could take longer in the evolution of the work.

At this point I had studied with the great choreographer Meredith Monk. Because I am also a singer, and she has an approach that is music in theatre, what she does interested me a lot. I actually performed in her piece *Quarry*, a revival of probably her most famous and biggest piece, at the Spoleto Festival in 2003.

In terms of bringing a choreographer in, I've always refused to buy a pre-existing work. It's often cheaper if you do that – a dancer can come, set the steps – dancers learn steps very quickly, that's part of their trade. But I've insisted that whatever we do is made here on the bodies and the people who are here. I do bring dancers in from other countries when we don't have enough people. They come here, spend time, breathe the air here, get on the buses, get rained upon, drink Guinness and do the living in Ireland thing. They become part of where we are, who we are and what we do.

We started to travel internationally in 1996. We've been to France, New York in Danspace Project, Norway, Sweden, Bulgaria, Turkey and Estonia. So the work is now starting to go out to other places. I worked with a French choreographer, Fabrice Dugied, in 1997; Sean Curran in 1998; John Jasperse in 2002; Thomas Lehmann, a German choreographer, in 2004; and soon Chris Yon and Sara Rudner from New York. These people are all innovators in their own field and in their own form, bringing new things to dance.

What excites me is that dance has never had much of a history in Ireland, yet I brought these people here to evolve their own work. After Sean Curran made *That Place Those People* on us, he was then going to set it on his own company in New York. He sent his dancer to see us perform in New York to learn the spirit of the work. I have seen a choreographer bringing a videotape of their work, and saying, "Look at this, the spirit is in it, see how this dancer moves, try and capture that." With *That Place Those People* we reversed that. We go to New York, the capital of dance in the world, with a piece made in Ireland, in cold freezing dance halls by a part-time company. And the American dancers come to learn our nuances and to find out who we are so they can perform the work better.

When I first became exposed to dance the two main companies in Ireland were

Photo: Chris Nash

John Scott in Bowing Dance

Irish National Ballet and Dublin City Ballet. They were companies where everyone was young, thin and physically strong. That's what people expected to see when they came to see dance. Yes, the clichés of men in tights, and *pointe* shoes and tutus. What has happened is that dance in Ireland has grown up. Even though we didn't have our middle history, in some ways we are catching up.

The Dance Festival, of which I'm a board member, brings in outside people who can change the preconceptions of dance and educate critics, audiences and practitioners.

Now there are different types of bodies performing in dance. I often work with Joanna Banks, whom I brought back on stage after she retired from a great international career as a ballerina with the National Ballet of Canada, the Royal Ballet, Ballet Rambert and Irish National Ballet. She had gone into teaching and became Artistic Director of the Irish College of Dance. What she gives now is so extraordinary. She is not a young dancer of a certain type, jumping around the place. The dance is more than the young dancer who can lift her leg up to her ears or dance high. Older dancers have so many rich and beautiful things to give.

I work best when I work with older dancers, or dancers who are experienced in different ways. They might come from different technical backgrounds: maybe someone has more of a history of performing in musicals and has a certain way of presenting their body; or someone who has a history of release technique, which is a much floppier way of moving; or someone who has a history of ballet, ballet, ballet all their lives. What these older, more mature people bring to the work is so rich that I've been able to minimise what I put into my own work and allow them to create something where they and their bodies speak much more of what is inside them. Somehow I make work that finds a trigger where what is inside comes out.

Working with torture survivors since 2003 has also greatly affected my work. Many of these people are natural performers and fit uncannily and automatically into the world my work inhabits.

When I started out, the ballet companies performed in the Abbey, the Olympia, and the Gaiety, with 18 to 20 dancers. Now companies generally have casts of four to seven dancers, so they are smaller productions in terms of cast size. But nearly all of the choreographers are Irish-based. It is original work. So it is the development of its own genre in a way that didn't exist previously. Maybe you play smaller venues, with a capacity of 150 to 200, but the work is deeper and richer now.

In the earlier days the choreography was by international choreographers. The international perception of dance in Ireland was that it was not of the same standard as it was in other countries. Irish companies did not travel abroad. There were very few known Irish choreographers: Joan Denise Moriarty and Irish National Ballet, then later Joan Davis, Anne Courtney and Mary Nunan. Ireland was not a place that had many choreographers working, really.

Now through the determination of all of us working here collectively in Ireland in our own ways and in our own pursuits, we have created a group of choreographers. We have produced bodies of work – for better or worse.

Now through the determination of all of us working here collectively in Ireland in our own ways and in our own pursuits, we have created a group of choreographers. We have produced bodies of work – for better or worse. Personally I can handpick four or five of my pieces that I feel are very important, that we continue to perform and revive. Our work is being accepted internationally.

I think some of the critics here are getting a much broader and more enlightened view of what dance is. I remember in the early '80s in the theatre festival Bill T. Jones came over and his work was completely misunderstood and torn to shreds. He still talks about the critical roasting he got in Ireland. At the same time he was performing in London, New York and Paris to full houses, getting awards, rave reviews. I went every night and sat in a little theatre with 50 people in Trinity College. Everywhere else in the world his work was exploding.

The audience you'd get in would love it, but the problem was getting them in the door. When they came they said, "Wow, this is fantastic." Now with the International Dance Festival, dance is beginning to attract a good public. They're coming for Merce Cunningham, Mark Morris, Joseph Nadj and Thomas Lehmann. The perception of dance as being the men in tights and the girls in *pointe* shoes is going a little and maybe – I hate talking about Ireland catching up and opening up because it's such a tired cliché . . . but in dance, at least, it's true.

David Bolger
Founder, CoisCéim Dance Theatre

*D*ancer and choreographer David Bolger is founder and artistic director of CoisCéim Dance Theatre. Below he recounts how after some quasi-clandestine ballet classes, his professional career began when he landed a role in HMS Pinafore at the Gaiety Theatre upon leaving school, and transferred to the prestigious Old Vic Theatre in London. That illustrious beginning fed into his natural penchant for the theatrical, which he has developed throughout his diverse choreographic oeuvre, spanning contemporary dance, theatre, film and opera.

Originally I just wanted to run away with the circus. When I was quite young I was fascinated with performance and the make-believe world that kids have, which is a great play world. Luckily I had visiting circus troupes near me. I became fascinated by circus, terrified of clowns, and absolutely besotted by trapeze artists and the way they moved. I thought, "Wow – these people are flying!"

For several summers I did actually manage to run away with the circus part-time. I used to go every single day, groom the horses and get to know the performers. What was interesting about the circus people was that they don't mind you being around a little bit, but they don't want to teach you their tricks. It's very difficult to become a trapeze artist on your own. I would sling up a rope on the goal post at the back of our house, try and make a swing and imitate trapeze acts I had seen in the circus.

But one day the whole thing went wrong. I hadn't tied the knot to the cross bar tight enough, and while upside-down I had a little bit of a fall straight on my head. I thought I had cracked something in my neck. Thankfully I didn't – I had whiplash. But it scared me away from trapeze. I thought, if I was only five feet off the ground at that point, what would it be like at the top of a tent?

Photo: Dylan Vaughan

Miguel Angel and Emma O'Kane in Chamber Made

So I started looking for other ways of expressing that side of myself. My sisters were going to tap-dancing lessons in the local hall – unfortunately boys weren't allowed. They used to go to the lessons, I'd wait outside, hear them all tapping, then we'd go home and destroy the lino in the kitchen with them teaching me how to tap dance. I became really fascinated by rhythms, movement and the theatre.

Luckily, I lived on a very theatrical road – Strand Road in Sandymount – with well-known actors and people in the theatre such as Christopher Cassen, Agnes Bernelle and Andy O'Mahony. There were a lot of people who worked in film and television who were familiar with the area. We got friendly with Agnes, and went to the Project Arts Centre to see her performances several times. Then I started to go to acting classes. I just got a love for theatre and performance, very early in my life.

When I was 16, I got involved in the musical and drama department in my school, Marian College. I was very active in that. My father asked me what I wanted to do when I grew up. I said, "Oh, I want to be a dancer." To my horror he turned around and said, "Well, if you want to be a dancer, you'll have to go to ballet." "Ballet? No way. I'm not interested in ballet. I want to do tap dancing." He said, "But every great dancer has had classical training." And my father wasn't from a theatre background at all, so it shocked me that he was saying this!

He did some research on it, and discovered the National College of Dance in Blackrock. It was part of Dublin City Ballet. He enrolled me into classes there. Because I was a boy they grabbed

Because I was a boy they grabbed me when I walked in the door and said, "You are going straight to master class."

me when I walked in the door and said, "You are going straight to master class." So my first ballet class was with all these girls who had trained in ballet since they were eight years of age. I was absolutely terrible at it, but because I was a boy they were pushing me towards it. So from 16 to 18 I used to go after school every day and do classical ballet. So I kind of fell into dance in a way. It must have been in my blood.

It is nice though that, now I am working as a choreographer in theatre, I can draw upon all those things that have been in my life. I still have a fascination with circus performance. I love physical theatre, classical ballet and contemporary dance. I have a very rounded appreciation and love for that form of theatre. It has been a great journey, and there is still lots to learn. That's the thing about theatre – you never know enough. You are constantly moving on. And because you are getting older and your body is changing you move in a different way. You are attracted to different things.

When I was leaving Marian College I won the Liguri Award, presented by Noel Pearson. He interviewed us all and asked us what we wanted to do. I said I wanted to be a dancer. He said, "Don't become a dancer, go to the bank, do anything

Ben Dunk and Marian Ribon in Rite of Spring

Photo: Dylan Vaughan

else, don't become involved in theatre." I got really angry at him because I had been training in classical ballet kind of secretly – only a few people in school knew I was doing this. Coming to classical ballet at 16 – your bones are beginning to set – you really have to work very hard. I said, "I'm going for this career, thanks very much, and I'll see you again." Just as I put my hand on the door – it was so dramatic – he called me back and said, "Wait, David, wait. I'm actually doing *HMS Pinafore* in the Gaiety this summer and we are auditioning for male dancers, would you like to come along?" I said, "Absolutely!" He set up an audition.

So I went along to the Gaiety and auditioned with Mavis Ascott, who was choreographing the show, and Pat Conway, the assistant choreographer. They auditioned me on the Gaiety stage and taught me some dances from the show, and after an hour or so offered me a job in the production. I went straight from school into *HMS Pinafore* at the Gaiety. It transferred from the Gaiety to the Old Vic Theatre in London. A very rare thing, a first professional job landing in a West End!

I was very interested in contemporary dance as well. When I was in London people such as Michael Clarke and Mathew Hawkins were on the scene. They were all teaching workshops because they were looking for new dancers. I was really interested in the idea of contemporary dance rather than classical. I felt that classical had a certain restriction to it, which is great, but I wanted to express myself in a different way. So I was able to look at all these people who were developing their own techniques.

I finished *HMS Pinafore* in London and decided to come back to Ireland. I started taking class here again. I wanted to keep doing shows. I did *West Side Story* in the Olympia, which featured the original Jerome Robbins's choreography, and several big musicals. I was interested in dance and pursuing just a dance career. I joined Irish Modern Dance Theatre and danced with John Scott for several years. I also danced with Fiona Quilligan's company, Rubato, and Adrienne Browne's New Balance Dance Company.

Photo: Kip Carroll

David Bolger (left) and Sean Jeremy Parker in Boxes

Then the annual New Music/ New Dance festival started in Project. A choreographer was able to submit to choreograph a new piece with new music. In 1993–94, I created my first choreography, *Silent Scream*, on Charlie Chaplin. I was very attracted to Chaplin and the fact that he did silent cinema – that he was able to do very elaborate pieces without sticking up the cards that told you what he was saying. I made the dance work based on his life, his exile from America, the whole communism issue and the way America turned its back on him.

Over the following two years I made two other pieces for the New Music/New Dance festival. So that was my training in presenting work, which was a fantastic opportunity. Eventually in '94/'95 I went up on the train with a video under my arm to the Old Museum Arts Centre in Belfast, and asked would they be interested in presenting some work for me. They said, "Yes we would; unfortunately we've no money but we'd like to programme you in our late winter season."

I decided I would need a company to present this work. A lot of the artists that were working at the time came together and we set up CoisCéim Dance Theatre. We did *Dances with Intent*, our first show, in the Old Museum Arts Centre. Subsequently that show went to the Galway Arts Festival that year, and to the Dublin

Theatre Festival. The year 1995 was extraordinary, taking a leap, and saying, "This is what we believe in, let's try it." That's how the company came into existence.

We were ten years old in February 2005 and to date we have created 17 new works and a dance film, and toured extensively in Ireland and internationally to four continents. We've had extraordinary support from our funders, the Irish Arts Council. We've also had sponsorship from ESB for our dance awareness programme "Ezi-Motion", a pilot programme which we set up in five venues around the country. The aim was to demystify dance by starting very gently with creative workshops. Rather than teaching people steps, we were trying to get people to look at dance in a way that they could read it back and realise that it wasn't a million miles from them.

> *When you work in dance theatre you try to look back to that language you learned when you were a child, and bring that more forward.*

I do believe that as children, body language is the first thing we understand. Then we learn to speak, the words come, and maybe movement and body language starts to take a back seat. When you work in dance theatre you try to look back to that language you learned when you were a child, and bring that more forward. That's the area I've been interested in. There is movement everywhere.

Performing to people who have some context for what they are reading into is a major concern for all of us. You want to be able to perform to people who have some background for what they are seeing. The International Dance Festival is fantastic to bring big dance companies like Mark Morris to Dublin, so people here can see these household names perform.

There are lots of wonderful dancers in this country. Up to a point people had to either train here or train abroad and stay abroad because the work wasn't here. Now I see a lot of dancers who are here and are staying here. We need to start having pride in our own voice and what it is we do. We need to make our own models.

I think everyone learns from each other and I've learned an awful lot from everyone I've worked with. It works both ways. You hopefully are continually learning and trying

Photo: Hugo Glendenning

Emma O'Kane, Muirne Bloomer and Rebecca Reilly in Mermaids to create dance in a new way or refine what it is you do, asking, "What is it I do? What is that dance I make?"

There is always an element of movement or dance in plays. What usually happens is, somebody gets asked to choreograph the party scene. But I've worked as a movement director on several productions where you're not just in to choreograph the three minutes of dance, but you can work with the actors quite a bit for the whole play. So your input is working side by side with the director's vision. You're not just coming in to look after that little bit and going home, thinking, "Hopefully they'll get it right."

I like working with any performers who are dedicated to what they do, be-

> *The minute you say, "I'm a choreographer" to a group of actors you just see their shoulders going up and thinking, "Oh my God!"*

cause then they're open. The minute you say, "I'm a choreographer" to a group of actors you just see their shoulders going up and thinking, "Oh my God!" But actually there are ways of breaking that down and saying, "Well, I'm interested in the way you move, I'm not going to try and teach you a different way of moving. I will work with the way you move to sculpt and choreograph that." I am interested in the way different people move – that's why we are different.

I have worked many times with Garry Hynes on several productions, including *The Playboy of the Western World*, and two John B. Keane plays, *Sive* and *Sharon's Grave*. In *Sharon's Grave* there are two characters who have huge physical presence within the play: Dinsy, a cripple, and Jack, his poor beaten younger brother who has to carry Dinsy around and literally be his legs while he is alive. It's an extraordinary creature that John B. Keane has written. When we were working on that we really tried to get the idea of this guy who is supposed to have limited mobility, yet when I read the script I thought, "He has to be the most mobile person on the stage, be-

Simone Litchfield in Ballads

cause you have to be terrified of him." This creation John B. Keane has written is really rather brave.

Movement is really important in these folk plays. Match how people move, where they are coming from in their lives, what they do for a living, the way their bodies are, with the lyricism of the language. If people speak in a certain way because of where they live they are also going to move in a certain way because of where they live. If they live up a hill they are going to move differently than if they live on flat land.

For a long time people had this notion that Irish drama is about kitchen sinks and there is no movement. But actually when you open up some of the lyricism and movement in the plays there is an extraordinary amount of movement. There is a notion of looking at these plays as rustic ballets, with plenty of movement.

What interests me in what Garry has been working on is opening them up to that and allowing people like myself freedom. But also having a very strong notion of the physical type of the piece and the way she wants it to flow. There are huge rhythms in these plays and I suppose that would be back down to my years tap dancing on the lino in the kitchen. Tap dancing is rhythm. So these things are all connected, and movement is not disconnected from speech. It's all very much part of our lives.

It is funny when people see contemporary dance, or dance that might be abstract, that they sometimes pull back from it because they don't understand it. But you should just allow it to do what it's doing to you. You may love it or hate it, but that is a reaction. All I can do with people who say they don't understand dance, and therefore don't go, is urge them to go and see it. Allow yourself to be taken into that world when we were kids and we understood. Before anyone could speak we understood movement.

> *All I can do with people who say they don't understand dance, and therefore don't go, is urge them to go and see it. Allow yourself to be taken into that world when we were kids and we understood.*

Tarry Flynn, at the Abbey in 1997, was extraordinary. Conall Morrison asked me did I know the novel by Patrick Kavanagh, and I didn't. I subsequently read it and loved it. I was so happy to be brought this thing. He had adapted the novel into a new script. He was so brave – all of the animals were played by the actors. There were chickens, cows, calves, people lepping around the place, people cycling up and down hills on bicycles. Conall wanted a hugely physical approach to the play and to storytelling. Again, I suppose it's down to Mummer's plays and this folk tradition I've been talking about. He was embracing this type of storytelling to tell this wonderful novel that talks about the landscape, the dunghill, the calves being born and the movement therein.

There were several trained dancers in the production mixed with actors. We put them all together and said, "look, this is the way it's going to be – I'm going to presume that all of you can do everything. Until we can't do it." That was on the first day, and I think by the second week I had made a lot of people work pretty hard. We worked extraordinarily long hours, because it was a four-week rehearsal period for an all-singing, all-dancing, all-acting extravaganza. It was a very big piece to take on for four weeks. I think the actors found it tough. The reward from all that was when the whole piece came together, it really did start to come alive. It was almost like there was a new approach in this theatre of words and movement.

We went to the Glenroe farm to study some of the animals, like the chickens, and how they moved; and the calves and the sheep. Just trying to watch animals, and how animals react among themselves. So instead of saying, "Well, I am playing chicken number three", it was "You are playing this kind of character within the pack." When you start to watch animals closely you notice the pecking order and how they react to each other. How they are scared of one, if there is a cheeky one, or whatever. We tried to bring that in. It wasn't just trying to mimic chickens, it was trying to understand that idea. With a sense of fun as well – because after all they were humans playing chickens, hopping around the table.

In 1998 we developed *Toupées and Snare Drums* with the writer Gina Moxley. It was a co-production between CoisCéim Dance Theatre and the Peacock Theatre. We were looking at the showband years in Ireland and how people in Ireland in the '60s used to dance every weekend to showbands. Also how during lent all the dancehalls would close down, and then open back up on Easter Sunday, and what that must have been like. After abstaining from dance all that time, then suddenly on Easter Sunday not only could you eat chocolate, but you could dance again and have fun. We started to look into the rumours about the devil appearing in the dance halls. These were rumours spread by other promoters to stop people from going to one hall, and going to the other. The script was developed with that in mind, and with the fact that we were going to use a mixture of actors and dancers together.

On the night the dance hall was called Dizzy Duffy's Dance Hall. We developed the idea that when the devil came in the whole communication would be just move-ment – all the dialogue would stop. It was a big learning curve, and a very big piece with sixteen performers in it. We toured Ireland. It was very successful around the country, because a lot of people remembered the era. People came to see the show who remembered some of the songs because we used Brendan Boyar songs, Dickie Rock songs, and performed the original Hucklebuck. One of the original Huckle-buck dancers, Bernie Keogh, recreated it for us. There were some wonderful nos-talgic moments. It was really nice to be performing to new audiences around the country who probably would never go to a dance performance. But the fact that they had some knowledge of the world that the production was set in opened the door of physical expression, theatre and dance.

Liz Roche
Co-founder, Rex Levitates Dance Company

*D*ancer and choreographer Liz Roche is co-founder of Rex Levitates Dance Theatre, along with her sister dancer Jenny Roche. The most highly regarded up-and-coming choreographer of the second generation in Ireland's contemporary dance scene, Liz here recounts how her work and vision were nurtured as a young dancer, bringing it to its current blossoming.

My parents were classical and ballet music people, so my sister Jenny and I were sent to the school of Dublin City Ballet, at the Irish National College of Dance in Blackrock. When I was seven in 1982–83 they did productions of *The Nutcracker* and *Copelia*, for which they needed kids. We were given a month off school, and were performing all the time. We were already showbizzy, but that clinched it. I really adored backstage – putting on makeup and getting ready. I was very competitive, and happy to be put at the front.

Jenny went full on into classical ballet. She was 13 when Dublin City Ballet did a production of *Giselle*, and then began dancing in the corps.

At age 15, after the Intermediate Certificate, I was utterly disinterested in school. I gave up, and did the foundation course at the College of Dance in Dublin for a year and a half. They did ballet, contemporary, jazz, tap, acting and singing. We had brilliant teachers, and there were only eight of us in our year. It was the third year the course was in existence. I really enjoyed it.

Then I went to London Contemporary Dance School. I was 17 and was living in a flat in London. I did a special dance-focused training course, without writing. You were meant to be over 20. In retrospect years later I could see what I got from it, but at the time I utterly didn't appreciate it. It was a huge school. There were 35 in my class, and 90 in the year. I was

Photo: Fïonn McCann

Katherine O'Malley, Nicola Curry, Liz Roche and Jenny Roche in Senses used to being in a place where people knew who you were. If you were slacking they'd get on to you . . . maybe. My year was a strong ballet year; I didn't understand why we were all competing to be good at ballet. After the first term I was confused by it. By the second term I gave up ballet for more contemporary classes and that started to make more sense.

Photo: Fionn McCann

Liz Roche in Senses

After a year I came home, and became an apprentice with John Scott's Irish Modern Dance Theatre. In 1994, I co-choreographed a piece for the New Music/New Dance platform for emerging choreographers. That was the beginning of making dance work.

Then, at about 19 I danced in *Deserts D'Amour* by the French choreographer Dominique Bagouet, for Dance Theatre of Ireland. Working with the Carnets Bagouet who re-staged the piece, their style, way of doing things and belief was my education. It was really eye-opening. Work with them was intense. We seemed to be together a long time. They came in '95 and we did an extract from *Deserts d'Amour*. In '96 we did the full-length piece, and then performed in the Montpelier Festival. In '97 we did *Strange Days* (*Jours Etranges*), which we performed in the 1999 Paris Biennale. Then I went to work for a company called Cie La Camionetta in Montpelier, run by ex-Bagouet dancers Helene Cathala and Fabrice Ramalingom, in 1999 and again in 2001. Because of these experiences in my early 20s, I feel very influenced by these French choreographers.

In 1995 I started to get busy work-wise. I worked with a company in Belfast called In Transit. Then I ran into David Bolger one day in the Dance Centre café, and was giving out about something. He said, "Well, why don't you do this next piece with me?" That began quite a relationship with David and CoisCéim Dance Theatre. I danced in about eight pieces over the years and was associate choreographer to the company for a time.

When I think of the environment then, if you were any good you got noticed, and you got work. It was exciting in that there was a sense that the choreographers were also excited. I certainly wasn't confident enough to go and live in London and do the three million auditions every week.

Choreographing became very integrated into who I was. I would dance for people, but they would know that I sometimes made pieces, and that was something that I really loved to do. In 1995 Dance Theatre of Ireland commissioned me to make a piece. In 1996 I made *Dragons and Tonics* with CoisCéim. It all grew together. I was also dancing a lot in a company in Vienna called 2nd Nature/Christine Gaigg. I would dance for CoisCéim for a while, then I might do a piece with DTI, then I might do my own piece, and then I might go to Vienna for three months. It was quite varied.

There have been times when I really wanted to be able just to follow somebody, and stay in one company all the time. But when I think of it, there was something very rounded about my experiences always being very different and varied, and me being in different levels of responsibility.

I felt fostered as a choreographer – which was quite unique. Even today there are not so many people being commissioned by other companies in Ireland. But they did it with me. It never felt like I had a big "coming out" into choreography. It was

> *. . . there was something very rounded about my experiences always being very different and varied, and me being in different levels of responsibility.*

gradual and organic. For example, when I was working with David it wasn't just him saying "do this", "do that"; they were his ideas but we worked together as a group to realise his vision. I didn't have to bend my dancing style to anybody else's will, but I still got to hang out with and learn from other people.

When I started to work a little bit more in mainland Europe, it was an interesting time because people really wanted you to be an interpretive artist and to bend to their way of doing things. That was sometimes quite difficult for me.

I started to have ideas about pieces and I figured that I would really want to make at least one piece a year, so it would be good to solidify something separate. Even though it is great to be commissioned by a company, and they look after a lot, there were times when I was commissioned by companies abroad and I had to use dancers I didn't really want to use. You get to the point where you just want to use the people you really want to use, at the time of year you want to do it.

When my sister Jenny and I started Rex Levitates in 1999, I was 25. Jenny had been travelling a lot, and had been going through a lot of different experiences dance-wise. Through the company, we could do what we were always doing, but now we were calling it Rex Levitates.

Regarding myself, Jenny, and our brother Denis working together, we don't think alike as individuals necessarily, but there is a sense of aesthetic agreement – a base-line of connection. When I listen to Denis's music there is something that resonates deep down. We've had to work very hard to not kill each other over the years – especially myself and Jenny working so closely together. It was hard at the beginning. If I wanted her to do a step a different way, I'd need to make sure it wasn't because she annoyed me when I was twelve, and vice-versa. Also when people would come in and work with us, we would not want to make our sister relationship the main relationship in the studio all the time. Over the years we have built a very strong core group of dancers, whom we love working with again and again.

It's silly to think that things aren't changing all the time. I've never had tunnel vision. I do know there are choreographers who stick to their guns and go about perfecting one thing. Even though I have a base-line aesthetic or idiosyncratic way of doing things, I feel that my pieces have changed. For one piece I might want to make a really theatrical event, like in 2001 when we made *Over the Rainbow* in the Gallery of Photography. I really didn't focus on the normal aspects of how I would make movement. I just wanted to say a certain thing, and not get into the abstract concepts of contemporary dance. But then six months or a year later I may want to look at another aspect of the process.

I feel a lot more confident about work I've made in the last couple of years. Sometimes, though, I go back and look at a piece like *Dragons and Tonics* from 1996 and think, "that was really great for someone of that age". But I would have gone through years where I couldn't bear to look at it.

Dragons and Tonics was a definite reference point. It's a place that I can look back and say that I was definitely into something then, and I can see a development now. *Salt Cycle* in 2000 as well, even though I see it was quite confused as a piece, and I was quite overwhelmed in the making of it.

I felt I cracked something with *Bread and Circus* in 2003, *Their Thoughts are Thinking Them* in 2002, *Resuscitate* in 2004, and the piece I made in China, *Catalyst* in 2004. What I really wanted to say and what I really believed in was emerging on a stage, as opposed to me always looking at a piece and wondering, "Why can't I just say the thing I want to say?"

When I started *Bread and Circus*, we had just done *Their Thoughts are Thinking Them*, and I had made a duet, *These Two People Forgot in Silence*, for the National Gallery of Ireland during the Dublin Fringe Festival 2002. That was a big success, because it was in a different environment, and people just followed it through the gallery. We were broke at the time, so we were carrying a ghetto blaster that I had hired. That was the beginning of not pretending. Up until then we had done quite big shows in big settings in Temple Bar. There were a lot of favours, so we looked better off than we were. Normally when people are starting off they do duets. But the first thing we did with Rex Levitates was with six people. People did it for very little money. I think there was an impression maybe that we were a big company. So when we did *Thoughts* . . . we were just on a project grant,

> *What I really wanted to say and what I really believed in was emerging on a stage, as opposed to me always looking at a piece and wondering, "Why can't I just say the thing I want to say?"*

and we didn't have any money to do it, but we did it anyway and didn't apologise for it. That felt much clearer.

For me, it doesn't follow a creation process. Sometimes I'd be washing my hair and get an image of something. I might get a really strong choreographic pattern in my head. Or I might see something happen, a pattern. Then I start to think about what the pattern means, and ideas grow out of that. Then I imagine a very strong lighting image, or a very strong colour to a show – and it just begins. It always comes after the premiere of another show. On the second or third night of watching a show that I've just done, I get a flash of something. That always somehow informs the next piece.

I've danced for choreographers who do the whole mathematical thing, and conceptualise. I would prefer to keep things more instinctive, or more with a heart-energy about it. But I also have a basic fascination with the grounding, and the expression of these concepts through the body. My work is through the body.

There have been times when I've tried to tell a story, but I've moved further away from things like projection or devices to narrate. While some people come to me and say, "Please, could you just have a narrative?", others say it is such a relief that there is no narrative. I'm a dance-maker above everything else, within a theatrical setting. I still really get the buzz off a theatrical setting. But I'm also really interested in non-theatrical settings. Over the last couple of years I have realised that when you are in the theatre you have to stick to the rules of the theatre, and embrace them, instead of trying to change them or turn everything on its head. Just get into it, because there is such a beautiful tradition and history within that. *Bread and Circus* in 2003 was an embracing of a theatrical setting.

> *While some people come to me and say, "Please, could you just have a narrative?", others say it is such a relief that there is no narrative.*

Even though my body would fall apart every now and then, I still stay dancing, because I learn a lot through dancing with people. I have worked as a dancer for another choreographer for at least three or four months of every year since I was 20. I feel very influenced by people when I dance with them. But also, for example, with Rosemary Butcher who mentored me as part of the first International Dance Festival Ireland in 2002, we just talked. As you get older a chat with somebody can be more beneficial than a three-week workshop, or working with them for four months. Then you really need to process that chat for a long time afterwards.

In 2004 I was dancing for John Jasperse. Because what John does is so complex movement-wise, you just need to dance the steps, and this huge amount of information and physical intelligence is communicated and taken on. If you haven't sorted out exactly every weight change, it just doesn't work. You can't even begin to work it out when you're doing it. Now, eight months later I'm really starting to see how he starts to come out of you. That's really exciting. It also shows how somebody else's solution to something can really help you find your own solution.

I think there is an Irish energy, but not necessarily an Irish way of dancing. There are lots of people performing here now who have that strength on stage or a kind of a confidence or openness that you don't see elsewhere. You can pick that openness out in a room of hundreds.

> *I think there is an Irish energy, but not necessarily an Irish way of dancing. There are lots of people performing here now who have that strength on stage or a kind of a confidence or openness that you don't see elsewhere. You can pick that openness out in a room of hundreds.*

It is hard financially to work full-time in Ireland. I have found that you can't really hitch yourself to one company, because there wouldn't be enough work to go around. So you have to get inventive about how you are going to survive.

For me, continuity is success. I'm trying to be slightly less ambitious now while focusing on doing it. For the last year I've been very focussed on getting things on the international scene. It's very difficult to get touring abroad. Also dance isn't really the fashion any more. It's much more physical theatre, experimental, and sometimes they are looking for a bigger event.

Of course, there is that part of me that wants the work to be successful, for people to know about it, and for the company to get bigger and better and more touring. But I would not prioritise that over the integrity of the work, or over me being able to make what I want to make – in the environment that I want to make it in.

I have never consciously compromised, in that I have never made a piece to keep somebody happy, or to keep an audience happy. I remember thinking as far back as *Dragons and Tonics*, "Well, they are going to hate it but they are going to have to just sit through it." I've always had a deep understanding of "that's what's coming out of me at the moment, so that's what I have to do . . ."

Michael Keegan Dolan
Founder, Fabulous Beast Dance Theatre

*C*horeographer Michael Keegan Dolan is founder of Fabulous Beast Dance Theatre. Here he recounts the circuitous story of how, from playing rugby and signing up for law at Trinity College Dublin, he followed the Billy Barry urge and wound up, via London's Central School of Ballet, working with the likes of Sir Peter Hall at Epidaurus, Chris Cunningham at the Royal Academy of Art Apocalypse Show, eventually founding his own company, fostering his own aesthetic and producing original new work.

My mother used to bring me to see the panto at the Gaiety each Christmas. Every time we went I saw the Billy Barry kids and would want join them and learn how to dance. I would ask my mother to take me but I never got to go. I don't think she realised just how serious I was about it. I also used to love watching Gene Kelly and Fred Astaire movies with my mum. I loved *West Side Story*, *American in Paris* and *Seven Brides for Seven Brothers*, which would be shown occasionally on the television. There was nothing in my environment that would allow this curiosity with dance to develop into anything, or so you would have thought. Then suddenly I was a teenager and we would go to meet girls and dance at our school's "socials", and at the Grove, a sort of disco on the northside of Dublin. I was good at the dancing part. I got into David Byrne of Talking Heads and tried very hard to copy his movements. It could be pretty dangerous for a young man to attempt to express himself that way, with dance, while growing up on the northside of Dublin in the '80s. Very often I had to make fast exits and run all the way home. Fortunately for me, as well as been a good mover I was a very fast runner over 100 metres!

Photo: Ros Kavanagh

Olwen Fouere as Maeve in The Bull

Then we did a school show in our transition year with the girls from the convent up the road. There was dancing and singing and Billy Barry's daughter was the choreographer. That was really the end of me having any chance of living as a normal person. I danced, and I sung, and I was the MC. Actually I was best at being the MC. Then I finally did join Billy Barry, but as a 17-year-old. Shortly after this I took my first lesson in classical ballet in my rugby kit, surrounded by a load of six-year-old girls. I started taking jazz-ballet, and was a bit better at that. I did my Leaving Certificate, and deferred my entry into Trinity to do law; instead I went to do a foundation course in the new dance centre in Digge's Lane.

I completed a year there with Ian Montague teaching me ballet. Mick Dolan was on that course too. We became great friends around that time and have remained friends for the past 20 years. Then I did auditions in London and because they needed boys I managed to win a scholarship at the Central School of Ballet. I was not very good. Allegedly I was made to walk too soon by my brothers and sisters, because I was the last of a long line of kids, and I developed turned-in feet. At the age of six it had become so bad I was encouraged by orthopaedic doctors to wear my shoes on the wrong feet. So when I went to ballet school I had absolutely no rotation outwards. I walked like a pigeon. I had very stiff ankles from all the running I did. I had poor co-ordination. I really was not great at the ballet, but they still took me. Very early on I got into choreography and was clever enough to see that I could be good at that. That's how I started.

In retrospect ballet was completely the wrong way for me, for my body and for my fiercely independent and creative temperament. But I finished the three-year course and now I know how to hold a conversation about ballet. I paid my dues there.

I graduated in 1991 when I was 21. I couldn't get a job, because I was technically confused. So I set up my own company, called Cartoon Dance Theatre, and produced an evening of work at The Place in the first Resolutions' season. In those days they would give you a whole evening, and I presented four 15-minute pieces.

As a result of that evening I succeeded in getting a place as a choreographer on the Gulbenkian course for choreographers and composers. In the meantime I

Photo: Ros Kavanagh

Daphne Strothman in Giselle

did get a job dancing in *Carousel*, the musical, at the Royal National Theatre, choreographed by Sir Kenneth Macmillan, and directed by Nicholas Hytner. So I started to get in some quite good company. The choreography course was led by Robert Cohen from London Contemporary Dance Theatre who knew Macmillan. Unbelievably and sadly Macmillan died during the rehearsals, and at the age of 23 along with Simon Rice I got asked to choreograph the last number, which he had not yet choreographed. I remember after this, Christopher Gable, who was my mentor at Central School of Ballet, offered me a job as his assistant choreographer at Northern Ballet Theatre but I was not ready for that.

I decided to work as a dancer for a while. I was in *The Kosh*, a physical theatre company – nine months of that really messed up my body, it was so tough. I guess I wanted to get the practical experience. I knew certain things intuitively. I knew you couldn't be a choreographer really without having been a dancer first. So I danced for as long as I could.

In 1996 I choreographed the dances in Handel's *Ariodante* at the English National Opera and it went well. Then I got a job with Sir Peter Hall as a movement director working with a large chorus of masked actors on the Oedipus plays. We premiered at the ancient theatre of Epidaurus in Greece.

Then I had to stop for a while after that. Well, I couldn't get any work. I was really confused by Peter Hall and the National. I thought, "If that's it, then I'm not interested." I tried to get into the Royal Veterinary College but they wouldn't have me.

Mary Brady of the Institute of Choreography and Dance in Cork called me up and suggested that I should come and make a piece at the Firkin Crane. I made *Sunday Lunch* in 1997 and founded The Fabulous Beast Dance Theatre Company. I reworked *Sunday Lunch* in 1998 as part of the Dublin Fringe Festival. I was awarded money by the Arts Council of Ireland to create *Fragile* in 1999, then *The Flowerbed* in 2000, *The Christmas Show* in 2001, and then *Giselle* in 2003. And in 2005, I made *The Bull*.

It's unconscious, I don't put too much thought into it, but I can look back and see what has influenced the development of my aesthetic. I worked as a cloakroom attendant at the Coliseum, home of English National Opera, while I was a ballet student, and during this period I saw about 30 productions over two years. Richard Jones, David Alden and David Poutney were doing great things with these huge pieces on that huge stage at that time. That must have affected me because my instinct is always to go big. I've always pushed for that – even when I have had no money. With *Fragile* I had €12,000 for the entire project and I wanted an enormous set. That made things very difficult because I could not afford a crew, or a production manager. I'd end up carrying objects like glass tanks that weighed almost half a ton on my back down stairs at three o'clock in the morning. I'd end up working extremely hard, while other choreographers were working with three dancers and a roll of dance floor and being much more successful.

Photo: Ros Kavanagh

Emanuel Obeya, Vadislav Benito Soltys (as Colm Cullen), Angelo Smimmo and Bill Lengfelder in The Bull

When I used to draw as a child everything would have to have hard black lines defining their edges. I love hard edges. Cycloramas which I use in *The Bull* and *Giselle*, for example, define movement very well, they give it a hard edged quality.

When I'm making a piece the images come like in a daydream and I just respond to them. So if it looks like performance art it's not conscious. The unconscious is very complex, and I think that I create from this place. Perhaps this is why I use narrative to help give it all structure; without a structure it just becomes too weird. Sometimes one's capacity for imagining can leave the audience completely out of it. My approach is to be fairly controlled with the narrative structure, and then unleash the unconscious inside that structure. So there is always a shape there to pull you back to earth.

I did work with video artist Chris Cunningham in 2000 – he's very clever. It was a positive informative experience, which lasted about two weeks. I learned a lot about video. He picked me because he saw a video of *Fragile* and asked me to work on *Flex*, which was part of the Apocalypse Exhibition at the Royal Academy of Art in London in 2000. He was well out of his comfort zone trying to cast that project and find the artists he wanted to work with. So I stepped in and helped him a little.

With *The Bull* there were six new people, but I do have a core of about eight people I try to consistently work with. Ensemble is imperative to my process. It's

Photo: Ros Kavanagh

Colin Dunne as Fergus in The Bull

my feeling that when people feel safe and harmonised, they are much more creative. Other people disagree with that. I know opera directors who believe that chaos and fear produces the creativity. But for me I like to feel that no-one's going to give me too hard a time while creating. You can't force that, you have to pick people carefully.

Initially, with *Giselle* I asked interested artists to do a week of yoga with me and my teacher and we observed how they reacted to it. There's definitely a quality of openness that I'm looking for. Performers are often very damaged by their past, because they do get messed around a lot – badly treated and badly paid. So it's a bit like trying to work with horses who have been badly treated. It can be very difficult sometimes, because they can be very twitchy.

I really don't feel I'm part of any tradition, although my grand-uncle, Edward Keegan, was an actor at the National Theatre. He was a also a 1916 rebel but wasn't famous. I have photographs of him acting with Countess Markiewicz. I guess that's where the gift comes from.

Personally I'm pretty wired. I recently taught a Dublin Youth Theatre workshop to a group of 18-year-olds and things have definitely changed. Their inner tension is very different to yours or mine. When I was 18 I was wound up like a spring. These young people were so completely chilled out they were almost on the floor. Then there are people like the rugby player Brian O'Driscoll, who is a genius physically, as good as it gets in his field. There is power, speed, co-ordination and the confidence which comes with the new age we live in.

At school we were encouraged to play football and to be very physically abrasive with the people we played against. The culture I was brought up

Photo: Inpho Photography

Brian O'Driscoll

in felt quite violent. My father, however, was a very gentle man, but quite wound-up mentally. My mother has had no problem with the violence in my work. She does have a problem with the bad language, and anything to do with the Catholic Church. Violence in theatre doesn't even register with her. You could smash somebody's head open on the stage and she wouldn't have a problem, but bring on a nun and she'll freak out.

How could being Irish not inform my work? I am a product of the 18 years I spent here, the 18 years I spent away being Irish in England, and then there is my obsession and love for the place, and now I'm back here to explore it further.

In *The Bull* Maeve says to Fergus, played by Colin Dunne, "Stick to the prancing around, and leave the serious stuff to us." That's really the attitude to choreographers. I've worked a lot with directors, and to directors it's a case of "The entertainment comes in". You could compare us to prostitutes, we come in, we make it all good, and we go. That's a really big misunderstanding. I think a choreographer is a higher state of existence than a director.

Eclecticism is part of the aesthetic. The singing is from all the opera work I did. So I'm comfortable with music. I can't sing particularly well, but I've no problem playing with it. I can't dance particularly well, or act particularly well. I've got good-ish rhythm but I've no problem engaging with it.

I've been doing shadow yoga for four years, since *Giselle* in 2003. It does inform my work. A substantial part of all I know about theatre and dance now that is of any goodness or quality, I have learned through my yoga practice. I do martial arts practice as well. With yoga and Japanese sword, it's all so functional and practical. Everything works – how to build up and dissipate tension. It's all about breathing. You need to be very very focused, very clear and very centred. I apply all those rules to how we work. The results are *Giselle* and *The Bull*. Love them or hate them, they are pretty good pieces of work.

When you get balanced between the head and the body, that's when something really extraordinary starts to happen. It's very hard to find performers who can do both. One of my ambitions would be to have a company in ten years' time and to create a style of performer and performance. People could come and have a really exciting experience at the theatre and want to come back for more.

For me, it's all therapy. I'm motivated by my own crap and it is very fertile. Movement and theatre are in my blood. I can't escape them.

Photo: Ros Kavanagh

Final tableau of The Bull

Catherine Nunes
Director, International Dance Festival Ireland

*D*irector *of the International Dance Festival Ireland, Catherine Nunes under-went an arduous journey to achieve her vision of an international dance fes-tival for Ireland, which finally came to fruition in 2002. It was a task that neces-sitated clear vision, tenacity and an intimate knowledge of the dance world. Here she relates what motivated her, how she stuck with it and how under her steward-ship the International Dance Festival Ireland eventually came to be.*

In 1994 I was working as Associate Director of Dance Umbrella in London, and was invited to Dublin by the then Dance Council to give a talk about dance festivals. At the time, nothing came of it. It was very soon after the 1989 Arts Council cuts, and 1994 was the beginning of the long climb back to recognition for dance as an art form. By 1998, when the proposal for an International Dance Festival in Ireland went in to the Arts Council, there was a whole different climate for dance here. There were a lot of companies by then – Dance Theatre of Ireland, Irish Modern Dance Theatre, Daghdha Dance Company and CoisCéim Dance Theatre. There was obviously a will to do something.

To initiate an international dance festival here was something that I had always wanted to do. I was really aware of the lack of a festival here. I had also started a dance festival in Newcastle, England, under the auspices of Dance Umbrella. It was very interesting watching how the festival worked in a little developed or under-developed dance culture. I thought the potential in Ireland could be enormous. Festivals raise the profile, confidence and visibility of an art form, all of which could only benefit the culture here. It was something that I had at the back of my mind, but I wasn't living in Ireland when it was in the back of my mind. However, when I came back to Ireland in 1997, at the time it did seem to be right.

On the back of the Theatre Festival not finding audiences for dance, they had begun to stop programming dance. But according to my research and from my own experience internationally, that didn't seem legitimate. They had programmed dance within the context of no other dance happening. Without focus on the dance itself it was very hard to find an audience within the context of a theatre festival.

I felt that in a different context if we really put the spotlight on dance we could find an audience. Especially because it was really growing as an art form. It was clear that Ireland at some point would have to embrace international dance if it was to become any sort of globally recognised major player in terms of culture generally. It had to start showing what was happening abroad, and raise the bar for Irish dance. If it hadn't happened by now we'd be really behind the races.

I have always been involved in dance so I was very aware of its development in Ireland. When I was studying Modern English and French at Trinity College I did dance classes with Dublin Contemporary Dance Theatre

> *It was clear that Ireland at some point would have to embrace international dance if it was to become any sort of globally recognised major player in terms of culture generally. It had to start showing what was happening abroad, and raise the bar for Irish dance.*

– Joan Davis's company on Molesworth Street. I did one of the summer seasons in dance at Digge's Lane. Mick Dolan and Michael Keegan Dolan were also on it. After Trinity, I studied dance in the Laban Centre in London, and did a postgraduate diploma in dance there. I went to New York for a year and danced there. I taught and performed dance in London after my time at the Laban Centre. But because I missed those crucial years as a teenager while I was at boarding school in Ireland, I realised that I would never be the dancer that I would want to be, or satisfy myself in terms of any career options. I then got sidetracked into programming, for which dancing was a great background. It makes you a different kind of programmer – not necessarily better, but if you have danced yourself you have a different feel for it.

I did the initial feasibility study for what is now the International Dance Festival Ireland in 1997. There was input from the Association of Professional Dancers of Ireland, Gaye Tanham at the Arts Council, choreographers and people from Northern Ireland. We put together a steering committee and made a proposal to the Arts Council to make the dance festival happen, on the basis that our research had shown that Ireland was ready for it. However, despite this, the Arts Council rejected it on the grounds that it felt Ireland wasn't ready for a dance festival.

Then, on the basis of very close dialogue with the Arts Council, we explored the notion of a festival some more, and came up with a more negotiated proposal. We worked for another year getting that proposal together. It was ready just at the end of 2000, and was accepted. Subsequently, there was very little planning time before the first festival, which happened in May 2002.

I'm really happy with how the Dance Festival has been going since then. A lot of people have commented on the fact that it feels like it has been around for a lot longer than it has been. It feels like it has slipped in without too much effort, controversy or fanfare around it. Often, to get things off the ground there is a huge heave-ho, it's very controversial, and people are throwing mud at it for a while. But we seemed to receive almost immediate approval.

The natural Irish theatre audience is very narrative-based. I always think that the biggest crossover audience is from the visual arts, because of its abstract nature. Having said that, with the headline act of the first festival, Merce Cunningham, dance had not been on the Abbey stage for fifteen years. And while many from a purely theatrical background – playwrights and actors – acknowledged that it was alien territory to them in many ways, yet they greatly appreciated

> *The natural Irish theatre audience is very narrative-based. I always think that the biggest crossover audience is from the visual arts, because of its abstract nature.*

its excellence and artistic integrity. They were genuinely excited and really had that sense of something important taking place.

You can measure success by audience figures, and maybe by how many dancers come to masterclasses, but I think a far more interesting way of measuring the impact is how it changes thinking, and people's perspective, which is far more anecdotal and hard to measure.

A lot of people come to the dance festival because of interest either in the body or in visual aesthetics. But you also have the people who are already converted, who love the body, and might dance themselves – mainly women. Many of them have done dance classes or have been involved in dance. There is also the theatre audience, who have seen dance theatre. Irish audiences are actually quite experimental in their taste, they love imagination and are quite open. There are the other ones who are a little more nervous, and haven't made their minds up, who might go along, and say, "well I didn't get it", and be quite intimidated by by the fact that they can't explain what they saw. What was the meaning? It's not like going to see Shakespeare. They don't feel confident enough to relax with it and say, "well I loved the idea, the colours, or the music". There are different avenues into dance. For example, DV8 Physical Theatre, which is possibly more accessible. Or you might get the more visual-arts-oriented audience going to Rosemary Butcher.

An interesting reflection of our attitude to the body is the fact that in 2004 a legal case was taken against the festival by one member of the public who reacted strongly to Jerome Bel's choreography at Project during the first festival. This man tried to sue us for €30,000 for personal injury. His case failed and he had to pay his own costs. The judge told him he had no case, but that he was clearly a nice, honest man, so they didn't charge him all the costs. Despite our clear innocence – and despite the fact that we were not required to speak in our defence because there simply was no legal case to answer – we still had to pay out our own costs, and it cost us quite a lot. I think that case

Pichet Klunchen and Myself, by Jerome Bel (right) at 2006 International Dance Festival Ireland

raised profound questions about art and Irish society, and about the issue that anybody can take a notion – even on a sort of personal whim or neurosis – and end up costing an artist or arts organisation dearly. That was the only time we encountered a reaction to that extreme of being taken to court.

But the case brought up a lot of thinking around it. We weren't particularly happy with how it was reported in the media, and felt it was unbalanced. It brought

> *. . . people were saying, "You call that art do you? It was profanity." Headlines in the paper were all, "Shock horror! Urination on stage!" and, "Is this art?" It just got ridiculous.*

up the whole issue of repression and the question of where we are at the moment as a society. We would get comments like, "We are a family paper so we don't believe we can print what you want to say about the piece." It was quite interesting. Then there was the Joe Duffy show controversy, where people were saying, "You call that art do you? It was profanity." Headlines in the paper were all, "Shock horror! Urination on stage!" and "Is this art?" It just got ridiculous. At the end of the day it did bring up big issues, not only around censorship but also about freedom of expression. And where are we in terms of how we respond to very gentle nudity on stage? With a paying public coming to see a show in an alternative arts venue with a very explicit pre-publicity image. It's a very interesting case. There is that element that the body is taboo. Stuff like this can really stop an audience from developing.

But that is the extreme end. We have this burgeoning audience now. It shows there has been a change in the attitude to the body. The reception to dance from the wider public has been fantastic. The Irish dance companies have been doing great things to build their own audiences. They've built a community.

Now the dance festival audience is between 5,000 and 7,000. One of my main motivations in creating the festival was to try to broaden the perception of dance among the general public. And to take it away from received notions – that it's very obscure, very elitist, with very dark corners on stages – which have maybe prevented people from going to see dance.

Very few dancers from Ireland partook in the workshops we offered in the first festival, and I couldn't understand why. But by the second festival they knew what it was, because the first dance festival was an unknown quantity. So more people had confidence to get involved in it – especially after Liz Roche's residency, and mentoring by Rosemary Butcher was very successful. That was very process-oriented, had been handled quite sensitively, and was an opportunity she might not have otherwise had. It did culminate in a performance, but there was no pressure on her for that to happen. It was definitely a great opportunity for a dance-artist that would not have been there otherwise.

The festival is educating and building an Irish dance audience. It's building an awareness, a confidence and a profile for dance and that can only have a positive effect for the indigenous dance scene in Ireland. As well as seeing an international palette of work, there is also an opportunity to take workshops, get involved in learning about dance on camera and to see what opportunities there might be. It gives a perspective on a wider section of dance, and the wider opportunites within dance as an art form – dance for camera, dance for film, dance writing, and dance at the Ark for children. In time people will have confidence in dance, will take the baton and run with it. That's a great example of a growth in confidence that there is an audience, it is a valuable art form, and it should definintely be embraced within Ireland's wider cultural landscape.

The traditional Irish dancing strand is an attempt to explore my own personal hypothesis that in going back to our own authentic roots we may discover a dance language for ourselves – in a non-prescriptive way. I do think there is a distance to be gone with that. Over time I think a very British dance language, a very French

Summerspace *by Merce Cunningham at first International Dance Festival Ireland, 2002*

dance language, and a very American dance language have evolved – I don't think a very Irish dance language has yet evolved. We still have quite an eclectic mix of dance languages in Ireland.

I'd love to see the festival becoming an annual event [this happened with the 2006 festival]. The biennual model was a good one to start with. It works in Montreal and in Holland. But in a relatively dance-poor environment, which we still are, the International Dance Festival is a difficult one to sustain because it's hard to keep up the momentum. The audience definitely want it to happen in the intervening year. We had DV8 Physical Theatre this year, which was totally sold out. Loads of people were turned away from the door. We did a big survey about whether people would like an annual event and the astounding response was yes.

As an annual event there would be a lot more possibility for exciting things like commissions, and to really develop a relationship with artists. If you have to let them go every year, it's quite hard to pick up all the different pieces again on a biennial basis. It would be a lot more alive and more immediately relevant to the dance community and the audience if it was annual. Within that another ambition would be to really develop the international links, which a lot of other cities have managed to do. A lot of the most interesting dance-creation and co-production is through international networks. It's hard for Ireland to take its place in that on a biennial level. If we are creating work in Ireland it doesn't have to be Irish work. There is an inherent value in having an international artist create work here – that's how it happens in Europe. Then Ireland will be recognised internationally as a player. People from abroad will recognise that Ireland is a place you can go to for international dialogue, exchange and cross-fertilisation.

If the festival became annual the difficulty would be trying not to make it a niche festival. No one is making really "dance-y" dance anymore. It's becoming much more conceptual, and crossing over with performance art, live art and cropping dance with other art forms. I'm very interested in how little pure dance – just a dancer moving in space – is to be seen in dance festivals in Europe. There is a shift. This festival is about looking for the best of what's out there. It depends on what's out there, in terms of what you programme. The third festival has a little more conceptual work than the previous two festivals, and I think that reflects the climate internationally.

I wouldn't be too anxious that Ireland only sees new work, because I think we do have some catching-up to do, and there is an education to take place to be able to put what we are seeing in a context of what is happening out there and of dance history. If the festival becomes annual it will automatically become more current. Merce Cunningham, for example, whom we had as the headline act for the first festival, has been around a while. *Biped* was a new piece, but people liked *Rainforest* which was a very old piece. Similarly with Mark Morris, who was our headline act for the second festival, we presented one new piece and some old pieces.

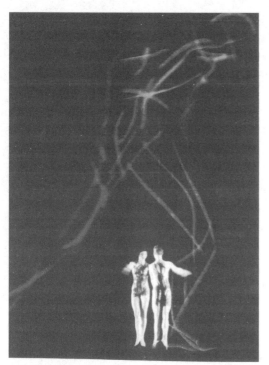

Biped *by Merce Cunningham at first International Dance Festival Ireland, 2002*

International artists are really keen to come over here. Ireland has such a romantic image abroad. Joyce and Beckett are people they would have read, and who would have influenced their thinking. Certainly Joyce would have inspired how Merce Cunnigham made dance. So he was really keen on performing in Ireland, and was really thrilled with the response. He knew he was the first act in the first festival and that he was coming to a virgin audience. He went back saying great things about Ireland. It's starting to seep through into the international consciousness. Ireland is a bigger player now because of this dance festival trilogy – people have a whole different sense of Ireland.

A lot of the impact is hard to measure. It's a slow burner – slow and steady. We really need to give the dance festival a longer life to see the full impact of it. The original plan was to have three festivals and then to evaluate how it was going and how to move forward from there.

In a practical sense we are in a really difficult position due to lack of depth on Irish stages. We have to make massive compromises, because of stage measurements, in presenting whatever large-scale acts we present. Then we are beholden to venues like the Abbey who charge us an absolute fortune to use their stage. Places like the Gaiety are programmed so far in advance, and their rentals are prohibitive. What we need is a flexible stage that is big enough to accommodate the larger-scale companies and maybe 800 people in the auditorium. You wouldn't believe the amount of talking you have to do to convince these companies it can work on a stage of five metres or less in depth. They don't want to compromise artistically. It eliminates companies like Pina Bausch, and you are restricting what is available for Irish audiences.

Dance is internationally an incredibly happening art form, not only as an art form but also as a commentary of where we are at in the twenty-first century. Dance grew as an art form in Britain by 68 per cent in the last ten years, whereas theatre only grew by five per cent. If the public is going to have a cultural experience of Irish life and society and international life, dance has to be part of that.

In terms of breaking down taboos around the body, I think it is one small way of doing that. People who are coming to see dance in the dance festival are people who want to look at the body differently. They want to see the body celebrated, and enjoy a freedom of expression that is emerging out of its previous repression. It's something new and exciting and something to be celebrated within Irish art.

It's quite freeing to be able to go and see something and realise, "I don't have to explain it. I can just enjoy it." A physical response is enough, and that is a very liberating thing. I can only imagine that if people move beyond their creaky-feeted notions of needing mental stimulation and verbal text and narrative – there is actually a great freedom to be had from it. That could lead to a confidence in the body that probably wasn't previously there – an ability to stand up and talk about the body, and to write about the body – cultivating a very positive and celebratory attitude to the body.

> *It's quite freeing to be able to go and see something and realise, "I don't have to explain it. I can just enjoy it". A physical response is enough, and that is a very liberating thing.*

The dance festival has definitely reached a new audience, because we have a wider audience than the Irish companies get for their shows. For example, in our surveys 60 per cent said they had never been to a dance performance before. So people are looking for a new way of physical expression, and looking for new experiences in theatre.

As well as a new confidence in the body, there is a desire to find for themselves a new way of talking about and contemplating the body. This is happening in tandem with a new sexuality emerging from the new generation. It's important that this new attitude is reinforced very positively – through cultural experiences. After so many years of repression you think that it could go a little bit perverted somehow, but there are things that will help that positively, encouraging confidence about the body. Nudity on stage is not shocking. It's actually something to be embraced, that we are able to look at the body in a positive way now, without all those taboos around it.

Very good dance is so valuable, getting to a truth that lies beyond narrative, beyond words, and beyond text. There is a truth in the body, and in the physical expression of the human body, which carries with it the truth of our ancestors, our current experience, our emotional experience and our physical experience. In any physical act we are giving expression in some way to our inner worlds. We see that exposed in dance. There is a raw honesty in dance because it is purely physical, and not faked in text. That is priceless.

Because we were so repressed we mightn't even have explored the possibilities of our inner selves through the body. All of those things that come with physical expression, whether it be sexual, dance or sport. That physical expression holds within it a profound amount of truth about who we are, what we are and how we function in the world. If you try to divorce your physical experience from your intellectual or emotional experience you are actually devaluing the body again. It's about the integration of the physical experience, whatever it is, with what is within.

With text, we hide from the body. Now the body is rising out of that text-based thing to be celebrated in a positive way. Probably it is reflected in Irish society coming out of being so text-based. It's no accident that the dance festival is taking root at the same time. We probably still have a way to go in breaking down those fears, and the boundaries that hold those fears in – text and intellect, literature and control – to dancing it, feeling it physically and valuing it.

It's amazing how you can see the truth of a person through the body, without them having to speak any language. Physical expression in dance offers an immediate and powerful way in to our inner worlds. A good choreographer will expose what is most vulnerable to us all, and there is an unutterable truth in that. That's where dance speaks to us, at a level that is way beyond our consciousness. A profound communication – that's the true power and value of it.

Notes

[1] Paul Johnson went on to found his own company, Mandance, and to be choreographer in residence at Project Theatre (1998–2000), culminating in the production *Without Hope of Fear*, and the publication *Fine Lines on Shifting Ground*.

[2] For further reading on contemporary dance practitioners in Ireland that are omitted here (for example, Cindy Cummings, Jools Gilson Ellis, Fergus O'Conchuir, Cathy O'Kennedy, Adrienne Browne and more), please consult *Dancing on the Edge of Europe: Irish Choreographers in Conversation,* published by the Institute of Contemporary Dance in Cork, and edited by Diana Theodores (2003); Theodores' "Report – Dance Critic in Ireland" in *Dance Chronicle: Studies in Dance and the Related Arts*, vol. 19, 1996, pp. 191–211; and *Fine Lines on Shifting Ground: Reflections on a Choreographic Process*, by Paul Johnson and published by Project Press in 2000.

Chapter 5

Chapter 5

Physical Theatre

Physical theatre is "a theatre piece in which the physical aspects of the performance are as important as the dialogue, if not more so".[1] As well as "theatre of the image", the term has been used to describe Tom Mac Intyre's mid-1980s plays at the Peacock Theatre. These plays heralded the development of a new idiom in Irish theatre, with an equally weighted verbal, gestural and visual score, even if the language was mostly incantatory as opposed to anecdotal or narrative in the traditional sense.

However, despite the traditionally static, neck-up "stand and deliver" Abbey acting style, which was used to deliver the typical wordy, cerebral Abbey script, there had been previous efforts to give the entire body its rightful place in the language of theatre. Not only did Yeats conduct his visionary theatrical experiments with Michio Ito and Ninette de Valois, but there had also been Erina Brady's erased collaborations with the likes of George Fitzmaurice and Austin Clarke at the Peacock Theatre in the 1940s.

It wasn't until the 1990s that physical theatre really began to take hold in Ireland, beginning, in 1993, with Barabbas the Company [clowning, mime, and Jacques le Coq-influenced]. Barabbas devised material, like the 1994 *Half Eight Mass of a Tuesday*, and gave new perspectives on traditional material, for example in their wonderful production of Lennox Robinson's *The Whiteheaded Boy*.

"Physical theatre", may now be ubiquitous and integrated into the mainstream Irish theatre landscape, but it was still in its infancy when Conall Morrison's boisterous 1997 adaptation of Kavanagh's novel *Tarry Flynn* burst onto the Abbey stage. Realised with the assistance of choreographer David Bolger, Morrison used four dancers and one mime artist in a cast of 29 to help embody the creatures of Tarry Flynn's imagination. Following suit were Corn Exchange's Chicago-style Commedia dell'Arte-charged productions (for example, *The Cherry Orchard*), and Niall Henry's work with Blue Raincoat Theatre Company in Sligo. *Toupées and Snare*

Drums, playwright Gina Moxley's 1998 collaboration with David Bolger and Cois-Céim Dance Theatre at the Peacock was another watershed production – integrating the entire body more fully into the language of Irish theatre.

In the meantime, quietly pre-dating all this activity, a less boisterous form of physical theatre, where "the physical aspects of the performance are as important as the dialogue, if not more so", would have to be the sparsely-worded and tightly choreographed theatre work of Samuel Beckett (since the 1950s). Theatre director Walter Asmus, many-time director of *Waiting for Godot*, among other Beckett works, sheds some light in this chapter on this notion of Beckett as choreographer.

Also out in the international arena (along with Beckett), "physical theatre" has been used to describe the work of Meyerhold, inventor of "biomechanics"; of Grotowski, whose laboratory theatre involved extensive physical training; and of Lloyd Newsom's DV8 Physical Theatre, who premiered *Just for Show* in Dublin, as part of the International Dance Festival Ireland interim year in 2005. The term "physical theatre" is also applied to a broader spectrum of work like that by Théâtre de Complicité, or even the physical language employed in John Breen's rugby play *Alone it Stands* (the story of when Munster beat the All-Blacks) in which the performer training in such disciplines as clowning, mime and *commedia dell'arte* infuses new life into traditional subjects.

Nowadays, however, as comfortable in their bodies as Leopold Bloom, most actors (like Tom Hickey, below) are fully trained in and open to the many disciplines and possibilities physical theatre has to offer and embody.

Tom Mac Intyre
Writer

*B*orn in Cavan, Tom Mac Intyre is one of Ireland's best-known playwrights and poets. Dance and a heightened sense of the physical have always informed his oeuvre. He worked with Calck Hook Dance Theatre in Paris in the 1970s, and has written about and been inspired by Pina Bausch and her Wuppertal Dance Theatre. His mid-1980s plays at the Peacock Theatre, in which he collaborated with director Patrick Mason and actor Tom Hickey, forged a new physical idiom and are widely regarded as a watershed in Irish theatrical history. They were The Great Hunger (1983), The Bearded Lady (1984), Rise Up Lovely Sweeney (1985), Dance for Your Daddy (1987) and Snow White (1988). Here he talks about dance, the body and where his aesthetic comes from.*

Initially the magic of the choreography got into my system with my journey from the womb into the world. The reason I say that is that at my mother's funeral, when I kissed her lips, while she lay dead in the coffin, I had an extraordinary replay of that experience. It's not to be described, but it is never to be forgotten. You forget the first invasion of your lungs by oxygen, but you don't forget a replay of that. And your attitude to the physical is altered forever, it seems to me.

Just as it is altered when you grow up in a society where fair day every month is full of intense physical theatre. You can't take your eyes off of it. The climactic. The dual cameo of that world being the dance of the Tangler. Tangler is the name given to a man produced by that world who, when it seemed that a bargain was about to be struck between buyer and seller, would move in, with a magnificently theatrical *spiel*, a waving of hands, a spitting on hands, and pulling on hands, a three-cornered dance, that was extraordinary to view.

After that I think my next intense and intense forever choreographic taste of bliss was to do with the movements of women. The woman you loved, the woman you are pursuing, women in the grip of the sensual, women in the grip of love, women in the grip of the sexual, extraordinary magic to me. Especially since men resist savagely getting into their bodies, and women by and large find that a natural inheritance.

It started before Calck Hook Dance Company in the '70s, though that was a crucial early adventure. I was a very timid thirty-year-old, hiding from the world in Clongowes Wood College. And, in some fooshtering-fashion, earning a living. With

Conal Kearney, Tom Hickey and Fiona MacAnna in The Great Hunger, *1983*

Photo: Fergus Bourke

terrible squealing of brakes and roaring of tyres, I got out of that world, and decided that if I didn't sit down to write and address that energy inside me I would explode. Or be taken away quietly, or something between the two, but I certainly wouldn't be permitted to abuse a gift which everyone recognised I had, and I knew I had.

So I get into the writing game. And in that Ireland, writing meant short stories. The short story was the dominant form. But quickly – because I'm Irish, because of my background, the theatre attracted me. Looking at the theatre, all I could see was a theatre where three or four people were standing on a stage talking. I said, "There's got to be more to theatre than this."

I could hear all around me, not especially in Ireland but in books I read – Meyerhold say – going to off-Broadway Theatre: Richard Foreman; La Mama; Meredith Monk; and related dance work in Manhattan of the late '60s and early '70s; that, yes, there is another kind of theatre. I discovered a whole new language, to do with the body and gesture. You didn't have to rely entirely on words. In fact words could even be secondary. So therefore my itch was to write in that new mode

> I discovered a whole new language, to do with the body and gesture. You didn't have to rely entirely on words. In fact words could even be secondary.

which was gradually becoming available to me through my fevered study of that kind of work.

Now we come to *The Great Hunger*, really. I'm skipping Calck Hook. I shouldn't skip it. Like many other Irish men then and since, I was enraptured by American women. I fell in with a number of them who were in the dance world and we landed in Paris, where you have to land at some stage. All the better if you are in love, and I was before long. But I was with a young American dance company in Paris, being taught the rudiments of modern dance theatre. I had great fun with them, and then it was over, as happens. That was in the late '70s.

There had been a lot of talk for the previous ten to fifteen years about a famous Irish poem and how

Conal Kearney, Tom Hickey, Fiona MacAnna, Bríd Ní Neachtáin and Martina Stanley in The Great Hunger, *1983*

you might get it on to the stage – *The Great Hunger*. Nobody could resolve it. I was very interested in solving that problem. I didn't know how, but I had an instinct that it might have to do with bringing what I knew about dance theatre and the whole movement theatre and image-based theatre into play. That might help.

I remember, I was in Boston – I was often in the States at that time. It was the era of Freddie Laker flights for $70 across the Atlantic. I'm in a gallery, I think it's the Isabella Gardner Museum in Boston. There is a Pissarro exhibition on, and I am wandering through it. I look up and there is a Pissarro drawing of men and women in a hayfield making hay. Pitch-forks and the hay and *pi-choing!* Something struck me. I said, "Now I had it. I could go and write the script of *The Great Hunger*". That's what I did. Then we were on our way.

The Abbey was immediately welcoming. Joe Dowling was in charge. I sent in the script. And *en passant* when talking to people in Dublin about it, I said, "I wonder who will I get to play Paddy Maguire?" They all said there is only one actor who could possibly take that role, and that's Hickey – whom I hadn't met at that stage. But I met him soon enough. We have been working and arguing and singing ever since.

Patrick Mason had an interest in that kind of theatre. He was quickly on the scene as the director. We were careful to pick actors for the most part who had some experience of movement. And then we went to work. The piece was intensely collaborative – as I fancy that kind of theatre has to be, and all vital theatre has to be.

We were given the run of the Peacock for five or six years, and had a great time. From *The Great Hunger* in 1983, its revival in 1986, *The Bearded Lady* in 1984, to *Rise Up Lovely Sweeney* in 1985. Then it was over. *Sin é an scéal*. That's the world.

I think the sensual and the erotic are still missing from Irish theatre. Irish theatre is a Daddy theatre for a Daddy audience, and this is lamentable. It follows instantly from that, that the erotic and the sensual are banished. They are banned. That's the position.

What to do about it? Well, if you are an artist who believes in that, given what I've said already about my passion for movement-oriented theatre, and the imagistic, by definition you are on the fringe. You don't complain about that. That's fine. It's my nature to be on the fringe. That's where I want to be. There is great liberty in being on the fringe.

My whole dark side wants to be in the heart of the establishment. I was brought up in a good middle class household in East Cavan of the 1930s, '40s and '50s. And believe you me, that was a Gestapo-istic climate. So I'm sure my insistence, my pursuit of articulating the erotic, the sensual, the sexy in theatre has a great deal to do with the Hitler-censored world into which I was born and reared.

The body was not to be mentioned in '30s, '40s and '50s Ireland. The young people nowadays have an attitude of freedom and openness with regard to the sensual – whether they have the capacity to handle it is another matter entirely. Because the magic, the mystery, the explosive colours of the sensual, the sexual, of love, are one of the great challenges in our lives. I'd have thought storytelling all the time is about that. Trying to learn how to love. Trying to learn how to make love. There is nothing more challenging.

For me the theatre experience – to try and articulate my thoughts on that, my on-the-skin feelings on that, plus writing fiction, plus writing poems – are my road to sanity, are my road to getting up in the morning.

I do not for a moment believe in a theatre, a literature, a dance, an anything that isn't informed by the sacral. I was in the Abbey inside the last twelve months, I was a speaker in a discussion on Sean O'Casey. I said, straight off – and I was glad of the opportunity to say it – that I had been working in the Abbey Theatre for the last 30 That's a failure of nerve. That's going with the secular surround. That's the death of magic. There is no magic without the sacral.

I was brought up in a society which for all its crimes was haunted. It had a sense of the sacral. All storytelling, it followed, was informed by the sacral. If you couldn't haunt the listener, go home and mind the tongs from the fire. That's why Kavanagh in the next county beside Cavan was rapture for us. We were brought up on Kavanagh. Our parents and everybody along the block recognised instantly that when Kavanagh wrote, "I only know that I was there, with hayseed on my hair, lying on the shady side of a haycock in July", that the door to the other world was being opened. I think the catastrophe of contemporary writing and contemporary theatre in this country is its facile acceptance of the secular as a way of thought and feeling.

Photo: Fergus Bourke

Tom Hickey (centre) in Dance for Your Daddy, *1987*

Establishing a record of my theatre work doesn't worry me tuppence. My worries are other. My worries are when I get up at eight in the morning, and I'm heading for my desk, to be in tip-top shape, on the page. The magic and seeking to get it on the page. To be in tip-top shape at that hour seven days a week requires, need I say, constant attention. That's the challenge of magical writing as far as I'm concerned. In short, it's a spirit journey.

That's what excites me about Pina Bausch. You look at that woman, and you could tell from ten thousand miles away that she is haunted. It's coming off her in waves. Was born haunted, is haunted, will always be haunted, and that informs her work. Don't ask me to go to the theatre or read the novel or the poem that hasn't that classic note of Irish literature from the year dot – the creak of the door between the two worlds. The whisper, the haunting, echoing whisper that exists in the creak of the door between the two worlds – that is the Irish voice at its best. That's what I seek to articulate. Whether it's in theatre or poetry.

> *That's what excites me about Pina Bausch. You look at that woman, and you could tell from ten thousand miles away that she is haunted. It's coming off her in waves. Was born haunted, is haunted, will always be haunted, and that informs her work.*

To play with that in theatre in terms of the physical, to try and express the spirit magic through the magic of the body – that is one of the beautiful challenges.

Tom Hickey
Actor

*F*or many years, Tom Hickey was best known nationwide as Benjy in the television series The Riordans. *This versatile actor, a legend among Irish actors, trained in the Stanislavski method at Deirdre O'Connell's Focus Theatre, where he did much experimental work. He describes, below, how this led him to a more physical style of acting, "we don't know from why", and in particular his fruitful collaboration with Tom Mac Intyre and Patrick Mason at the Peacock Theatre in* The Great Hunger, Dance for Your Daddy, Rise Up Lovely Sweeney, Snow White *and* The Bearded Lady. *As well as consistently performing in productions by Ireland's major playwrights at the Abbey Theatre, Tom has played Drosselmeier in CoisCéim Dance Theatre's production,* Nutcracker.

It was a coincidence that I finally met Mac Intyre. But even before I met Mac Intyre, I was in the Stanislavski studio at The Focus Theatre with Deirdre O'Connell. That was during the time when it wasn't popular for acting schools to be around. I think the general opinion was that inspiration was all, and you needed no more than talent and inspiration. Workshops, or work on the body and the voice, were frowned upon. "High-falutin'" is the word that probably was in currency at the time.

Within the Stanislavski studio, the actor's instrument is the body, the voice and the inner instrument – the imagination, the emotions, the dark side. The heart of the matter is that the body and the voice express whatever is going on inside. So therefore you need plasticity of body, and flexibility of voice. That's the nuts and bolts of what I learned at that time.

We used to do improvisations in the Stanislavski studio, where I had been one of the first pupils. But because I was learning so much, and because I was part of the scene, I became like a permanent student for years. I used to do these one-man improvisations, which became more and more bizarre. You improvised dialogue and movement, but a lot of the movement became quite surreal and very strange. I remember Deirdre saying to me once, "Thomas, these are very strange things you're doing.". Deirdre was more literary-based.

Tom Hickey as Drosselmeier in Nutcracker
(CoisCéim Dance Theatre)

So that was the direction in which I was unconsciously heading in the Stanislavski studio. I worked subsequently with a well-known radio playwright, Lee Gallagher. We did two shows in the early '70s called *The Good-bye Machine* and *The Velvet Abattoir*. I directed one, and acted and played in another. They were very strange and surreal shows.

Then I was floating around for a while and I remember seeing Colin Blakely in the Abbey playing in *The Morning After Optimism*, by Tom Murphy. The physicality of this man's performance was extraordinary. I'll never forget it. Certainly it was influential, because it was something that I recognised. I didn't know what it was, but I recognised it.

In 1975 I did a play called *What a Bloody Circus*, by Ionesco. It was the English-language world premiere at the theatre festival, directed by a man called Patricka Ionesco – no relation. He was an extraordinary director. It confirmed something in the way I was going, in that he totally emphasised the instinctive side that's available to an actor, combined with the most extreme athleticism. He could just stand up on the table and do handstands. He was a graduate of the film and acting school in Romania, and an extraordinary man. The play went on for four and a half hours.

I remember him saying once, "Now you come in the door", and he did this amazing sort of physical stance. He saw the question in my eyes, and answered,

"We don't know from why." I knew immediately, "Fine, excellent, so you are operating from somewhere else."

I was also aware that if you were going to operate this way, you needed to be aware of the flexibility of the body. So I went to dance class to Miss Burchall on Stephen's Green. She was wonderful. "Thomas, Thomas your tendons are too tight", she would say. Well, that was the best I could do. So there was some sort of unconscious movement in me towards this area of physicality in acting or whatever.

I met Mac Intyre in 1983. We started work on *The Great Hunger* with Patrick Mason directing, and the mime boys Vincent O'Neill and Conall Kearney, who were just back from Paris. I hadn't seen this sort of script before, but I did recognise it.

Mac Intyre's way of articulating his script is that he has what he calls a "verbal score", and he has a physical or "gestural score". So I said, "Oh, okay, fine, right."

I said, "Tom, that line, where should I pitch it?" He answered, "Pitch it somewhere between the quotidian and the enigmatic, and you'll be alright." "Oh," I said, "Fine, that's great."

It wasn't easy in the beginning. I had a line in *The Great Hunger* which was, "Patrick Maguire went home and made cocoa." I didn't quite know where to pitch it or what to do with it. I'd only known him a week at this stage. I said, "Tom, that line, where should I pitch it?" He answered, "Pitch it somewhere between the quotidian and the enigmatic, and you'll be alright." "Oh," I said, "Fine, that's great." I didn't understand it, but I recognised it in the sense that, "he's not being dictatorial, you'll find it, it'll be found".

One of the great benefits from working with the mime boys was that they had a whole series of physical exercises. These were formal, mechanical, physical exer-

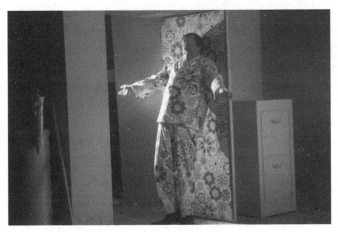

Tom Hickey as Drosselmeier in Nutcracker

cises which we used in warm-up exercises, and before improvising things. So now I had found something that was certainly a help. At that time, in the '80s, it would have been unheard of for actors to go out and do a warm-up on the stage before the audience come in, vocally and physically. To my memory that started with the Mac Intyre shows we did in the '80s. It never happened before that. All this is taken for granted now.

In the script, the physical score would be described in very long stage directions. For example: "Patrick Maguire comes in, he has a bag apron, he relates to the mother . . ." There was a whole series of stage directions like this. What we had to do, in conjunction with him of course, was to find out "What's the scene really about?" It consisted just of unconnected poetic text and a description of physicality. What we would do was to take the scene apart and improvise to find out what basically was going on. Then we would go back to the beginning again and it would have altered. Some of what seemed to be most important in the scene might have gone, and something that was quite innocuous would now come up front.

It's the old story of play: It's by play that you reach whatever you are going for. It's not an intellectual exercise. It's exploring with body and voice. You know what ballpark you are in, in relation to the play. You take the scene apart and then put it back together again with the insight you have gained by doing, and necessarily even discussing. We used to do some fairly extreme things I can tell you.

Tom Hickey as Drosselmeier in Nutcracker

I came to the conclusion that it was dancing. There would be a central, firm, choreographic shape. That didn't exclude variations, but it was like steel up the middle. The trick was that it's fresh, it's open, despite this track that is laid down.

Sometimes things happen – objects that one is using start behaving in a particular way. You might make some sort of discovery – Mac Intyre would attend every show, and he might say, "We'll keep that". So even objects could tell you things – objects do all sorts of strange things. In rehearsal some of the basic objects that were in the stage directions simply wouldn't stay. They'd walk out the door and some innocuous object that didn't seem important would come centre stage. So it was all about finding out, and listening to what we were all doing to find the end result.

It's a question of emphasis. For me the central principle of what I am doing is that I have a body, a voice and an inner instrument – to reveal the life or soul of somebody. That's the same whether it's Patrick Maguire in a Mac Intyre play or Firs in *The Cherry Orchard*. You're still doing the same exercise, but the emphasis is different. Where language is sparse and poetic you understand that the emphasis then becomes on the physicality because that's the nature of the beast. The objective is the same – to reveal the unconscious. It's the same with any art form. And this is very difficult. It's the same journey, but with a different emphasis – to reveal the unconscious so that some wisdom emerges.

In this surreal, imagistic work there were, and there should be, laughs in the audience. But there were also shocked silences I can assure you. We went to Edinburgh in 1986 with a revival of *The Great Hunger*. For the opening performance the burghers of Edinburgh were there on comps. We were fifteen, maybe twenty minutes into it when the seats began to go *click, click* as they all left. By the time we reached the interval I would say we had a third of the audience that we started with. It was a really tough and unnerving experience, a vote of no confidence in what we were doing. *The Great Hunger* was original, powerful and surreal, and made severe demands on an audience. One needed to re-align one's confidence. I remember saying to myself, "We've got to keep going through with whatever we have arranged to do and not be intimidated". And we did. The third of the audience that stayed until the end gave it a wonderful reception. It played to full houses for the rest of the time and won a Fringe First Award. It was just the wrong audience on opening night.

> The Great Hunger *was original, powerful and surreal, and made severe demands on an audience.*

As time went on – we were working from 1983 until 1989 – we developed an audience. It wasn't huge. We did one show per year in those times. One of the interesting aspects was that in the previews Tom Mac Intyre and Patrick Mason would do a discussion with the audience. We did learn a great deal from the audience. If there was something that wasn't working, we would be able to clarify that. We got a lot of abuse as well.

People thought they were coming in to a normal play. But, you know, Mac Intyre doesn't believe in a beginning, a middle and an end, in that order. So it's not appealing to the brain. It's going straight for the gut, or the heart, or the insides. I believe that people were being affected by it, but they couldn't understand what was going on. They couldn't understand it with their brains, but it was doing something to them somewhere else, in a visceral way. Some people were very upset about that, and they gave out shit.

Mac Intyre had spent time in Manhattan and had seen Merce Cunningham, and Kantor from Poland. I was always fascinated by Fellini and Bergman. So there was a whole American/European influence floating around in the rehearsal room. And there was Grotowski whom I didn't know much about. But I was aware he defined theatre as sacred and holy, which I believe it is. It's a ritual containing elements of "play".

The poetic text and gestural score in a Mac Intyre script can't be addressed in a naturalistic, conventional way. The celebrants must have a poetic vista. The language has to be treasured and spoken as poetic language. You've got that discipline, and you've got a physical discipline, so it's very demanding. It's very, very demanding work.

Patrick Mason
Theatre Director

After Manchester University where he studied theatre, Patrick Mason first arrived at the Abbey Theatre as a voice coach. This was the start of a long, fruitful association during which Mason brought many major new works in the Irish canon to life on the Abbey stage, including works by Frank McGuinness, Tom Kilroy, Tom Murphy, Hugh Leonard, Brian Friel and Tom Mac Intyre. Between 1982 and 1986 he developed a new theatrical idiom with Tom Mac Intyre and Tom Hickey at the Peacock Theatre in the plays The Great Hunger, Rise Up Lovely Sweeney, Dance for Your Daddy, The Bearded Lady *and* Snow White. *In 1990 he directed Brian Friel's* Dancing at Lughnasa, *which won him a Tony Award for best director. Patrick Mason was Artistic Director of the Abbey Theatre from 1993 to 1999. Here he offers some insights into his 1980s work with Mac Intyre and the notion of the dance in Friel's* Dancing at Lughnasa.

From the beginning – I mean in the aftermath of Edwardianism, and then in the Free State, and the Catholic state – there has been such a repression of the body and everything to do with the body in Ireland, that "head-energy" and linguistic skills have dominated. In the last 35 years that I have been working in the Irish theatre I think there has been a huge re-awakening of interest in the body of the performer. There have been efforts – my own work with Tom Mac Intyre and Tom Hickey in the '80s, other companies in the '90s, like Barabbas the Company, and the emergence of significant choreographers, like David Bolger's work with CoisCéim. All this has contributed to an awareness both in training and the preparation of the Irish performer in the importance of the body. But having said that, it's all modest enough.

Tom Mac Intyre came to me through the good offices of Tomas MacAnna and Joe Dowling, saying, "I think you are the only one to do this, what can we do?" And we started from there. Hickey was on board, which was absolutely pivotal to the whole thing. There were a handful of people who had training. By that time, the early '80s, the Marcel Marceau thing happened, and he had a huge influence. At the same time there was a Paris connection, with others going to the Le Coq School. That started to filter back. We are only talking about handfuls of people but it was significant in its time. Vincent O'Neill and Conall Kearney, who had been with Marceau, came into the group that we were forming around Mac Intyre and Tom Hickey, and we were able to use their skills. But we had our own problems with that classical mime aesthetic – we wanted to do something different. But if someone has a physical training – a trained body – be it in Martha Graham, Marceau, Le Coq, whatever, they have the ability to use their bodies.

There was quite a lot of resistance internally and externally to the work. It was seen as being pornographic. I remember when we were in the States in 1985, with *The Great Hunger* – we went to Russia, and to the US – and the Ancient Order of Hibernians lobbied the government to recall us because we were "a disgrace to the nation". And it was all to do with Tom Hickey and those bellows!

Look, you don't do it deliberately. You do it because it's part of that landscape. How do you deal with "The Great Hunger"? How do you deal with the sexuality of that blighted land, if you don't actually explore, as Patrick Kavanagh did, images of masturbation, and lusting after young ones in the grass and all this sort of stuff? It's in that landscape, so what are you supposed to do? Kind of politely pretend it didn't happen?

The interesting thing was, it was Tom Hickey with a pair of bellows. We used to say well what's the problem? It's a man with a pair of bellows – what's your problem? I mean, you'd know exactly what the problem was. The force of it was, you had made something happen in their imagination.

Photo: Fergus Bourke

Dearbhla Molloy, Bríd Brennan, Catherine Byrne and Bríd Ní Neachtáin
in Dancing at Lughnasa, *1991*

Then there was *Dancing at Lughnasa*. Gosh – what a beautiful and subtle play, and what a master Brian Friel is. Because what is always astonishing about that play is that he is touching on so many sensibilities. And yet it is done with such charm and subtlety that sometimes audiences don't even realise until after the event what has been going on, and quite how subversive that play is. And it is a very subversive play. But it's a great celebratory play as well.

Agnes: Wouldn't it be good if we all went?

Chris: Went where?

Agnes: To the harvest dance.

Chris: Aggie!

Agnes: Just like we used to. All dressed up. I think I'd go.

Rose: I'd go too Aggie! I'd go with you!

Kate: For heaven's sake you're not serious, Agnes – are you?

Agnes: I think I am.

Kate: Hah! There's more than Ballybeg off its head.

Agnes: I think we should all go.

Kate: Have you any idea what it'll be like? – Crawling with cheeky young brats that I taught years ago.

Photo: Fergus Bourke

Robert Gwilym, Bríd Brennan, Catherine Byrne and Rosaleen Linehan
in Dancing at Lughnasa

Agnes: I'm game.

Chris: We couldn't, Aggie – could we?

Kate: And all the riff-raff of the countryside.

Agnes: I'm game.

Chris: Oh God, you know how I loved dancing, Aggie.

(Act One, *Dancing at Lughnasa*)

There is "the dance", the big dance in the kitchen. There is the romantic dance of seduction in the garden, but then of course there is this extraordinary final vision of these figures swaying in the golden light of the past, as if it was dancing.

Michael: When I remember it, I think of it as dancing. Dancing with eyes half closed because to open them would break the spell. Dancing as if language had surrendered to movement – as if this ritual, this wordless ceremony, was now the way to speak, to whisper private and sacred things, to be in touch with some otherness. Dancing as if the very heart of life and all its hopes might be found in those assuaging notes and those hushed rhythms and in those silent and hypnotic movements. Dancing as if language no longer existed because words were no longer necessary.

(Final scene, *Dancing at Lughnasa*)

In Friel's play the dance becomes not just the literal dance but the cosmic dance. It sounds pretentious when you put it like that. But the great genius of the play is that it doesn't sound the least bit pretentious when it's said. It's so exciting, that moment when the radio comes on, it's just suddenly these characters start . . .

What's beautiful about it too is how Friel's description of the dance is utterly rooted in character. Just taking the particular physical nuances of that particular Aunt Kate, that particular Aunt Maggie, or whoever. And it was really following what Friel had put in his text. The dance aspect of the play was not just that you suddenly did a routine. It was organic to the character. It had to come absolutely out of the character.

Conall Morrison
Theatre Director

Conall Morrisson has directed many large-scale physical productions at the Abbey Theatre, including most significantly, his own adaptation of Patrick Kavanagh's novel Tarry Flynn *in 1997, featuring a 29-strong cast of dancers, actors and mime artists, and choreographed by David Bolger. Conall is currently an associate director of the Abbey Theatre. Here he explains the sense of physicality in his work.*

The body has come more centre stage. The old Abbey tradition was that they stood and delivered. In the Fay tradition, they were very obsessed with "the voice beautiful", because there was a great emphasis on the writers, and the primacy of the text. The voice beautiful – and you would just stand there and give all the focus to whoever was speaking. The rules were that you didn't move, and you didn't pull focus while somebody else was talking. It was very regimented. That then probably filtered out into the other theatre companies – "Well, if that is what the Abbey tradition is, the lauded Abbey way, then that is what we should do." So while that had its benefits, and put great focus on the text, I presume it also put a set of clamps on the body for a while.

That leads to the fact that I think the Irish actor didn't really open up the full range of their possibilities until relatively recently. We just specialise on characterisation, being able to do good impersonations of the range of characters that you would see around the place. In many ways it wasn't a million miles away from what you would do in the pub, or what you would do entertaining your friends. In terms of really opening up how far the actor can go, and how expressive the actor can be with their body – that's a relatively recent development.

It's also partly happening because theatre is having to ask itself tough questions. What is our *raison d'être* in this environment where film and TV can do so much, and in the world of special effects, which is almost infinite in what it can achieve. What is it that the body can achieve? The body and its expressiveness and how it connects with the imagination, in a live environment, what is that, that's different and better?

We all know about boring shows we've seen. But the really memorable moments are when we've been there in the live environment and something happens that is expressive in a way that you don't get in any other art form.

We know we have the writers, we know we have the texts, we know we have the musicality in the voice, but the great unexplored is the actor, and the body in space. It's there in dances and the choreography of "work". Friel uses it brilliantly in the choreography of domestic work in *Dancing at Lughnasa*, but now we are becoming much more self-aware about it, bringing the range of possibilities centre-stage and saying, "What can we do with this?"

It's partly to do with a confidence in what the theatre community can do. Also theatre needs to keep on constantly re-inventing itself, re-assessing itself, asking, "Why do we exist as an art form, what is it that we have to offer that film and television don't?" And that's about the live moment, the body in space, the imagination and inventiveness. One of the things that doesn't come out of your TV screen is the exchange of energies you get whenever you watch the body in motion, or physical inventiveness, in that live environment, as it's happening.

So I think this past fifteen years has seen a very noticeable marrying of different traditions – of language, what people can do in terms of their characterisations and narrative skills, but also using great physical inventiveness, and what it is that makes an event truly theatrical.

A lot of my inspiration would have come from shows that I have seen. I went over to live in Edinburgh when I was about 18 and I saw a lot of shows, including a lot of dance shows at the Festival.

I don't want to be a film director. I'm interested in what kind of languages you can use in the theatre, be it through spoken language or music or movement or design. I think movement is physical poetry in the theatre. You can say a huge amount of things, but not necessarily say them in a leaden, naturalistic, prescriptive way.

I'm interested in how you take different forms and fit them with different contents. So various pieces just seem to suggest themselves as texts that are going to want a physical manifestation or exploration. They are often about the imagination. Or about just digging into the subconscious or the unconscious and finding images that seem to express the idea better than a literal description, the well-turned phrase. But it's all about the search for the ultimate expression of the idea. Sometimes that is in the word alone, sometimes in a physical image, sometimes it's in a fusion of the two. Or any other element. It's not so much that I'm just interested in physical theatre as such. I like to think that it's an ongoing search for the ultimate theatrical expression of whatever idea I'm trying to explore.

Tarry Flynn came from the text first. I took as my keynote a line from the novel, that says that "any act or any incident can contain within it the energy of the imagination".

Photo: Amelia Stein

James Kennedy as Tarry Flynn (centre),
Eugene O'Brien (left) in Tarry Flynn, *1997*

That Tarry as the poet, and obviously as a thinly disguised portrait of Kavanagh, just saw poetry everywhere in everyday life. Be it in the action of a rusty gate or in the weather on a mountainside or in dragging a drain. Within all those actions or entities he saw poetry.

The question was how to animate that. Although he is the peasant subsistence farmer, he has an incredibly rich animistic imaginative life. So I was trying to find physical and visual languages that would demonstrate that. The idea struck me to have the choric energies of the novel played by actors who were playing animals, the idea being that a lot of the characters in the book, and in that society, are not a massive journey away from animality. They have speech and thought, but they are scratching away there at a very bare, rugged, rough existence.

That's there in a lot of plays. For example, John B. Keane's "The Bull" McCabe. Or "the bird" or "the ram". It's a given in Irish life to identify people with their animals. It's also an actorial training tradition that you identify what the animal is within you, or the animal that is behind a character, like I mentioned, "The Bull" McCabe. Whenever Anthony Hopkins did King Lear at the National, he based it on a bull. Again, you don't iron out all the complexities of a character, but do identify a physical type and a set of animal urges.

My key was to have the animals as chorus. They had more cop-on than a lot of the characters, who were actually close to "animal" in many respects. There was a blur and a bleed between the two. Not all of it satirical. There is the idea that if you get back in touch with your animal you'll have a much more open and celebratory relationship with the earth and your environment, and that's what Tarry was trying to tell them. Become your own physical poet. It's comic, unsentimental rough-edged stuff, but it's poetry no less. As Kavanagh said himself, "Find the poetry in every blooming thing."

> *Become your own physical poet. It's comic, unsentimental rough-edged stuff, but it's poetry no less. As Kavanagh said himself, "Find the poetry in every blooming thing."*

It was a very big cast. Patrick Mason was behind the whole enterprise. He said, "If you think it's absolutely necessary to the piece, I'll supply the resources to allow you to have a big cast." Which allowed me to get dancers, a lot of whom had never been on the Abbey or any kind of "traditional" stage before, up to wonderful older character actors like Derry Power on the other end. So I had that entire scale of community, which was very important, so you had the sense of a community against Tarry, how he related to them, but also to have that full range of physical types.

So the two worlds are blurred, with animals coming out of the drains, or actors playing tufts of grass, heifers, and all those kind of shape-shifting entities that are in the book. It was great having those performers, and that range of physical skills at my disposal.

It was an interesting struggle with tradition – again always with Patrick's backing. This was a language I would have used in other shows, or felt much more at ease using in other venues. But there was something about the heavy-handed tradition in the Abbey that did give me pause for thought. You could kind of feel Ernest Blythe's clammy fingers on your shoulder saying, "Now, boy, this isn't helping the National Cause! You can't be having talking chickens on the Abbey stage!"

But on the other side, there were other voices – including Mason's, and my own – urging, and saying, "This is exactly what the Abbey needs." It was a gamble that I like to think paid off. I had a visit from Kavanagh in a dream, which I was very surprised about. Initially he was complimentary about the adaptation. I didn't think he'd be on for it at all. But true to form at the end of it he just turned around and growled, "Ah would you ever fuck off!"

Tarry Flynn, *1997*

Photo: Amelia Stein

I'd long admired David Bolger's work. I think he's the best choreographer in Ireland at the moment, and the best theatrical choreographer as well. We get on very well and would share a theatrical language, to an extent. So when I was writing the adaptation, I was writing things knowing I was going to work with David on it. I was able to let my own imagination run riot, knowing that I had a top-quality choreographer there to help me realise the images. David really put the cast through their paces. In the same way that I was encouraging the dancers to develop their acting skills, and their capacity to characterise, David was really pushing those actors to do some movement and dances they wouldn't know they had in them. It was tough stuff. It was very demanding.

There's a large opening dance that goes on with a lot of pounding rhythms in it; it was tough, but they did it. I like to think that the cast entered the spirit of it. They got quite infected by the ethos behind the adaptation – that you can unlock the physical, the sensual, the musical, the linguistic poet within yourself given half a chance. Part of the problem in society is that we will suppress it – or we will accept it if it's in between Faber and Faber covers. But if we were to get on more easy, freewheeling terms with our own poet we'd maybe be a happier bunch. So the cast got in touch with that, and it made them more willing and more open to be rolling around like eejits on the floor, and to play with the material.

I think the audiences are changing, simply because they have been seeing more throughout the year. The time was when they would just see some stuff during the theatre festival, and go, "Well that's great, but that's what the foreigners do . . ." But always section it off like that.

Because it's come more into the mainstream, I think the audiences are much more educated, much more open, and then sometimes also much more critical about it. Either they've seen it before, or it's just another set of workshop exercises that maybe should have been left on the workshop floor. If you are going to raise the bar, you have to keep on challenging the audience's expectations.

But I think, in its own small way, having *Tarry Flynn* in the Abbey in 1997 had its own significance, because it was on *that* stage. Well, of course, Tomas MacAnna had done great big rambunctious shows, and there are forebears, but it actually had a very specific physicality to it, and a sort of brazenness – a great celebratory energy about the nature of physicality and that kind of expressiveness. I think it did lay down a little bit of a marker that said, "right come, this is a great area of theatre to explore".

I like to think that I plan according to the material, be it a one-man show or a big frothy musical. Again you are going to keep on asking hard questions about what it is that makes this a piece of theatre, of live performance. If that involves high physicality that's fine; if that involves standing in the corner with your head in a bucket, then so be it. The chances are that I am going to keep returning to more overt styles of physical theatre because I find them very exhilarating, very challenging, and very expressive. The variety is what I love. Theatre is like a big baggy accordion of an art form. It's got small enclosed little notes and then a big wheeze of a sound. I love exploring that range of it. But physicality is probably going to remain at the core of my work some way or another.

> *Theatre is like a big baggy accordion of an art form. It's got small enclosed little notes and then a big wheeze of a sound. I love exploring that range of it.*

I think it has taken Irish theatre longer to embrace physicality than elsewhere, as there are long traditions of actors just relying on the text. Pushing yourself further, you actually admit and confront the idea that you are a professional actor, and have a wonderful range of expressiveness – not just doing a set of voices and all-purpose characterisations. It's about pushing that and really opening up that huge envelope of possibilities. I think that has come quite late to Irish theatre, but at least it's coming now, and there are a generation who are up and running and at it. They are trained in a range of skills and are much more fluent in them and up for it. I think that change has happened and the development will continue.

Gina Moxley
Playwright and Actress

*B*orn in Cork where she studied painting at the Crawford School of Art, Gina
Moxley is a well-known actress and playwright. Her plays include Danti-
Dan, Tea Set, Dog House, *and* Toupées and Snare Drums, *with CoisCéim Dance
Theatre at the Peacock Theatre, which she discusses below.*

On *Toupées and Snare Drums* (1998):

David Bolger approached me to do a show with him. I previously had only written
straight plays for theatre and actors, no people moving at all hardly. So we tried to
come up with a scenario that could reasonably involve both actors and dancers – so
you could have dancers talking, and actors dancing.

I was interested in the '60s showband era. I loved the music, and the kitschness
of it. As far as I know that was the beginning of any sort of sexuality in Ireland.

So we decided on that era, and then muddled through fitting a story to it. It got a lot of actors off their arses. They'd never worked so hard. A lot of the dancing in the Showband era was quite formalised – there were routines, like the Huckle-buck. That was the beginning of it.

The story of *Toupées and Snare Drums* centred around "Dizzy Duffy's Dance Hall" – an old dance hall opening up after Lent. At that time there was no dancing allowed during Lent. It's bonkers to think of it now. A very big, swishier kind of Albert Reynolds dance hall had opened up down the road. It's the last night before Dizzy Duffy's closes down, and the band that are supposed to play

Photo: Amelia Stein

*Muirne Bloomer and Sean Kearns watching on
in Toupées and* Snare Drums

195

don't turn up. So the local band are forced to keep doing their three or four songs. It's basically about the small little hokey places, and the burgeoning sexuality of the women as well after Lent. They are gagging to be out, and the same old awful fellas are coming in and out the door.

There's a rural myth about the devil appearing in these places. It was a rumour put out by rival dance hall owners, apparently, and also the Church, so that nobody would be getting too hot under the collar. We had the devil appear in this dance hall. Of course he only appears to the girls. They are in their bras and pants by the end of the dance. That era was so buttoned-up and straight-laced in loads of ways. Even the men and the band were wearing five-piece suits. What are you talking about, you are going dancing for God's sake! It was just raw sex after Lent really, let's face it.

We tried to develop a meeting of languages between dance and acting. We didn't have any role models – not in this country anyway – so we were making it up as we went along. It was quite difficult because a lot of dancers had never been asked to speak on stage. And their beautiful lyrical bodies – how do you match that with being able to speak as well? Probably the hardest part of rehearsal was getting each discipline to do the other discipline. The blending of those disciplines was what we set out to do. We attracted all sorts of audiences that we never expected to get – pure dance, and pure theatre people. And then all of these women who remembered all the showband stuff. They were jiving in the aisles. It was fantastic.

It was bizarre that they got two different people to review the show in *The Irish Times*. The dance reviewer reviewed just the "dance" part of it, and the theatre reviewer just the "theatre". And our whole purpose was to meld the two disciplines!

Now people are trained to use their bodies more. And a lot of the directors now, like Conall Morrisson who did *Tarry Flynn*, a fantastically physical show, don't just rely on words. This kind of work is just much more vital and exciting. Parameters are broadened because people travel more and see more.

> People began to realise that the body is capable of such lyricism that you can't just rely on the verbals completely. I think, a lot of the time, that writers – and I'm to blame for this as well – just hear voices. I'm sorry I don't see the bodies.

People began to realise that the body is capable of such lyricism that you can't just rely on the verbals completely. I think, a lot of the time, that writers – and I'm to blame for this as well – just hear voices. I'm sorry I don't see the bodies. It's something you just have to force yourself to do more. But that kind of physical work takes much more rehearsal. It all becomes more expensive because people are only learning how to do it. So there are all sorts of reasons why we are not doing big huge shows like *Tarry Flynn*.

I really do think there has been a big sea-change though. Particularly when it can be applied to something as fundamentally Irish as *Tarry Flynn*. Seeing that, it just makes total sense.

Raymond Keane
Co-Artistic Director and Co-Founder of Barabbas

A long with Veronica Coburn and Mikel Murfi, Raymond Keane was a founder member of Barabbas the Company (www.barabbas.ie) in 1993. Raymond's *acting style is a great exponent of their clown-based aesthetics. As well as his journey as an an actor Raymond here explains, among other things, the relationship between holistic hairdressing and physical theatre.*

I didn't get into this business until I was in my mid- to late twenties. I had never even done a school show, though I did sing a song in a scouts' concert once. But I had no interest in theatre whatsoever. In fact, I was a hairdresser for many years.

Then one weekend in Paris in the late '80s I saw fellas doing mime on the street imitating people. Being from Dungarvan, a small town on the Southeast, I had never seen anything like that in my life. I thought, "What is that?", and "I want to do that." So I got myself a book, and started to teach myself mime in front of a mirror.

Then The Grapevine Theatre Company came to the Milky Way Theatre in Amsterdam, where I was living at the time. Thom McGinty (The Diceman), who headed up the company, told me to forget the book. He put some makeup on me and put me out on the streets of Amsterdam. That was my

Photo: Charlie O'Neill

Raymond Keane (left), Mikel Murfi and Veronica Coburn in Come Down from the Mountain John Clown

beginning in physical theatre. In the great lines of Steve Martin, "Some people have a way with words, and some people not have way." I was attracted to something that was physical, rather than words.

From there I got more and more interested. I was invited to set up my Hairwork studio at the Grapevine Exhibition space in Dublin. I had my first studio there, with a whole philosophical approach to hair and social consciousness, about unwaged prices and all that stuff. It fitted with their community arts, and the notion that hair could be a creative endeavour.

While I was there I worked with Kalichi, and his company No Dance, training and performing in dance-acting. We worked with all sorts of influences from Martha Graham to Isadora Duncan but they were mostly of Eastern origin, like t'ai chi, yoga, Japanese Noh, Butoh, the notion of the intelligent and efficient body and all the philosophies all that brings.

At the back of it all, though, I think this clown thing has always been a part of me. Later Charlie O'Neill and I had a comedy duo for years, "Morris Major and Morris Minor", and did a lot of street theatre. I learned as much as I could, and got more and more attracted towards the clown thing because it allowed me to be playful, have fun and be stupid. It just suited me.

In the mix of disciplines from different cultures, I was learning French mime with a Marcel Marceau background from Vincent O'Neill and Conall Kearney in their Oscar Mime Company. Soon I felt I was beginning to mime like a French person. Marceau had developed his own physical vocabulary and gesture and I was adopting it into mine, as you do.

Around that time I also spent seven years doing young people's television, when I would have hit off of Mikel Murfi and Veronica Coburn who were both working on different programmes in RTE. We soon found ourselves playing shows together in town.

Sometimes we joke about the fact that we were always cast as the "jumpy up and down person", in a play – the one who did the more bizarre physical things. This was because we could I suppose, and because we were up for acting the maggot.

Photo: Kate Horgan

Louis Lovett in God's Gift

So in 1993 we thought, "Why don't we form a company and dedicate ourselves to this jumping up and down theatre?" We found very fancy and sexy names for that of course. We had many influences from mime, dance, clown, *commedia dell'arte*, *bouffon*, puppetry, and all that eastern influence that I had. But at the centre of it all was this red-nosed clown. On top of that we wanted to make a theatre that was Irish – because we were Irish. We were interested in the Irish physicality, but inspired by the principles from a lot of European disciplines, and then trying to adopt those into a new form of Irish theatre, which would be a Barabbas theatre.

There is an Irish physicality, even if it was more pronounced 20 years ago than it is today with globalisation. We have the tipping of the cap, or the apologetic nature of our physicality. The 800 years of oppression if you like. Oppressive religious backgrounds perhaps smothered us. What is the make-up of your past that gives you your physicality, your outer self?

You could go right around the world. When the American cousins used to come to stay every summer I was so envious of them. They were big, tall, stood up straight, confident, loud, wore white socks, underarm spray, these things I thought, "I want them." When I was growing up, underarm spray didn't exist for boys. They had lovely clean white socks that they changed every day. One of the things that used to drive me nuts was that they could cross their legs in a way that I couldn't – loose physicality – putting one ankle on one knee. I'd try and imitate that and I'd get a pain in me hip doing it. It still fascinates me. I always felt that while the Americans were there taking up space in the kitchen, I was cowering in the corner. That was significant for me.

Raymond Keane in Half-eight Mass of a Tuesday

Photo: Charlie O'Neill

With Irish society coming of age, finally shedding the colonial past, new riches, Celtic tiger, success, arts, sport, whatever, I think we have straightened up as a society. We're heading on into the world saying, "Take us seriously."

I have been fascinated for years by the fact that we are all so culturally different. However, we are all starting to adopt each other's speech patterns, and each other's physicality. Particularly American culture: how many teenagers today are moving like the people in *Friends*? Forget the language, watching the physicality, it is extraordinary.

So, when we started with Barabbas first, we were totally obsessed with this Irish physicality. Mundane things interested us – the ordinariness of the Irish world. We were interested in the non-verbal, so the literary tradition wasn't really a huge influence. Although of course it always is, because you are what your past is. But we were interested in digging into this Irish psyche through a physical format. You make things from your own experience – so our experience was from growing up in 1960s, '70s, '80s Ireland.

I'll hang this on one show we made in particular – *Half-eight Mass of a Tuesday*. Now half eight of a Tuesday is a totally different mass than eleven o'clock mass on a Sunday morning. We set the show in a very small village, where a very small congregation would turn up for this mass. We wanted to represent that ritual in theatre. Of course the mass is a perfect dramatic structure. It allowed us to look at the kinds of quintessentially Irish people who would turn up some frosty morning in the middle of winter for half-eight mass of a Tuesday. It's also a perfect place to make a non-verbal piece of theatre, because people don't tend to talk during mass. They whisper or they pray. They also think a lot.

> If we look at our great masters, Yeats and Beckett, both put equal emphasis on the physical. Beckett would say he takes his inspiration from clown and silent movie actors. Yeats was interested in "total theatre". So we do have a strong tradition in it.

Physicality is not that foreign to us Irish. I think we have a great love for physical theatre. If we look at our great masters, Yeats and Beckett, both put equal emphasis on the physical. Beckett would say he takes his inspiration from clown and silent movie actors. Yeats was interested in "total theatre". So we do have a strong tradition in it.

We also have Irish dancing, which, personally, I think can be incredible. It's a lovely cultural thing to think that we move from the waist down. Other cultures would comment on Irish dancing with, "It's just the legs isn't it?" Stiff upper bodies – almost devoid of emotion. But then you watch old guys out in the west and they are mad dancers. They haven't learned the tradition of arms by your sides, straight torso and bouncing ringlets.

With Barabbas we decided to dedicate ourselves to the physical approach to theatre, but nowadays most theatre practitioners have that knowledge and experience.

Walter Asmus
Theatre Director, Specialist in Samuel Beckett's plays

*W*alter Asmus – long-time friend and colleague of Samuel Beckett, and professor of acting in Hanover – has been working on Beckett's theatrical opus on and off for over 30 years now. He first met Beckett in 1974 at Berlin's Schiller Theater, where Asmus was assisting the Nobel Prize-winner on his directorial debut with Waiting for Godot, *the play that has become synonymous with Beckett's hilarious and excruciating worldview. Walter has directed* Waiting for Godot *at Dublin's*

Gate Theatre four times since 1988, and is directing it again for the centenary of Beckett's birth this year (2006). Here he reflects upon the notion of Beckett as a choreographer, and the creator of the most eloquent Irish body on stage to date.

I met Beckett in Berlin in 1974 when he directed *Waiting for Godot* for the first time in his life. I was his assistant. As you may know, he often sat in rehearsals from the beginning. When Roger Blin directed in 1953, Beckett attended rehearsals, and Beckett himself was not a director. He had just started to write plays. I think he learned a lot from sitting in rehearsals.

One day he thought, "To do it the right way, the way I visualise it, I might as well do it mysel." He worked on *Waiting for Godot* for over a year before he came to Berlin, working out his script, writing out his play anew in these physical terms of movement, and choreography. For every scene he had a definite choreography. It wasn't this precise before.

He said, "I'm not a theatre director so I have to over-compensate. I have to sit for one year." And by the end of it he knew the text by heart in German. He was sitting in rehearsals like a conductor, knowing the score by heart. He would conduct the play, saying, "No, no, there is a pause"; "No, there is a wrong word". So it is absolutely like music with the timing

Photo courtesy the Gate Theatre

Alan Stanford as Pozzo in Waiting for Godot

and the rhythms, and very quick exchanges. Like one of the thieves was saved, and there is a crash and they come together.

When you read it thoroughly, the stage directions and so on, you see there is a definite vision of how it should be done. Approaches and crossings are in the script in the stage directions, as are the emotions. They have been adhered to since the play came out in the '50s. At times it was very staid. In terms of its psychology – once there was a stage direction "violently", and people would shout without motivation. There were no real links in it – so it became an absurd play, shouting out of the blue.

> *He [Beckett] was sitting in rehearsals like a conductor, knowing the score by heart. He would conduct the play, saying, "No, no, there is a pause"; "No, there is a wrong word". So it is absolutely like music with the timing and the rhythms . . .*

But as regards the movement, when Beckett came to Berlin in 1975 he himself said, "It's a mess of a play." He remarked how it was written very untidily, and with loose ends. That was long after he had written *Endgame*, which is a more structured play in terms of the script. It's really water-proof. In *Endgame* everything has an inner logic. When you read the text thoroughly you get the reasons why things have to happen at a certain point – from one thing the other follows.

So after Beckett had developed as an artist, looking back on *Waiting for Godot*, he found it untidy, and disorderly. He had to give it a structure. He sat down and worked out a definite structure for every movement of the actors with his Regisbook. It became a sort of ballet or choreography. In the very beginning of rehearsals he called it "balletic".

I remember the actors asking, "But if we do it balletic doesn't it become a formula? Or sterile?" Every actor is afraid of becoming formulaic. They found out that the blocking of the play is very logical and has very much to do with the psychology of the characters. For example, the repetition of Estragon and Vladimir moving away and coming together, he approaches step by step. "Are you hungry?"; "Look at me"; "Embrace me". Until there is an embrace, and he says, "You stink of garlic". "It's good for you." They are one character and they are two characters: the mind and the belly, the hat and the boots, and so on. These two characters act as if they were one character – very simple, very obvious.

I have always used Beckett's basic 1975 choreography and score, but it has changed tremendously. This Gate Theatre production came out in '91 with this cast. Before Tom Hickey was Vladimir and Barry McGovern was Estragon. But in terms of chemistry, Johnny Murphy and Barry McGovern are really the perfect couple for it. Yet it changes a lot because the actors have more confidence. They don't have to act so much. In the beginning the problem with this choreography is that actors try to be actors of course – and to show their capabilities. I think the more they can rely on this score and live in it without putting on too many things, the better.

With this choreography, precision, and music, you have to serve the play in a different way from some director putting on a Shakespeare and deconstructing *Lear*, for example. That is a completely different matter. It has happened with Beckett, but it is not my cup of tea. I am loyal to Beckett.

Barry McGovern as Vladimir in
Waiting for Godot

Perhaps I was a bit overawed before. I have directed *Waiting for Godot* seven times – in Germany, in New York, for television, and twice here in Dublin with different casts. My first *Waiting for Godot* was in 1978 at Brooklyn Academy of Music in New York. They wanted Beckett to direct it, and he said, "No, let Walter Asmus direct it." What a great gift and a trust on his side.

Then of course I was much more his master's voice, and wanted to do it right. But everyone thought he had to follow this "thing" in a much more abstract way. I think it has loosened a little, and now my vision of the characters has become much more mine. It is much more what I find in the play and what interests me from my experience and also the actors' experience from the streets – from our life and society.

It's not Stanislavski, or Brecht. It's a melange, a mix of all kinds of things. But Beckett had his vision, and that's

Photo courtesy the Gate Theatre

Barry McGovern and Johnny Murphy in Waiting for Godot

why Billie Whitelaw, as you say, was his medium. That worked very well. Others did not put their egos to serve the play. Billie tried to serve the play and serve Beckett. Not to try to improve Beckett, to make Beckett more bombastic than he is. In this work it's a danger to have actors who try to live their big egos on the stage.

You can't be esoteric of course. He tried to put across to the actors exactly how he wanted it by doing a line-reading. But they had to take over. In Berlin during the rehearsals of *Waiting for Godot* the actors did exactly what he wanted them to do in the quick exchanges, and for a long time it was just mechanical. Then by and by it came to life. In the end it was very realistic, and very down-to-earth. Beckett would sit there like a little boy, and *loved* it. But it was not his way to explain it to them, to say, "This character is this . . ."

Then by and by it came to life. In the end it was very realistic, and very down-to-earth. Beckett would sit there like a little boy, and loved *it. But it was not his way to explain it to them, to say, "This character is this . . ."*

I met a young Swedish director a while ago and he said "I love to work on Beckett, but especially with older actors because they don't try to show their acting capabilities anymore." They have the self-trust and self-confidence to just stand there on stage. They know what they have to say and what they have to do and they don't have to act out so much. Of course, a young actor always has the ambition to do a lot of things – unconsciously. And many actors are scared to do Beckett because of the nakedness of the plays. Just standing on stage and doing nothing. That's very hard.

I first came to Ireland in '88. I had to learn some things from the actors during rehearsals. The German was more "meaningful". Irish actors can just be more colloquial. Because this Irish-English language is more genuine, and they know what it is about. The Irish-ness is that they speak like this in real life so it tightens and is lighter than German or American productions.

Going to a pub in Ireland, it's a cacophony of talk – talking, talking, and people screaming in each other's ears. I think this Irish talking quality, telling stories, is what we were all enchanted by in the '50s, '60s, and '70s. Sitting in a pub drinking whiskey, and somebody would start to tell stories, and ghost stories. It is a talking thing.

> It's very funny – the play starts with the programmatic line, "nothing to be done". An Irish audience responds to the black humour of that immediately, because they recognise it has to do with their lives.

It's very funny – the play starts with the programmatic line, "Nothing to be done." An Irish audience responds to the black humour of that immediately, because they recognise it has to do with their lives. If things are getting too difficult, there is nothing to be done. That is my interpretation, but there must be something in Irish life which strikes a chord in the audience. It's a laugh. But *nichts zu machen* isn't a laugh in Germany. His boots shined, or nothing to be done?

I think Beckett was just writing dialogue. Of course there is a little bit of this philosophy of body and mind, the relationship, how body interferes with the mind, and how body out-does the mind, But once you start to explain the text in any way, it goes wrong. Beckett himself said, "It's all play. Nothing but play." That sounds very simple, but if you follow this line you will find that it tells thousands of things, by itself. Without imposing them on the audience.

Note

[1] Andrew Solway, p. 594, *The Continuum Companion to Twentieth Century Theatre*. London/NYC: Continuum, 2002

Chapter 6

Chapter 6

Ballet/Contemporary Crossover

I n dance, entities don't generally stay in their neat boxes. In Ireland, Joan
Denise Moriarty had begun mixing genres in her first full-length ballet based
on J.M. Synge's *The Playboy of the Western World*, with the now defunct Irish
National Ballet in Cork.

Moriarty was also probably the first to try to integrate Irish folk dance with ballet and contemporary dance in ballets such as *West Cork Ballad*, *Billy the Music*
and *Devil to Pay*, all based on Irish folk tales, together with *Lugh of the Golden
Arm*, based on Irish mythology. Even if, as Carolyn Swift who saw them opined that
"the Irish dances however stood out obstinately as inserted set pieces", Moriarty
definitely set a new movement style in motion.[1]

Later, Joanna Banks, whom Moriarty brought to Cork in 1974 with her impressive international background, would walk across from the ballet world into the
contemporary world too. Banks's dance pedigree stretches back rather neatly for the
purposes of *Irish Moves* to Ninette de Valois and the early days of the Royal Ballet
School in London. Her foray from there through Ballet Rambert, and then taking in
the Royal Canadian Ballet, Bat Dor Dance Company, Israel, and Bavarian State Ballet Munich before her arrival to Cork and the Irish National Ballet would eventually
culminate in her establishment, and ongoing directorship, of the College of Dance
in Monkstown, County Dublin. Joanna stayed in Ireland, and founded the school
at the urging of John Regan, a dancer with Mayo roots who had enjoyed an international career incluing dancing with Diaghilev's Ballets Russes.[2] More recently,
not unlike Mikhail Baryshnikov who sashayed across from the ballet world into the
more quirky arena of contemporary dance, Joanna Banks has become a performer
with John Scott's Irish Modern Dance Theatre, bringing her wealth of experience
to bear on Irish contemporary dance. Her life, traced out here in her own words,
exemplifies the open spirit that is so typical of the international dancer.

Joan Denise Moriarty
Founder, Irish National Ballet, 1973–1989

*B*orn in Mallow, County Cork, legendary dance pioneer Joan Denise Moriarty founded the amateur Cork Ballet Company in 1947, and in 1973 realised her dream of establishing the professional Irish Ballet Company, later to be the Irish National Ballet. The company thrived until 1988, a black year for dance in Ireland, when the Arts Council withdrew its funding. Here, in an extract from a 1979 radio interview with John Quinn, Moriarty explains how her passion for dance, and for founding a national dance company for Ireland, came about.

What is dance? A lot of people don't really understand what dancing is. After all, before we are born into this world we are moving. Inside the mother's womb we are moving. And when we are born, we move. From the very first minute we are brought into the world, we move.

Dance is only an extension of human moving. It's extending yourself, training you to further the movement that you do naturally. That's really what dance is all about. There has been dance in the world since the world started.

When I was about 12 or 13 I got scarlet fever very bad. I was a normal height up until then. But when I got out of bed after three months I had grown inches and inches. I remember getting out of bed, and seeing myself in the mirror, and crying, "I'll never be able to dance, I'll never be able to dance, I'm too big!"

Marie Rambert seemed to see something in me as a character. I don't quite know what my character was. And often during class – she used to take class herself – she used to scream at me: "Get out of my sight! There is too much of you there! If you were on a stage there would be room for nobody else!"

> And often during class — she used to take class herself — she used to scream at me: "Get out of my sight! There is too much of you there! If you were on a stage there would be room for nobody else!"

Well you can imagine, for a young girl, how humiliating that was. But she was a great friend. Because it did come to the time when I had to make up my mind what I was going to continue on and do. I had done a certain amount of stage work. But for England I was too tall, because the tradition in England is very small dancers in height. That stems from the fact that the only men they could get interested to train as dancers were small. So you can't have a towering ballerina and a small little male dancer.

I was home on holidays with my mother and we were in Cork, standing on Saint Patrick's bridge. My mother met a gentleman and a lady whom she knew and they were talking. They turned to me and the man said to me: "And what are you doing?" "I am training to be a dancer." "Oh, what kind of dancer?" "I'm training in ballet mostly at the moment." And he seemed to swell up and said: "Oh I can't stand it! I can't stand it!" I looked rather surprised as to why he was so violent about it. "Well the reason being – what is it? A man chasing a woman around the stage!" I was so furious. As I said, I've got red hair, which is inclined to give you a little bit of a temper. I remember thinking to myself: "I'll make you eat those words yet. I'm going to come back home one day and I'm going to start a ballet school, and a ballet company, and you will all accept it." And that is exactly what I did.

I spoke about it to Marie Rambert, and I said: "Look, what am I to do? Either I've got to go away altogether to America or Germany, for my own dancing career. And yet", I said, "I feel I want to go home and do something there." She is very tiny, a very petite little person, with a very foreign accent, even after all the years in England. And I can always remember her saying: "My dear, you go home. There are lots of dancers, you can always get dancers. But I feel you have something more besides that."

(From "Once in a Lifetime: Joan Denise Moriarty" in conversation with John Quinn, produced by John Quinn, 25 August 1979, RTÉ Radio One.)

Joanna Banks
Founder and Artistic Director,
The College of Dance, Dublin

*W*ith her impressive dance pedigree, Joanna Banks, Director of the College of Dance, Monkstown, has made an immense contribution to dance in Ireland since her arrival here in 1974. After a fascinating international career as a ballerina, which started at the age of three at the Royal Ballet School, Joanna found her way to Joan Denise Moriarty's Irish National Ballet in Cork, which led eventually to founding the College of Dance in Dublin. Similar to ballet legend Mikhail Baryshnikov, Joanna now brings her wealth of experience to the contemporary dance world via John Scott's Irish Modern Dance Theatre. Here, she recounts her fascinating life trajectory, which intertwines with the giants of twentieth-century dance, including our own Ninette de Valois.

It begins in London at the age of three. My mother sent me to dancing classes, more as a remedial proposition than anything else. I was the first born and walked in a slightly askew way. There was nothing wrong with me at all, but fussy mother thought I should be sent to ballet classes. Of course it wasn't ballet, it was creative movement. The rest is history. I just never wanted to do anything else. It may go back to a grandfather who was addicted to Tchaikovsky, who was around when I was in the pram. From there it became a serious obsession. My parents were extremely worried because I had come from an academic background, and dance – while they loved it – was not on the agenda as a career for me. Father particularly was saying, "Yes, this is fine, dancing classes, but you take your 11-plus, and then you go to grammar school, and then you go to university."

My career has really been a series of chances that have led me on a really weird and wonderful path. My parents knew nothing about the Royal Ballet School – it was Sadler's Wells School then. It had kicked off in 1947, and was a very small, but very good institute at that stage. My mother went to the dentist, read an article about this amazing school where you could combine education with ballet training, wrote off for a prospectus, I went for an audition, and at the age of seven I was accepted as a junior associate. I think my mother would have been up for child neglect these days because it necessitated getting leave of absence from my junior school from the education authority to travel up on the train after school to do these classes. I did this on my own.

I remember being absolutely terrified. My mother used to make me a little packed tea. There was a Kit-Kat biscuit and a round of sandwiches, and I could hardly eat these because I was terrified I wouldn't be able to open the doors on the London underground. In those days they weren't automatic, you had to actually force them apart on the district line. But I did it because the dancing was the absolute thing that was important. So I put myself through this and went up three times a week to classes. The only concession was, when I got off the bus if it was dark my dad would meet me.

Then when I was coming up to eleven, I auditioned for the main school. My agreement with my father was that if I got into the main school he would reluctantly allow me to go. And I was accepted. Father actually went up and demanded an interview with Arnold Haskell, who was the director of the school at the time, to see if the educational side would be alright for his daughter. Fortunately they were both rather shy men who smoked pipes, and everything was fine. In fact the education was fine because it was a very small school. We were in classes with approximately 20 to begin with and that got refined down because you were assessed every single year.

> *Dame Ninette de Valois would come, watch classes for a week in the spring term, and after that you watched the post every morning with horror because if your parents got a letter to come and talk things over it meant you were for the chop.*

Dame Ninette de Valois would come, watch classes for a week in the spring term, and after that you watched the post every morning with horror because if your parents got a letter to come and talk things over it meant you were for the chop. And they were ruthless. People grew too tall, developed knee problems, slight back problems, and they were all annihilated, for their own sake. The Royal knew they could only accept so many into the company each year. We were absolutely hand-picked. So it was a bit traumatic, but you learned to live with stress even at the age of twelve and a half. I progressed. We had absolutely amazing teachers. One of my main teachers was a wonderful woman called Winifred Edwards who had danced with Pavlova's company. She was a grey-haired, beautifully elegant elderly lady with the most amazing feet. She could still demonstrate most of the barre-work absolutely beautifully. It was the old generation – they had sticks. I'm not saying they hit us, but it was a very strict discipline.

I used to be chosen every year to do the summer school, which meant you got extra coaching with Winifred Edwards. So during the summer holiday you continued on with classes at the Royal Ballet School. Teachers came from all over the world. De Valois had her own syllabus. It wasn't Royal Academy of Dancing, it was a specific syllabus, slightly Russian-influenced, because de Valois had worked with the Diaghilev company. So her influences were very wide. We demonstrated this amazing ballet dance syllabus for all these international teachers.

You shook in your shoes physically when Ninette de Valois walked into the room. She was a very tough lady but she couldn't have done what she did had she not been unbelievably strong. She had an amazing presence. She believed in what

> *She [de Valois] had an amazing presence. She believed in what she was doing with an absolute passion. That's why it succeeded. And I think there was that wonderful Irish streak to her nature.*

she was doing with an absolute passion. That's why it succeeded. And I think there was that wonderful Irish streak to her nature. She was born in County Wicklow, and I think Ireland should be incredibly proud of her. She took the French name for her stage career at a time when her other name wouldn't have been suitable.

I got to know her later when I was dancing in the company. There was a hugely human side to her. She had to have the authority and the discipline. Don't forget she was a woman in a tough world. Dealing with the powers-that-be in Covent Garden Opera House, which was very male-oriented, must have been incredibly difficult.

She came on tour on one occasion and we were all sick with the flu. She knew we had a matinee the following day in the Grand Theatre in Leeds. She went off to Boots and came up to the dressing room before the matinee with a bag-load of cough-lozenge, linctuses and aspirin. She was just like a lovely mother hen. She was always very kind to us when we were doing her summer schools. You would be nervous that you had to do your absolute best for Madam. But then she would come out into the garden at the back of the Royal Ballet School while you were eating your lunch and be like anybody's granny. She was a lovely person, I have a huge amount of respect for her.

The other lovely thing was that years later when I thought that Dame Ninette would have completely forgotten me, I was dancing with the Irish National Ballet

Company in Cork, with Joan Denise Moriarty, and de Valois came on a very rare visit. I thought, look, so much water has passed under the bridge, this is years on, she won't remember me. But she remembered the little blonde girl, and we had a lovely chat, and a big hug in the stalls in the opera house in Cork. I think it inspired me to do one of the best *pas de trois* la Ventana that evening. I felt that the wheel had come full circle, because I was dancing in her country.

De Valois was a true international. When you work in the area of dance, nationality is probably important in some ways, but I think the dance community embraces all nationalities. She was too broadly based a woman to narrow herself down. She was a woman of the world, and way ahead of her time.

So I was accepted into the Royal Ballet, and toured with the company. I was actually accepted into the company after only a year in the senior school. And that was extremely unusual. Then I suppose I felt that the Royal Ballet was an enormously big company, and the awful thing was I wasn't particularly happy. I found it very scary, quite intimidating. I was only seventeen when I joined the company. That was a year earlier than usually happens, so I left all my friends behind in the Royal Ballet School, and I really knew nobody when I joined the company. So I'm afraid that coloured my unhappiness. I stayed a year with the company. It was a very difficult time in my life because my ideal had been to be a dancer with the Royal Ballet, and here I was in the Royal Ballet, finding that I wasn't particularly happy. So I left.

I went to the Ballet Rambert, which was a smaller company. Although Madam Rambert was temperamental and extremely difficult to live with, she was an extraordinary woman, and I found my niche there. I spent many happy years with the Ballet Rambert. It was an outrageously interesting company, full of creativity. A smaller company, we did an enormous amount of performing. We toured extensively in the UK and also got to do some very interesting assignments overseas because the British Council would send the Royal Ballet to the bigger places but they would send Ballet Rambert to places like Malta. We actually re-opened the little Manoel opera house in Valletta Malta after the war. We did a fantastic tour to the Middle East, giving a gala for the Shah of Iran before the revolution, and got to shake his hand. He was devastatingly good-looking and we were swooning at his feet. We had the privilege to dance in the lovely opera

Joanna Banks in Raymonda *by Marius Petipa (arr: Ballanchine), 1978*

212

house in Cairo, which is where the first production of *Aida* was staged. Sadly it was destroyed by fire afterwards, but we did amazing performances there. It was infested with cockroaches backstage, and that caused a few problems because they got inside the layers of tulle of the long ballet dresses for *Les Sylphides*. But worse still we were doing *Coppélia*, and at that stage I was still a character dancer. You learned that you had to shake out your character boots before putting them on for Act One or you might find a cockroach in your boot. But we were young and it was exciting. We just loved the foreign tours. Rambert was an amazing artist. She would stimulate you, exasperate you, be very cruel, but she was such a woman of the theatre that one learned so much about stagecraft and theatre that I wouldn't have it otherwise. She was an amazing influence on my life.

> *Rambert was an amazing artist. She would stimulate you, exasperate you, be very cruel, but she was such a woman of the theatre that one learned so much about stagecraft and theatre that I wouldn't have it otherwise.*

Certainly never a dull moment with "Mim", as she was known. She was quite outrageous. She would watch every performance, and if something wasn't quite right, you would hear the click of the pass door and she would be in the wings screaming at you on stage. They don't come like that any more. It had its good side and its bad side. She never ever paid you a compliment without qualifying it. She would say, "Joanna, that was very good, BUT . . .". And then the "but" completely annihilated anything that had gone before. She cut you down to size. But after the classical company had changed I met her at Covent Garden several years later and she said, "I am so happy that you are still dancing". She paid me the nicest compliment of my life, saying, "You are a wonderful dancer." I thought, "Well, yes, I wish you had said that while I was in your company." It was a compliment I treasured, because she didn't pay compliments lightly.

Then Rambert became a contemporary company. I didn't want to go that route at that time. There were periods of being out of work, and desperation, and working with some amazing teachers in London from whom I learned a lot. I joined a small company, which toured in Europe. And that was a case of doing one night stands all over Germany, Switzerland, France and Austria – hair-raising touring, but I needed a job, and I learned a lot. From there I eventually got a contract with the Canadian National Ballet Company. And I spent a very exciting year, based in Toronto, working under Celia Franka – an ex-Royal Ballet person. Touring coast-to-coast in Canada, dancing lovely things, but the problem with being in a Canadian company was that they are all much taller than I am. I was like the midget, and I replaced a midget.

Oh, the lifestyle was amazing. I was paid more than I had ever been paid in Europe. There were expectations of what a dancer's salary should be. You had your own apartment. But I suppose I am obstinate, and I really wanted to dance. By this time I wanted to have a career that continued to be creative. I frankly didn't want to go on being a cygnet, and dancing *pas de trois* in *Cinderella* for the rest of my days. It was a very difficult decision, but after eight months I went to talk to Franka. I said that reluctantly I had decided not to accept another contract with the company because I felt that I would still be dancing cygnets for the rest of my life, and there had to be more to a career than that. If I stayed another year I would get terribly used to the good money, and the lovely lifestyle, become complacent, and I wouldn't be able to dig myself out.

> Oh, the lifestyle was amazing. I was paid more than I had ever been paid in Europe. There were expectations of what a dancer's salary should be. You had your own apartment. But I suppose I am obstinate, and I really wanted to dance.

I had a terrific season. Roland Petit came to create a very strange work called *Krannert*, with which we opened in the New Arts Centre in Ottawa. That was very exciting. It was an electronic score by Jannis Xenakis plus full symphony orchestra. Weird designs, the whole thing was black and white. We were in all-over black and white body-stockings. It was modern ballet. This would have been around '69 probably. Roland Petit happened to like me because I am small and easy to partner. So he worked out a lot of stuff on myself because he could flip me up on his shoulder. I would have died for him. So I left on a high.

I came back to Europe and the phone rang almost immediately. I was invited to go to Israel to work with the Bat Dor Company. I was supposed to be a classical dancer and do the classical roles, but when I got out there I was thrown straight into a Graham class. I had never done a contemporary class in my life. So one just makes the best of these situations. It was an interesting year because it was funded by Rothschild money so they could buy in literally any choreographer in the world that they fancied. Choreographers would come, virtually for a working holiday. Batsheba de Rothschild would treat them very well. I worked with Lucas Hoving and Norman Walker. Peter Wright came out and did a very strange balletic piece. But I knew that it wasn't for me in the long term. So I came out of that after a year.

Then I spent a little bit of time in London – to get my bearings back. I felt the ballet classes, which are a dancer's lifeline, were not the best in Israel. I had lost a certain amount of technique, and I went to my mentor Eileen Ward who gave professional dance classes in London and talked things over with her. Eileen said, "Look, I could get you into a company in Germany tomorrow, but I think if you want to just chill out for a little while, we can strengthen your technique and then you will have a lot of options." When I had been working with Eileen for about a month, the Kirov came to London. Natalia Makarova defected, she goes into hiding for a couple of days, and where does she come to class but with Eileen Ward. I had this amazing Kirov-trained role model in front of me on the barre, and actually distraught in the dressing room because she wants to borrow a pair of scissors, and she doesn't know the English for scissors. So I taught her the English word for scissors. She would not actually go across from the corner doing turns on her own for the first few classes. She would just drag me, because I had been friendly to her in the dressing room. I'm a good dancer, but I'm not an international ballerina. I just had to get on and do it. It was just very inspiring to have her around. I learned an enormous amount.

Then I got offered two contracts simultaneously. This is how it works in the dance world. You are uselessly unemployed, and then suddenly you get two contracts at once. David Poole liked my work very much, and invited me to go to South Africa. I was very anti-apartheid, and I knew my father would probably never speak to me again if I took up that contract for that reason. But within a couple of weeks I had been offered a contract to go to the state theatre in Munich, where the artistic director, Ronald Nynd, was ex-Royal Ballet. So I headed for Munich, where I spent a very happy three years in the State theatre. Once you get into the German system you are paid extremely well, looked after extremely well, and had I stayed there I would be putting my feet up now, bored stiff, and drawing my pension.

Then Ronnie left; he had been trying to build the company up to what John Cranko had done in Stuttgart, but unfortunately the Intendant of the house at the time was a big opera man. Gunther Rennert thought that ballet

> *Once you get into the German system you are paid extremely well, looked after extremely well, and had I stayed there I would be putting my feet up now, bored stiff, and drawing my pension.*

was something that decorated his operas, and he wasn't interested in the ballet company having its own identity. After three years Ronnie decided that he couldn't fight the establishment anymore. We were left in dire straits because we had all signed our contracts, in true German manner in February, for the following September. The following September we were inflicted with a very unfortunate narrow-minded German director who didn't like the *Ausländer*. He made a point that he felt there were far too many foreigners in the company. Unfortunately, his German girlfriend was exactly my size, and all of a sudden all my little roles are being taken away. And then funnily enough she couldn't cope with them, so all of a sudden I am being told, "Oh yes, but you are doing cygnets on Wednesday." I said, "On Tuesday I wasn't good enough, so why am I doing it on Wednesday?" I was told, "Oh, well, Joanna you've signed your contract, you're a dancer, you do what you're told." I think there comes a time in one's life – I was into my thirties by this time – when you start saying, "I may be a dancer, but I am also an intelligent woman who thinks for herself and I don't need to be treated like this."

I was looking around for a change of scene, and again, by chance, I'm reading a dance journal, I see in the stop press at the back page that Domy Reiter-Soffer whom I had worked with previously in a small company was coming as Joan Denise Moriarty's assistant with the newly formed Irish Ballet Company in Cork. I thought, well, this is probably my escape route, because Domy and I had danced with a very small company in the Gate Theatre about ten years prior to this and he had said, "If the things get off the ground in Ireland, would you be interested?"

Photo: personal archive

Joanna Banks and Wayne Aspinall in Raymonda, *1978*

So I wrote to Domy, who was not a good correspondent. I didn't hear anything, but he passed my details on to Muriel Large, who was the excellent administrator of the Irish Ballet Company in Cork. She contacted me, and very wisely she suggested that I came to Cork. She said, "We are very interested, with your background we would love to have you, but I think you should come to Cork." When I came to Cork I could see why, because I had to see for myself the contrast at that time between Munich, which had just been made to look extraordinarily beautiful for the Olympic Games, and Cork where I arrived in June on a Sunday night and there was literally wall-to-wall litter blowing down McCurtain Street, and it was raining. It was going to be a big cultural shock, apart from a big financial shock. But I liked the spirit. I went to the studio on the Monday morning, and did class with the company, who were very young. There weren't many experienced dancers. But I was full of enthusiasm for this pioneering spirit. I thought, this is wonderful, it's what I want to do. I've had a great life, I've had some very well-paid jobs in my time, maybe it's about time to start giving something back. They were very keen to have me – so I went back to Munich, finished out the season, and arrived in Cork in September of 1974.

My first encounter with Joan Denise Moriarty was very interesting. She had come to watch me do class with the company. She was absolutely delightful. We talked, and I was delighted to go and talk with the administrator and accept the offer of a contract to come to Ireland.

In fact, Joan Denise did not have a lot to do with the professional company. She was absolutely devoted to her school, which took a lot of her time, and she also had the amateur company – The Cork Ballet Company – which did a big classical production every year. I really do respect Joan Denise, and a huge debt needs to be paid to her, but as far as the professional company was concerned, it really wasn't her first love. I think she had struggled to get government backing for a company, and when it finally came we always felt she was a little intimidated by the professional dancers. Some of us who came from international backgrounds had obviously done a lot more than she had done – in a way it was a slightly fraught situation. I do have a huge respect for her work and I think dance in Ireland wouldn't be where it's at today without her.

> *I really do respect Joan Denise, and a huge debt needs to be paid to her, but as far as the professional company was concerned, it really wasn't her first love.*

Within her own parameters she worked tirelessly for dance in this country. But I feel it was sad what happened to the Irish National Ballet Company. It's very easy to talk retrospectively but there needed to be a high calibre school in place that would feed young Irish dancers into the company. There also needed to be more of an outreach programme into schools, which happened latterly. And, I'm going to be very controversial here but I personally feel that we could have reached a far wider public if the company had been based in Dublin. The finances of the Irish National Ballet Company were crucified because we had to be paid a *per diem*, had to be put up in hotels, and rather than the National Ballet Company having as much exposure as possible to the capital, we were restricted to one season a year.

I arrived in the second year of their existence, and left in 1985. We celebrated the tenth anniversary. I spent ten happy years with the company. In the early years we did very interesting work. Latterly funding was becoming tight. The company was trying to establish its new home in the Firkin Crane. I think money had to go into the building project.

In the early days it was very exciting because Muriel Large, the administrator, had connections with the Scottish Ballet Company. Peter Darrell, a very good choreographer, mounted quite a few works on the company. Peter's works were very theatrical. They were ideal for the compa-

Photo: personal archive

Joanna Banks in Pas de Quatre
(Chor: Anton Dolin), 1978

ny because they were small cast works, interesting musically, and interesting choreographically. We had the wonderful 20-minute version of *Othello*, which says it all in twenty minutes and is an absolutely magnificent piece for a cast of five people. I danced the Emilia role in that. That was riveting, really good theatre.

Anton Dolin (Patrick Healy Kaye) came over to mount his famous *Pas de Quatre*. It was a wonderful experience to work with Pat. And of course Pat Dolin has his Irish roots and he was delighted to come back to Ireland to give us *Pas de Quatre* – one of the few ballets that was actually filmed by RTÉ.

We also had connections with a wonderful 80-year-old Hans Brenner who was a veteran of the Royal Danish Ballet. He mounted two works from the Bournonville repertoire and actually came and gave a Bournonville class and mounted *La Ventana* and *Konservatoriet*. So on the classical side we had the small-scale classical works that suited the company.

Domy was doing some extraordinarily interesting theatre pieces. His version of Lorca's *Yerma* was riveting. He did some less successful full-length pieces. He did one on the life of Colette, and an interesting version of *The Lady of the Camelias*. I was involved in both those productions. Sadly, when money gets tight you can't afford to bring in top rank choreographers, or even third-rate choreographers. When you start scraping the bottom of the barrel it's amazing how the audience senses that this isn't wonderful quality work. It was very sad to see the work go down. Although we had Charles Czarny working with us (*Sunny Days* and *Concerto* – memorable pieces), one could see that the future was not rosy.

Sean Cunningham (Christy) and Anna Donovan (Pegeen) in Irish National Ballet's Playboy of the Western World

The Playboy of the Western World with the Chieftains playing live was Joan Denise at her best. She used a mix of Irish dancing and ballet. That really took off. The Chieftains were amazing to work with, and we integrated terribly well. We rehearsed it to tape in the studio. It was a very exhausting piece to do because Joan Denise took the scene at the races, which takes place offstage, and made that into a major dancing piece. It was extremely tough on the girls, because they were on stage the whole time. The boys were the horses so they shot across the stage, took their breath, and came back again. But we were literally doing Irish jigs for what seemed like ten hours. It was probably more like twenty minutes, but it was very tough on the legs.

I found it extremely embarrassing doing the jigs because I wasn't terribly good at the footwork. There was one particular step where I had to be hidden at the back because I couldn't do it competently. I played one of the four girls who comes to visit Christy. We came with our chicken and our bits and pieces. That was nicknamed "chicken and chips" in company law. The strange thing is when you are rehearsing something like that you have no idea whether it is going to work and the closer you get to the opening – which was for the Olympia Theatre in the theatre festival – we couldn't see that this was going to work. We were overtired and over-stressed and we were terrified. Then we got into the Olympia and suddenly the Chieftains were in the pit and the whole thing just took off. We could have Irish-jigged all night, it was just so inspiring. We began to think "Hey, there is some magic component happening here." We had a standing ovation on opening night. It's the only time I can remember when people queued for return tickets around the block for the Irish Ballet Company.

> *I found it extremely embarrassing doing the jigs because I wasn't terribly good at the footwork. There was one particular step where I had to be hidden at the back because I couldn't do it competently.*

Photo: Fergus Bourke

Irish National Ballet's Playboy of the Western World

Joan Denise worked very closely with Paddy Moloney, and their choice was extraordinary. They got such a contrast of moods in the pieces they used. It seemed to flow seamlessly, one thing into the next. It was a brilliantly worked-out collage of Irish music. Not a word was spoken. RTÉ filmed it latterly.

Sean Cunningham, a wonderful Irish dancer who had a career with the Ballet Gulbenkian in Portugal, played Christy. He was perfect for the role. That may have influenced why it happened. Anna Donovan – a very strong dramatic dancer – danced Pegeen. They were two very strong leaders.

There were always a few Irish dancers, but it saddened me that there weren't more. I felt it should be a company for Irish dancers. At that stage there was really not sufficiently good training in Ireland. There were certain teachers in certain places, pockets of good training, but there was no way of becoming a professional dancer. It was very hit and miss.

That's one of the reasons I stayed on in Ireland. Constantly on our tours we would meet lovely children in Ireland. There just wasn't the possibility for them to learn. I left the Ballet Company, somewhat disillusioned with how things were going. Unfortunately within a few years the funding had been cut. We hit that awful period of doom and gloom in dance in Ireland where everyone was scrabbling around. All the best dancers left, because there was no work here. Everything had been annihilated, the contemporary company had gone, Dublin City Ballet had gone, Irish Ballet had gone.

I was very lucky in that I had moved up to Dublin, and worked with Roy Galvin. We must have been mad – we worked freelance. Because we were desperate for work, Roy managed to get us in with the Gaiety Theatre as leading dancers with the Gaiety pantomime. I had the wonderful opportunity to work with the late Maureen Potter. Maureen was a wonderful professional to work alongside and was so appreciative of dance. It was a very happy season.

Then in very quick succession I met the late John Regan who became my partner in life. John had an extraordinary pedigree. He came from an Anglo-Irish family, but he had danced with the Diaghilev ballet. The family had moved away and he was brought up in England. He had got into dance late and sideways, but wound up studying with Cecchetti, and dancing in the last days of the Diaghilev company.

Then John toured the world, coming back to Ireland, probably to die here. But he liked my work and he choreographed a very special programme of pieces for me. I did a one-woman show with John in the old Project Theatre, which was just entitled *Ballet*. John knew my weaknesses and strengths and he probably choreographed things that suited me better than anybody else. That's a memorable period in my life. Then John became ill, and I nursed him as long as possible at home. He then died in St Vincent's. Before he died he said, "Jo, you stay here and you make something happen." He and I had often said, look, if anything is going to happen in this country we have to have a school. I suppose I've spent the rest of my life doing just that.

I started the College in 1990. There had been a loosely based dancing course in the old dance centre in Digge's Lane. The owner of that centre, Mark Archer, approached me, with my colleague Anna Donovan who at that stage was out of work after the demise of the Irish Ballet Company. He said, "I have no money; you'll be paid for the classes you teach, but I would really like you to structure something here." So we worked together and were joined by Gavin Dorian who was ex-Scottish ballet. It was tough going, we were really pioneering. Anna then went to work with the Dallas Ballet. Gavin and I worked away together.

Carolyn Swift was always in the wings saying, "Look, you have to do this." When I would get down, and thought it just wasn't working, she would say, "Stick at it." An absolute rock. She was elected to be chair of our board of directors. It was so hairy and so tough in those days, I don't think we would have survived without Carolyn reminding me of my promise to John, saying "Hang in there." We also had to cater for the needs of the Irish dancers. The college has progressed, and it is a very broadly based training. A very good foundation course.

> *Carolyn Swift was always in the wings saying, "Look, you have to do this." When I would get down, and thought it just wasn't working, she would say, "Stick at it." An absolute rock.*

We have to take on board that most of our dancers don't get to us until they have done their Leaving Certificate. So the ballet option is not going to be one they can follow. They will go into contemporary dance or musical theatre. They will need strong ballet anyway. Occasionally we get an amazing child in transition year who is very strong in ballet, like Therese Schweppe, who won a scholarship to the Central School of Ballet in London and danced in the English National Ballet at Albert Hall last summer. But that is really the exception to the rule. There are a few very brave Irish children in ballet schools, but it means going abroad to a boarding school to do your ballet training at age 11. That is tough.

Lizzie Roche was obviously very talented, even at an early stage. She managed to choreograph everyone else's solos for the bursary auditions as well as her own. She went to London School of Contemporary Dance, and is now back here running her own very successful dance company, Rex Levitates. She is back with huge commitment to work in this country and she is going to make things happen. Ella Clarke is working freelance in the contemporary area, and also Niamh Condron, Becky Reilly. Jessica and Megan Kennedy. They all have to go away to finish their training, but they come back.

Now I have extended my career to a lunatic level. I had retired from performing. When I started the school, and after John's death, I really didn't want to dance anymore. I hadn't danced for eight years when John Scott approached me. I was probably very difficult. I said, "Look John, I have retired for eight years, I'm per-fectly happy running the college, and I don't need this." But he came up with a very exciting proposition. He was doing a very interesting production called *Macalla*, in the RHA. It was fortuitously going to happen in a holiday period. We struck a deal and I said "I will come to a few rehearsals and if you feel it's working out alright, then OK, but if you think I am just a fish out of water, well then I'm quite happy if you say no. Likewise, if I am uncomfortable with what you want me to do, we'll call it quits." But it worked very well. I'll never forget the opening night because your nerves get worse as you get older. I stood at the top of the steps near the sculpture garden, physically shaking in a pair of high-heel boots, and a long astrakhan col-lared coat. But when I got on, and started doing it, the buzz was back, and I had a ball. John kept adding in a lot more vignettes during the week. So I ended up doing a lot more by the Friday night than I was doing at the beginning of the week. John and I have a great respect for each other. Sometimes if he is doing very energetic work it obviously doesn't suit an old lady like me, so I don't do it. I love working with John. Irish Modern Dance Theatre went to Estonia in May 2005, where we performed in Tallin and also in a barn converted into an Arts Centre. So the career goes on I'm afraid.

I was also in John Scott's *Rough Air* which I love because it's a very personal piece. I've been given an awful lot of leeway. If you analyse it I don't do an awful lot – I sort of walk around the place – but you walk around the place creating certain atmospheres. It's wonderful because you are not fixed, and it comes out differently every time. That is the glory of working with John. It's not set and cast in stone. I like that concept. You are never bored. You may hate it, you may love it, but it always stimulates some sort of audience reaction.

The more Irish people are ex-posed to dance – ballet and con-temporary – the better the audi-ence will be. It's important that the dance parameters are set very wide. Dance is an interna-tional art form, and the more you are exposed to, the better.

The more Irish people are exposed to dance – ballet and contemporary – the better the audience will be. It's important that the dance parameters are set very wide. Dance is an international art form, and the more you are exposed to, the better.

Carolyn Swift
Former Irish Times Dance Critic

*C*arolyn Swift's place in Irish cultural history was assured when the moral uptightness of the Irish state infamously caused the demise of the Pike Theatre (1953–1964), which she co-founded with her then husband Alan Simpson. She went on to champion dance, then a beleaguered and misunderstood artform, by giving it voice in writing, first as ballet critic of the Sunday Independent, and then as dance correspondent of The Irish Times *from 1979 to 2001.*

Swift's own debacle with the state when Alan Simpson was arrested for "producing for gain an indecent and profane performance"[3] *– Tennessee Williams's* The Rose Tattoo *– parallels the moral atmosphere towards dance and the body in John Charles McQuaid's and de Valera's Ireland. In fact, June Fryer, Ireland's first modern dancer who trained in Erina Brady's ill-fated Irish School of Dance Art in the 1940s (another casualty of that moral climate), worked as a choreographer in the Pike Theatre at Herbert Lane. A prolific writer and producer, Swift's contribution to the arts in Ireland was manifold, from staging the first Irish production of* Waiting for Godot, *to the invention of* Wanderly Wagon *and the writing of children's books.*

Acutely aware of the lack of documentation on dance, in her last years Swift undertook to write a history of dance in Ireland that was intended for publication. Along with Jacqueline Robinson's memoir of dance in 1940s Dublin, given to her by John Scott, she passed her unpublished manuscript on to me. Here, in polemic form on RTÉ Radio One, is how Carolyn Swift responded to the Arts Council's axing of the Irish National Ballet in 1988.

The £420,000 of a grant [the Irish National Ballet] got from the Arts Council is the bulk of their funding. I cannot understand it. It's most extraordinary. Adrian Munnelly, the Director of the Arts Council, is reported as saying that the Council has no further confidence in the company, and dance hasn't been developing in this country as the Arts Council would have expected. I cannot understand his grounds for saying that, because there is nobody in fact on the Arts Council who is in a position to judge this. Nobody has ever been appointed to the board of the Arts Council with expertise in dance. None of the officers of the Arts Council has particular expertise in dance.[4]

I think the Arts Council recognised that when they got Peter Brinson to do this report for them in 1985 called "The Dancer and the Dance". In it Peter Brinson says there is no question but that an Irish National Ballet should exist. A standard has been achieved, there is a repertory on which to build, even with reduced numbers.

Whatever criticisms may be made of Irish National Ballet, Ireland has nothing else in theatrical dance remotely comparable in quality.

(Carolyn Swift on "Appraisal Music, Ballet, Contemporary Dance", 24 March 1988 on RTE Radio One; Produced by Michael Johnston)

Notes

[1] For further reading, see *Joan Denise Moriarty*, ed. Ruth Fleischmann, Dublin: Mercier Press, 1998.

[2] Born in Mulrany, County Mayo in 1905, John Regan had trained with both Cechetti and Legat, both former dancers at the Maryinski Theatre and teachers at the Imperial Ballet School in St. Petersburg. He had not only danced with Diaghilev's, de Basil's, Woizikowski's and Balanchine's Ballets Russes, Nijinska's Warsaw Ballet and the Markova-Dolin Ballet, but was the only foreigner ever to dance with the Georgian State Dancers. In 1937 he formed his own company, International Ballet Company of London, later Les Ballets Trois Arts. His series "Ballet for Beginners" ran for four years on BBC TV and he appeared in many films, notably *The Red Shoes*, in which he was principal dancer. He returned to Ireland in 1977, founding the Limerick School of Classical Ballet and Mid-West Ballet Workshop. In 1982 he founded "Theatre Omnibus" (members included Jon Kenny, of d'Unbelievables), teaching, choreographing and occasionally performing until his death in 1988. (Carolyn Swift, "Dance in Ireland", unpublished manuscript.)

[3] Documented in *Spiked: Church-State Intrigue and the Rose Tattoo* by Carolyn Swift and Gerard Whelan (Dublin: New Island, 2002).

[4] Gaye Tanham (Youth Arts and Dance Officer, incorporating education: 1996–1998; Dance and Opera Officer: 1999–2003), was the first officer with a background in dance at the Arts Council. Previous to that, Arthur Lappin (Drama and Dance Officer 1979–1985) had a background in theatre; and Martin Drury (Education and Dance Officer 1986–1990) had a background in education. Since 2003, former dancer Finola Cronin has been Dance Specialist at the Arts Council. Dancer Paul Johnston also serves on the Arts Council, as Artists' Services Manager; while Mary Nunan is a Council Member.

Chapter 7

Chapter 7

Developments Out of Riverdance and Siamsa Tíre

Irish dancing was acclaimed worldwide long before *Riverdance*, according to longtime *Irish Times* dance correspondent Carolyn Swift in her unpublished history of dance in Ireland. This was courtesy of a priest, no less, Fr Patrick Ahern, born on a farm in North Kerry, who began to experiment with occupational songs and dances in 1964 when he was director of Tralee's St John's Parish Choir. Under this priest's direction (most unlike the aforementioned *sagart paróiste* in Chapter One), butter churning, threshing, milking, feeding calves and twisting *súgán* ropes were performed to music, leading to a folk pageant in 1966, an RTÉ television series in 1968, and twice-weekly performances under the name of Siamsa. Overseas visitors flocked in their thousands, the shows toured to Dublin's Abbey Theatre, Germany, and London, and on 9 February 1974, Fr Ahern founded Siamsa Tíre National Folk Theatre. More extensive global touring ensued, across the US, to Paris, Bonn, Brittany, London, Toronto and Australia.

By 1991 with *Ding Dong Dederó, Forging the Dance*, based on the life of North Kerry dancing master Jerry "Munnix" Molyneaux, the son of a blacksmith, dance had become a major element of Siamsa Tíre shows. Carolyn Swift praised "Fr. Ahern's efforts to forge traditional and modern dance". He had attempted this fusion previously in his 1986 Christmas show with Jonathan Burnett, a former soloist with Irish National Ballet, but according to Swift, it wasn't until Mary Nunan's choreography of *Clann Lir* for Siamsa Tíre in 1999 that the two came together successfully. "The choreography successfully combines the footwork of Irish folk dance with contemporary arm and body movement . . ." she wrote. "At last, one hundred years after it had chosen to isolate itself on nationalistic grounds, Irish traditional dance had been successfully united with 'foreign dance'."[1] Since then Siamsa Tíre has continued to collaborate with contemporary choreographers, like John Scott and Cindy Cummings, stretching the limits of the dance form.

In the meantime, on a more legendary scale, *Riverdance: the Show* was born out of the sensational 1994 intermission act for the Eurovision song contest. John Mc-

Colgan and Moya Doherty mortgaged their home to turn this intermission act, starring Michael Flatley and Jean Butler, into a major dance show at the Point Theatre, and hence succeeded in catapulting hitherto minority interest Irish dancing onto an international platform. Suddenly Irish dancing, and the Irish (even if they were American-Irish) became sexy, international currency – the Celtic Tiger in motion. Re-introducing "foreign" dance elements – for example flamenco, with Maria Pages, and American tap, with Tariq Winston, in the humorous as well as skilful "trading taps" – helped to loosen up the upper body slightly from the competitive dance strait-jacket effect. But probably most importantly, *Riverdance* lead dancers Colin Dunne, Jean Butler and Breandán de Gallaí went on exploring the form, testing its limits and its possibilities, infusing it with the principles of contemporary dance, storytelling, theatre, film, capoeira and other eclectic disciplines – and are still doing so today. Where it will go remains to be seen. Here, along with Micheal Ó Súilleabháin's musings on the meeting of traditional Irish dancing and contemporary dance, and the "green shoot" sprouting up through the tarmacadam, is a snapshot of their respective aesthetic journeys recollected, and their thought in progress.

Micheál Ó Súilleabháin
Director, Irish World Academy of Music and Dance, University of Limerick

*A*cclaimed composer and musician Micheál Ó Súilleabháin is Director of the Irish World Academy of Music and Dance at the University of Limerick. He has composed for Siamsa Tíre National Folk Theatre, and for Colin Dunne, and also admits to dancing himself in his spare time. Here he offers a meditation on the interplay between the "Irish body" and Irish traditional music, Irish traditional dance, and the brave new world of contemporary dance which made its first indelible impression on him via Domy Reiter-Soffer's choreography with the Irish National Ballet Company in the 1970s.

In a reincarnation I would be a dancer, because when I'm performing I feel a huge connection between gesture and sound. I'm very interested in the connection in the musician's body movements – in other words, how gesture engenders sounds. I often feel that instead of dance being a response to music, music is a response to the initial gesture which creates the sound. You can't create a sound unless you make a gesture first. I know this from when I'm sitting at the piano. A sound comes from a gesture. Then a gesture may respond to the sound. So I'm interested in something that goes deeper than music or dance.

Secondly, because I feel genetically motivated or linked in with indigenous Irish sound and gesture, I feel I have an intimate knowledge, without it being experiential, of Irish traditional dance as an expression of the music.

I first became aware of contemporary dance in the 1970s in Cork with Joan Denise Moriarty's Irish National Ballet Company. Domy Reiter-Soffer, an Israeli choreographer, was there. I remember seeing his work and going "Wow!" The thing that hit me was that it was abstract. No story! No narration! Now Irish traditional dance is also abstract, but in a particularly different way. So I was just completely taken. From that moment right up to this I was completely mystified as to where the impulse was coming from to do these kinds of these things with your body. "Why?" is the question that is coming to me all the time. I am sitting there in absolute awe. Sometimes it is hitting me emotionally. But even when it doesn't hit me emotionally, I'm thinking, "Why do people do this?" They spend their entire lives refining the gesture. I know it's not a Morse Code. There is something about how the body moves through space that makes us want to do it. It's a universal thing.

I'm always amazed when people say that dance is undeveloped in Ireland. I think that's an unfortunately narrow point of view. What they mean is contemporary dance, or ballet, not dance. Club dancing and Irish traditional dance, the revival of non-competition dance, like *sean nós,* has been regenerated in teenagers. It's an improvised form. There's show-dance, and of course set dancing – quadrilles with four couples. Traditional dancers within competition culture don't do set dancing. It's a different culture. Set dancing is extremely Irish, and an extraordinary expression of contemporary culture. It is its own university. Like an Irish session, you can learn it on the hoof.

The term "step dancing" would apply to that primarily solo dancer, hard or soft shoe. Competition culture is 60 or 70 years old, and in a sense it unionised the tradition. As Dr Catherine Foley's research has shown, with an increase in competition there was a decrease in improvisation. It became more virtuosic, faster and less risk-taking. It's hard not to use value judgements.

Every time I see a *sean nós* dancer I always find myself smiling. It's humorous – like water – to do with creative flow. The upper body is quite loose. Like the water diviner who takes a hazel rod and practises divination. You can't learn water divination. That's like an artist. *Sean nós* culture is in touch with it, but competition culture feels like it has been tarmacadamed. The green fuse can come up through the tarmacadam but it's rare. There is almost something post-modern about the old style dancing. It has lasted so long that it

229

has out-paced modernism – like a digital recording of West Clare fiddling. Some of the contemporary dance people I know are nearer to whatever the Irish body is expressing in the non-competitive step-dancing tradition, old style, than with the competitive.

Riverdance could not have happened if the Michael Flatleys and the Colin Dunnes had not been prepared. Like Olympic athletes, that culture was preparing dancers like them for 60 years. The dance form was getting more and more refined, because of elements of the rigidity of its codification, and the necessity to be able to deliver. That's the Celtic Tiger of course. The brilliance of it was that someone threw it up on a sexy stage with top-class lighting. World champions doing the same thing to millisecond precision.

> Riverdance *could not have happened if the Michael Flatleys and the Colin Dunnes had not been prepared. Like Olympic athletes, that culture was preparing dancers like them for 60 years.*

On the other hand, there is that scene in *Dancing at Lughnasa*. There is no indication that any of the characters had learned to dance when they were young. The music takes hold of them and they start jigging around. I think if you are talking about the Irish body – this is an experience that I know myself – I find it unnatural to listen to certain trad musicians and bands without wanting to get up and move. It's very natural for those of us who have traditional music in the blood not to respond to music in that way. It's kind of "eejity" – to use a Hiberno-English word, and very funny. There's a lot of kicking and lepping and digging-in going on that I associate with the *agriculture* of dance in Ireland – the part of dance which is actually linked into the soil.

But I don't want to make claims for that for traditional dance as opposed to contemporary dance. I think what contemporary dance has got to do is to find a way of embracing the local. That's its big challenge. That's the secret of the global, I suppose – if you go down far enough you'll end up in Australia.

I do think the dance scene in Ireland is a lot healthier now. On the traditional side of things we have had a fascinating revival of *sean nós* dance and of set dance traditions even as the competition dancing continues. Over 30 years Siamsa Tíre under the inspiration of Fr Pat Ahern produced the first stirring of an Irish response to Eastern European and Russian National Folk Theatre. Those could be seen as the first intimations of an Irish show dance. *Riverdance* in a sense moved that up a few gears in the '90s, creatively breaking the ethnic boundaries of the dance.

On the contemporary dance side of things the '90s have been a revelation. The Arts Council took a significant ownership of the artform, even if it still was unable to find a way through to traditional dance – although all of that is set to change now with the proposed developments with the traditional arts.

The establishment of the International Dance Festival in Dublin is a huge indicator of an attempt to find new ways forward, even though I feel the dance community is still quite polarised and confused. Traditional dancers haven't got a clue what contemporary dancers are up to. They don't even know they are there. Contemporary dancers know the traditional dancers are there, but they are complex about it. Firstly, they're not sure whether it's art. Most of them think it isn't. I think they are wrong. So there is a problem of espousing informal dance forms from an egalitarian point of view, as of equal human validity to the others. You do find this phenomenon in classical music too, but less so.

The current Irish audience has an opportunity of viewing contemporary dance that it didn't have before. People have got to see it first. I know it's still very small, but the Dance Festival is making a massive contribution. If I hadn't seen Domy Reiter Soffer's choreography in the '70s in Cork that seed would not have been set. I would like to see intelligent bridges being built between the different dance forms in Ireland.

Contemporary dance sometimes goes for the goal as if other forms of dance don't exist – I sense they are embarrassed about other forms. It is possibly not mature enough yet to overcome possible elements of a post-colonial attitude in some cases. I won't even begin to talk about traditional dance and elements of cultural fundamentalism, which can be very apparent and equally disturbing. The traditional dance community doesn't want to talk about contemporary dance, because it doesn't have the discipline and the structure of Irish traditional dance. Ballet can be regarded with disdain – ironically given that traditional dance and ballet have a highly disciplined body in common!

The traditional dance community doesn't want to talk about contemporary dance, because it doesn't have the discipline and the structure of Irish traditional dance. Ballet can be regarded with disdain – ironically given that traditional dance and ballet have a highly disciplined body in common!

As regards the "Irish body", it's quite extraordinary that people like Jean Butler and Colin Dunne are opting to spend a year here in Limerick studying in the MA in Contemporary Dance Performance. However, there is no way one body in one year will solve the problem. For me, the personality of Ireland is reconfiguring itself in gesture. If it will ever happen – words like "fusion" or "crossover" are far too small; I'm talking about the underground cultural well that the diviner tips into. It will either take a kind of Colin/Jean figure walking across, or someone in the opposite direction – likely to release some aspect of the Irish body that will bring the two halves of it together again.

As far as the Irish World Academy of Music and Dance here at University of Limerick is concerned, what we have to offer is a space and time for things to germinate organically under controlled conditions.

We have Daghdha Dance Company in residence here. We appointed the first traditional dancer in residence in any university in the world – an eighty-year-old *sean nós* dancer! We have the first degree programme in contemporary dance and Irish traditional performance in the world, and we have the only full-time higher education appointment in ethnochoreology (the study of dance in culture) in Ireland. I believe this environment is one primed for the kind of creativity we are speaking of here.

Colin Dunne
Dancer and Choreographer

*B*orn in Birmingham to Irish parents, Colin Dunne is best-known for stepping into the shoes of an abdicating Michael Flatley in Riverdance. *Previously Colin was world champion Irish dancer for nine years, toured with the Chieftains, and subsequently created* Dancing on Dangerous Ground, *based on the Diarmuid and Gráinne legend, with Jean Butler in 1999 (he also qualified as an accountant). More recently he has taken a foray into the world of contemporary dance, doing the MA in Contemporary Dance at the University of Limerick, where he was dancer in residence in 2001–02. While there he created and performed several solo choreographies, as well as in Yoshiko Chuma's* The Yellow Room *with Daghdha Dance Company. Most recently Colin created and played the role of Fergus O'Rourke in Michael Keegan Dolan's modern version of* The Táin: The Story of the Bull. *Alongside his international teaching career, Colin has also participated in projects like* Dancing at the Depot, *a reality TV show in which he instructed Birmingham bus drivers in the art of Irish dancing. He received an Arts Council Bursary Award in 2004 and 2005. Here he reflects on the Irish dancing world he grew up in, and his hopes for the future of the dance form.*

Riverdance for me was the beginning of the journey I am on now. It started me asking questions of myself as a dancer. What place does dance have in my life? Where am I as a performer? How can I be a different performer? A better performer? How can this particular dance form be presented on a stage now in alternative ways?

Once we got over the initial euphoria of *Riverdance*, and that initial impact of "showing", I wondered what is beyond showing? What impact can it have? How can I deconstruct my own form and myself as a dancer and performer, finding other interesting ways to be on stage – ways that challenge me, and an audience as well? Maybe tip the whole thing upside down a little bit so something else about the dance and the dancer becomes revealed. Rather than, "Here I am, this is what I do because I have been training from a very young age, and aren't I great?"

I had a fairly typical upbringing in the world of Irish dance. My parents were Irish, they sent me to dance classes at the age of three in Birmingham, and it went from there. Competing up until the age of 21 or 22 at world championship level, and then going into teaching in the late '80s and early '90s when there were no real professional outlets for an Irish dancer. So you did your thing, you hung up your boots, or you went on tour. But then in the early '90s I started to tour with The Chieftains and Jean Butler, because she had moved to Birmingham to study drama. We had known each other through the competitive scene. So we toured with The Chieftains, we danced together a good few times, and then *Riverdance* happened.

My own experience of entering *Riverdance* was quite dramatic, with Michael leaving and me taking over in London in October '95. We were thrown onto a world stage – onto some of the biggest stages, and biggest theatres in the UK, and Radio City in New York. We were a bit naïve, I suppose, and a bit unprepared, but you got out and you did it. And we all know about the success of the show.

Until *Riverdance* I would never have considered myself in the same breath as the word "artist". I was a dancer who was adept at a particular technique of dance that I had

Photo: personal archive

Colin Dunne wins the 1982 boys' 11-13 World Championship Cup and Belt

learned from a very young age, and had been very successful at on a competitive level. *Riverdance* was really an opportunity for us as dancers to show the audience that level of skill we had all achieved within that small parochial world of Irish dance. It burst out of that, and we were suddenly on stage in front of these audiences, essentially "showing". It was a show and you were exhibiting virtuosity and form. It kind of loosened up a little bit – a bit of personality here and there. You could actually smile, which was a novelty.

As I started at such a young age, I was locked into this system of competing, and never really questioning the form itself. It was Irish dance. You put your music on, you put your shoes on, and isn't it great. I knew nothing about warm ups, had no real awareness of my body, how it worked or how to look after it. Very few of us did. It just wasn't part of the training. In *Riverdance* I had some great performances, and some really horrible ones. But I didn't initially have the performance skills to know why or how, or how to let the bad performances go. Of all the performing arts, dance really relies upon being in tune with the body – that whole body–mind connection thing. There is nothing worse than being on stage having to embody something which for whatever reason feels uncomfortable – where every bone and muscle from head to toe is screaming at you to stop and get off the stage! I had to learn those skills for myself on the job.

It's probably something that comes with age, and experience, having performed so much. I think when I got to 30, I thought, "Here is this thing that I have been doing for so long – why am I still doing it?" After those three years with *Riverdance* I realised that there was perhaps a different kind of performer inside of me, that wouldn't be appropriate for that show. It became necessary for me to find some other reason to be on stage other than, "This is what I do, and I'm good at it."

Photo: Chris Hill

Jean Butler and Colin Dunne in Riverdance

I had a revelation three or four years ago about the actual effect of the dance form on my own body. It is a very vertical dance form. The whole technique of step dance is down in the feet. I began to feel that the more emotional or intelligent parts of the body – your head, gut, stomach, heart, lungs and even your face – were somehow disconnected from the actual dance form. Your feet are so far away from that, and everything else is just stacked up on top.

You have this great foot thing going on underneath you, yet your face is out to the front and your body is pretty much straight. In *Riverdance* we started to decorate it with some arm movements, but these really didn't come from any impulses in the feet. They were essentially just stuck on top, to put it a little bit crudely. In certain performances I began to feel that I was on the outside of the performance experience, looking in. The actual dance form physically in me felt useless and not at all fulfilling.

At that time I had started coming here to the University of Limerick, and I'd been teaching on the Master's course in Irish dancing. I'd begun to talk to Mary Nunan who runs the Contemporary Dance Stream of the MA about my experience of dance, of choreographing dance and the whole journey throughout. Through really engaging in conversation with her as someone coming from the world of contemporary dance, I began to feel that the Masters here at UL would offer a place to submerge myself, and ask questions.

If anything it might be difficult to nail down what exactly contemporary dance is. Some people, myself included, used to think it was just a case of doing your own thing, whatever that may be. But within that there is an inherent tradition of asking questions about dance, movement and performance at all sorts of levels. At the physical level, the conscious level, the sub-conscious level, and the whole body—mind connection thing, which sometimes goes way too deep for me.

I thought that would be a great place to situate myself, and to begin to ask those questions about the form. Also about myself, and my own relationship with the form. I learned new systems of movement and of tracing movement through the body, finding impulses that were informed and free-flowing rather than adding or throwing "shape" on the body by imitating images of what I thought real dance should be! I began to consider possible new contexts for dance performance outside of the notion of a "show" – particularly in the area of solo dance performance. I realised that in *Riverdance*, as soloists we had it so easy! The company of dancers and the music did so much to build up to the solo performances, and to support what were relatively short solos on stage – of about a minute or even less. But how would I, the soloist, set up a dance whereby there was only myself in the production? How do I avoid pressing play, starting to dance when the music starts and finishing when the music demands that it ends?

I don't want to criticise the way Irish dance is taught, because I have been working recently within contemporary dance where dance and movement is taught from a very informed place. You talk about moving from your diaphragm, moving from your kidneys and all these weird and wonderful places.

Competitive Irish dance – certainly the form that I grew up with – was taught very informally. A lot of it was by imitation. When you go into a class as a kid you just watch the older kids and start picking up steps, and your teacher's style, by looking at other kids in the class.

Most of the focus of the training in Irish dancing would be down in the feet. It's about musicality, and where you put the feet. Not much attention is given to the upper body other than if your upper body is moving about, or if your arms are swinging. Heaven forbid that you should move the torso and engage with the music a bit. There is that notion that the arms are held to the side. Some teachers even had the sleeves of their dancers' costumes sewn to the bodice of their dresses or jack-

> *Most of the focus of the training in Irish dancing would be down in the feet. It's about musicality, and where you put the feet . . . Heaven forbid that you should move the torso and engage with the music a bit.*

ets so that they couldn't move their arms. At the time I was teaching and it wasn't a practice I engaged in, but I thought, "Okay, everyone is doing what they need to do

Jean Butler and Colin Dunne in Riverdance

for the dancer to win." But from the outside now I can see it's a case of something that got completely out of hand in a world where common sense is not present.

Personally, I used to have a problem with my left shoulder if I did a travelling step leading with the left foot. My left shoulder would dip. My teacher came up with the solution of putting extra padding in the left shoulder of the jacket. I didn't question it at the time. But looking back I think, "Why would you not just spend some time in the studio trying to address it physically from a dance-and-movement point of view, rather than cosmetically?" But that is the kind of crazy world it is. Now that I'm outside of it I just wish those of us who have left it could have an impact in a positive way on it. But I don't know if we'll ever have the chance.

The cousins of step-dance would be tap and flamenco, in that they are percussive dance forms. In my teenage years I watched the old Hollywood movies, Kelly, Astaire, without taking too much notice of the relationship. Later I was recording them, and rewinding. Particu-

> *Of all the important things that* Riverdance *did – in terms of those of us who had been dancing within this small self-contained world – it really snatched the dance out of this thing you might call tradition or the establishment.*

larly when the likes of Gregory Hines came along and that particular sense of black American, real rhythm tap. It was just so musical, and worked its way into my own lexicon of rhythm and step dance, in subtle ways. But certain members of the establishment would have frowned at it for not being "traditional".

Of all the important things that *Riverdance* did – in terms of those of us who had been dancing within this small self-contained world – it really snatched the dance out of this thing you might call tradition or the establishment. It really quite firmly threw it in our laps and handed the ownership of the dance over to the people who were actually dancing it, its practitioners. With that comes responsibility to take the dance and go off and find your own voice as a performer, choreographer, artist or dancer. I feel a little disappointed at the moment that that really hasn't happened. It's ten years on from *Riverdance* now and the dance itself is probably quite stagnant. In terms of its image, or the work that is being done with it, I feel that it's kind of back to

Photo: Mark Johnson

Colin Dunne

square one really in terms of work people are doing with it creatively. There have been numerous spin-offs. The pretensions that these shows are original or have something else to say is annoying, but that they should earn money and tour – why not?

I would like to see people beginning to find a voice and working in other ways. Whether it be on a conceptual level of choreographing for dance theatre, or even going back to the notion of the dancer as musician.

Traditional music is really well represented in this country and is quite healthy. There are great TV documentaries about *sean nos* and its roots and song – as there are for trad musicians. It's sad dance doesn't have its place in that. In a way, it's our own fault that we have placed ourselves somewhere else, as we traditionally have done. The competition aesthetic is very displaced from arts and culture. We have to really work to begin to find our own voices and to find a healthy place for the dance again.

> *Ten years on, Irish dancing is quite silent as a creative, artistic or even cultural force in this country. We have placed ourselves in a world of our own.*

Ten years on, Irish dancing is quite silent as a creative, artistic or even cultural force in this country. We have placed ourselves in a world of our own. The competitive scene is quite exclusive, uninviting, and alarming even, to those on the outside. Whether we are in that world or out of it, all we seem to talk about are wigs and costumes. The important thing – the dance itself – gets snowed underneath all the baggage.

Will the sane Irish dancer please stand up?

Jean Butler
Dancer

*F*rom *New York, Jean Butler is most widely known as the original lead dancer*
in Riverdance. *As a child Jean excelled in the competitive Irish dancing arena,*
winning several world champion titles. From there she went on to tour internation-
ally with The Chieftains, whose album, The Long Black Veil, *features the acoustic of*
Jean's hard-shoe dancing. In 1999 she choreographed and performed in Dancing on
Dangerous Ground *with Colin Dunne. More recently she completed her MA in Con-*
temporary Dance at the University of Limerick, where she was dancer in residence,
choreographing and performing her own solos. She has also acted in films. Jean
gives masterclasses internationally, and has just produced an Irish Dance Master-
class DVD. Here she reflects on her journey so far as a dancer.

My teacher Donald Golden was, and still is, extremely popular and respected on
the Irish dance scene in New York as a performer and teacher. He had an incredible
way of teaching the love of dance, music and rhythm. So I really learned to dance,
and to love to dance first, and to compete second.

I had done two years of ballet and tap before starting Irish dancing lessons
when I was about six years old. I then gave up the ballet and tap because I thought
Irish dancing was far more fun and accessible. My mother was born in Ireland and
she wanted to keep some Irish culture in the family.

Competitions soon followed as that is the world in which Irish dance mainly op-
erates. I went along to compete alongside my peers at regional, national and world
championship levels. It was very competitive, and we worked really hard, but it was
also great fun. My teacher had an unsung theory of "just do your best while you're
out there, and if you win, that's the icing on the cake".

Donny also gave a lot of workshops or master classes around the New York
area and I would go with him. There would typically be a performance at the end of
these workshops. So I was performing with Donny from the age of about 15 years
old, and really got a taste for it. It was different to performing for competition with
the three judges watching you. In shows with Donny, the line between audience and
performer or judges and dancer disappeared. I really enjoyed that. I was able to express myself freely without worrying what place I would come in. Eventually this led
me to a Chieftains tour, which led to another Chieftains tour, which led to six years
performing with the Chieftains. That led to a phone call from Moya Doherty asking if
I wanted to partake in this piece at the interval of the Eurovision Song Contest.

At the time, Eurovision didn't really change anything because I viewed it as
just another gig. But afterwards it changed everything. It was an enormous success
on many, many levels. My performance skills were honed and tuned during my

period with *Riverdance*. We played to huge audiences, travelled around the world, experienced different cultures, and brought the dance to different countries. As a performer and as a technical dancer it was certainly a challenge to keep up with the pace. But it certainly set me up for a few things after that. In hindsight it was also "the start" of something else.

After *Riverdance* I really needed to take stock of the entire experience. I started going into the studio with no agenda except to dance, to release, and in some ways shake off the last three years of performing and touring. I wanted to remind myself what Irish dancing was before my experience with *Riverdance*, before my experience with the Chieftains. I wanted to have a look at "the dance" itself. But it was precisely these experiences that informed the way I approached the dance at that moment.

Photo: Maurice Gunning

Jean Butler at University of Limerick

When Colin Dunne and I got together to do *Dancing on Dangerous Ground* (1999), I believe we had a sympathy for the fundamental technique that makes up the lexicon of Irish dancing. We really did study the line of the body, the weight shifts, the crossed position of the feet, the locked knees. It was certainly a time of questions, of experimenting. What emerged was a predilection to the extension of the natural boundaries of the technique. Feet became over-crossed, knees were allowed to bend, weight shifted, a lunge was achieved. And all by accident, in a way. When I say by accident, I mean more by intuition. I did not have the vocabulary then as I do now. I would not have been able to describe what was happening in a "dance literate" sense. What I see now was that we came off the vertical access, and started lowering our weight into the ground, albeit with one leg in front of the other. It was a step towards defining a particular stylisation of the Irish dance tradition, a style that the show became known for.

As the current (2003–2005) artist-in-residence at University of Limerick I am doing a Masters in Contemporary Dance. This experience alone, so far, has shed re-markable light on my life as a dancer and performer, and on my idea of what dance is or can be. I started this course out of a need to learn, to be a student, to give back to myself as an artist in order to see if I had more to give as a performer. I wanted to be educated in a dance tradition with practitioners and pioneers whose work has been studied and recorded. I wanted to be "dance literate" and to understand different techniques and theories of composition which I now have words for!

It's phenomenal because in *Dangerous Ground* I was trying to teach the dancers about "centre", which I certainly was not an expert on. It is remarkable that I got to the age of 30 as an Irish dancer and never once heard the word "centre" in any class, rehearsal or show I took part in. But I knew there was something there. I knew it was the basis of all movement. That and *breath*, another thing Irish dancers are not taught about. I was trying to teach myself and a company at the same time. One of the things this MA has allowed me is the ability to hone, refine and explore, so I am clearer teaching.

I think *Riverdance* achieved everything it set out to achieve, and that was to bring Irish dancing to the world globally. It did it triumphantly you might say, and is still doing it. But for me as an artist, I had to stop and take a step back from it, look at it again – and decide whether that is the only way Irish dance can be presented. Irish dancing is at such a beginning, still. Without the pioneering work of *Riverdance* we wouldn't be where we are today, but ten years on there is still so much work to do.

I don't have any idea yet how I am going to incorporate what I am learning now in the MA into my Irish dancing. At the moment it's a very strict schedule: Monday to Friday, 9.00–6.00. My goal is to process all the information on my own body first, before I transfer it to the Irish dancing. But even having an awareness of possibilities has just been extraordinary.

Irish dancers are vertical. They don't use any weight in soft-shoe dancing. The objective is to stay off the floor, to never even touch the floor – to leap higher and to dance very lightly around the floor. Now I'm flipping that on its head and I'm into the floor, I'm on the floor. Everything is on the floor. Where I came from and where I am at the moment is an amazing juxtaposition. I need a bit more time before I can see what the relationship between the two worlds will be.

> Irish dancers are vertical. . . . The objective is to stay off the floor, to never even touch the floor – to leap higher and to dance very lightly around the floor. Now I'm flipping that on its head and I'm into the floor, I'm on the floor. Everything is on the floor.

I would credit *Riverdance* with where I am today as a dancer, and very much as a person in a serendipitous way. I had no intention of continuing on as a dancer. The Chieftains was as good as it got for Irish dancers, and before *Riverdance* I looked towards theatre because I knew I wanted to perform and I thought I wouldn't be able to do so dancing. I always thought it was such a waste that I couldn't perform with a skill or talent that I had fostered for years. I had many hang-ups as an Irish dancer. It was such an odd existence in a way. I was single-minded about my dance, committed to the point of ignorance on most subjects unrelated to it, yet I knew at the time there was no future there.

Performing in *Riverdance* did open up different opportunities. Irish dancing used to exist in a very small world, a closeted world, almost a box, and the larger outside world didn't know anything about it. And then, all of a sudden we're on a London stage at a Royal Variety performance. We found ourselves among all these different performances going on from different disciplines. The exposure to different dance and theatre was intoxicating. Being there as an Irish dancer was also kind of terrifying. I was proud to be there, but I fought with the merits which got me there. I also envied the confidence of performers of more accepted art forms. I knew then that there were other things that I wanted and needed to explore.

My journey at the moment is very much about myself, and trying to find a truth in my original movement. I have no interest in trying to cross-fertilise Irish dancing and contemporary dance. The contemporary dance I have seen and the classes that I have taken to date have opened up a different world of physical opportunity. I now understand the difference between choreography and step-arrangement. A lot

Photo: Maurice Gunning

Jean Butler in Does She Take Sugar in Her Tea?, *2005*

of Irish dance is about step-arrangement and its musical counterpart. This is not meant critically. But what happens to an Irish dancer, to me, when you take away two compositional structures? What happens when you are conceiving a piece of dance that is not there to "entertain" in the general sense of the word? How do you choreograph something that isn't choreographed just to be viewed or enjoyed? Choreographing without music, and without mirrors – this territory is foreign to me. It seems to be more about you as an "artist" rather than as a technician. Irish dancing is extremely exciting because of the sheer virtuosity of the skills required to perform it. But one can also pose questions through dance, challenge assumptions, surprise and delight through a different application of the same virtuosity.

There is an enormous intellectual and conceptual skill involved. I wish I had started this ten years ago. But for the moment I can only take in things one at a time.

For example, something as simple as a *plié*. It is essential, can be so excitingly useful, and can be transferred into my work at any time, transforming the movement.

I think most of the upper body movement in *Riverdance* was either stylised or practical. When stylised, the arm movements were ornamentations. When practical, the arm movements aided balance.

In contemporary dance, however, there is no line drawn under "upper" or "lower" body work as there tends to be in Irish dance. There is an awareness of continuity within the flow of the energy in your body that is *not* dissected at your waist! This notion, although easy to comprehend intellectually, is not the same in physical practice – especially after years of keeping my spine erect! When I first started this course I forgot that my head was connected to my shoulders. So when my shoulders went down, my head automatically stayed up. I really needed to release the back of my neck, and my spine, and remember that I am all connected! Moving kinaesthetically opens up endless possibilities.

Physically it's extremely liberating, although I am still at the exploratory stage. It's not, maybe on a physical endorphin level, as cathartic as going in and putting on my jig shoes, and tapping around for an hour just to release some energy. But it is extremely challenging. At the end of a day in the studio it used to be that my legs were exhausted – now my brain and my body are utterly wiped! It is hard to explain. It is a different type of energy. It brings you straight into yourself really, and grounds you.

When people used to comment on how *Riverdance* put sex back into Irish dancing, I really couldn't see it. What is sexy to me is "energy". I would like to think that is what was being communicated in the show. There was so much energy on stage, and so much energy coming at you – coming off the stage into the audience. I don't think sexy is a pose or a head movement, or an arm movement. It's an overall thing, the *je ne sais quoi*, which one can't precisely name. I think of it as an energy that cannot be manufactured. There is nothing worse than a packaged "sexiness".

> *When people used to comment on how* Riverdance *put sex back into Irish dancing, I really couldn't see it. What is sexy to me is "energy". I would like to think that is what was being communicated in the show.*

As an Irish dancer I do consider myself fortunate in that I was taught "the love of the dance". This was very important in a world dominated by competition. I always felt that I was dancing from the inside-outwards, that I was trying to express something of myself. But this "outside" was so structured, so formal in technique, that as time went on it was difficult to continue that connection. The MA programme has enabled me to root myself within my body and experiment with movement that I know is unique to me. The value of that movement is yet to be seen. I am not passing judgement or aspirations. I am not ready for that. It's just process at the moment.

Breandán de Gallaí
Dancer and Choreographer

From Gaoth Dobhair in County Donegal, Breandán grew up speaking Ulster Irish, and started Irish dancing at the age of eight. He too excelled in the competitive dancing scene, procuring numerous national and international titles, including four world medals. This talent led him to tour the world with Riverdance, *in which he danced the lead role for many years. However in tandem with all this glamour, he managed to acquire an honours degree in applied physics from Dublin City University along the way. While appearing on and presenting many culture shows on TG4 and RTE, he is currently putting together his own large-scale Irish dance show,* Balor. *Here he shares his thoughts on, and experiences of, Irish dance.*

Irish dance has tremendous scope as an art form, and has yet to be explored properly. I think people assumed up until the Eurovision that it really had only one purpose – to have little ringletted Irish colleens entertaining Yankees wearing overly ornate dresses. *Riverdance* in the Eurovision transformed the Irish public's perception of Irish dance. Suddenly Irish dancing was sexy. Now, ten years later, the feeling has changed again: *Riverdance* is considered cheesy, and there is no room for manoeuvre in the art form. I would completely disagree with that.

I was teaching in Dublin when I got a call about *Riverdance* just before the 1994 Eurovision. They were shooting the six-minute interval act. I was brought in to audition, got the part, and was with the company until around April 2003, the last seven years as principal dancer.

Fortunately for me *Riverdance* was massive. A lot of my colleagues and I did very well out of it. It opened doors. However, it didn't allow me *carte blanche* with my own ideas once I left – from the point of view of people believing and allowing you to nurture what you want to do creatively.

I do hope that *Balor*, the project that I am working on at the moment, will prove there is so much more that can be done with Irish dance as an art form. I also hope that it will be a commercial success.

It is my intention, in creating *Balor*, to deconstruct the Irish dancer and rebuild them. The only thing that really needs to remain is that unique spirit which good passionate Irish dancers have: their love for rhythm, and their ability to create fantastic rhythms. I am not a big believer in the "the faster you dance percussively, the better a dancer you are". A lot of people who watch dance don't actually look at feet. Research has shown that audiences look at your chest and not the feet. In a way, that makes sense because that's where I feel the energy is coming from – your centre.

It is exciting to work with talented Irish dancers who are geniuses when it comes to producing rhythm with their feet. But what is more important to me is to nurture a more visceral approach to dance. To focus a lot more on what you feel inside, rather than what you can produce in a calculated, mathematical way, "X" amount of beats in "X" amount of time. It's more about the energy a dancer can expel in the execution of a step or movement.

Photo: Hugo Glendenning

Breandán de Gallaí in Riverdance

The idea behind *Balor* is that we are using Irish dancing the same way the *Ballets Russes* used ballet. It is there to tell a story. It's not only about the steps that are to be danced, but about the character you are playing. The purpose of the dance changes as a result, because you must allow your character to exist and develop.

I don't want people to focus too much on the fact that when we speak about *Balor* we use words like "classical influences" or "flamenco influences". They are not deliberate influences. It's not a case of "What gimmick would work? Well *Cirque du Soleil* seems very popular now, let's throw a bit of that in, so we could sell tickets." It's to do with where Irish dancers have arrived.

For example, what are the influences on dancers like me, who are coming out of the Irish dance competitive arena, and the *Riverdance* arena? I studied contemporary dance, jazz, ballet and tap in Chicago before I went to university, and therefore have some influences, which have been with me for the last 15 years. The Russian folk and the flamenco dancers whom I performed with in *Riverdance* have also influenced me. Flamenco is percussive, so it is no surprise that it's going to affect us.

I performed with a wonderful male flamenco dancer in the Royal Albert Hall once, and the minute we met, we had a special bond because we are similar. We are percussive dancers – with the same sort of fire inside us.

Though it did serve its purpose, I don't think *Riverdance* pushed Irish dancing forward as far as it could. The brief of *Riverdance* was "X", and Irish dancing in *Riverdance* fulfilled that brief. But I certainly don't think that is the be all and end all of Irish dance. But it seems that an awful lot of people associate only that image with Irish dancing. In fact, they don't call it Irish dancing, they call it *"Riverdancing"*. While *Riverdance* does what it intends very well, that is a very, very small aspect of what Irish dancing is capable of achieving.

Riverdance certainly raised the profile and opened doors for all Irish dancers, which is brilliant. But people don't realise that there is the traditional element too. Competitive dancers, and their level of skill and excellence, is way beyond what we do in *Riverdance*. What we did competitively required a different type of focus. Competition requires a lot of discipline and practice. Those children who dance in the world championships work night and day to get to that level. Of course there are other challenges in *Riverdance*; the speed with which we dance; we may kick higher; we move a little faster and further; but rhythmically and step-wise it isn't that much of a challenge.

As a result of dancing with *Riverdance* and collaborating with the flamenco and Russian dancers, I am moving forward. The way I dance is probably more similar to what would have been done in Ireland 200 years ago when the rules and regulations did not exist and people just danced to be happy or to celebrate. There was no pressure to cross feet, or to have good turnout. That evolved as a result of the Gaelic League and competitions.

I see Irish dancing moving forward now, and undoing a lot of the stuff that prevented us from expressing ourselves as we would like to. If you have a routine with eight bars of rhythm and you are concentrating on crossing your feet, keeping your knees together, and keeping your arms by your side, I feel that

Photo: Joan Marcus

Breandán de Gallai in Riverdance

impedes the expression and energy. Now my Irish dance colleagues and I might choose to do it a little bit differently. The Irish dance adjudicator may criticise because in competition certain boxes need to be ticked. Whereas somebody who enjoys dance for what it is would say, "God, that really moved me because I really felt something very unique there." That would be because it wasn't about the technical excellence, but about the spirit, or the emotion. They would feel, perhaps, what the dancer feels – which is a big thing for me as a dancer. I don't want you to go, "Wow, look how fast . . ." or "Look how precise . . .". I want you to feel what I feel when I perform. That is the stuff of excitement and invigoration. I often feel sorry for the audience because they may not get to feel what the dancer feels.

I took up dancing at about eight or nine, and was still competition dancing at 24. A lot of dancers start as early as three or four. At 18 I went to Chicago to do a full-time dance course and was very taken by contemporary dance. They always had a live musician. You would do barre, followed by a variety of routines in the centre. One of the things I loved to do was to jump, but because it was contemporary dance there was no pressure to land on the beat. I had a reputation for jumping high, and the musician used to play to me rather than me dancing to his beat. He was quite impressed at how high I could jump. I felt that I could stay in the air as long as the music would allow. I use to say, "I'll jump as high as you allow me to jump. The longer you hold the note, the longer I'll stay in the air." That is something that I want to introduce into Irish dancing.

When I was back in university in Dublin and back in competition, I would get an awful lot of grief about not landing in time. I was accused of having bad timing, but really I was just in my own little world experimenting with different ways of approaching Irish dancing. That was the only time I felt restricted. I suppose I was older then and I wanted to do something different. I was thinking, "The whole competition thing is limiting me now." It wasn't really a problem when I was 16. When I danced in competition, I didn't feel restricted by having my arms at my side.

Irish dancers who are born and bred in Ireland seem to have a natural flare. Maybe because they are exposed to it all the time from a very young age. My parents would have done *ceili* dancing at home in Donegal. Keeping my hands by my side was not a big deal because it seemed natural. In fact, when *Riverdance* burst on the scene people always joked about "the arms by the side" thing. But there are so many dance forms where you may not do certain things with the arms. Take flamenco for example. When they are doing their fancy rhythm, their arms do not move. They may not be down by their side, but they are in a static position. Flamenco dancers don't actually take away from their fast rhythm by doing a lot of arm movements. They punctuate phrases with their arms. I think it's unfair to be amazed by the fact that we don't use our arms. It is like saying that soccer is a ridiculous game because you are not allowed to lift the ball.

> *Irish dancers who are born and bred in Ireland seem to have a natural flare. Maybe because they are exposed to it all the time from a very young age.*

You could say that ballet is just as strict a dance form as Irish dancing. When it comes, for example to fifth position, it's either a good fifth position, or a bad fifth position. So it's exactly the same. It's just a way of doing something.

Jonathan Kelliher
Siamsa Tíre

*J*onathan Kelliher has been involved with Siamsa Tíre *since the age of eight.
He trained at the Teach* Siamsa *Training Centre for three years, and became
a professional member of the company in 1989. He has played leading roles in*
Siamsa *productions, and is directing the current show* Tarmon *(opening April
2006). Before he took over as acting artistic director in 2004, he was company
dancing master. He also lectures on* Siamsa Tíre's *dance style at the Institute of
Technology, Tralee.*

Siamsa means "entertainment", and *Tíre* means "country" or "land", so Siamsa Tíre
means "entertainment of the land". We are the National Folk Theatre of Ireland.

Siamsa Tíre is rooted in Irish dancing, but uses contemporary dance to develop
the dance we have, and to use the body. Contemporary is the body movement of our
Irish dance. It's the development of our feet into the body. Our "Munnix" style of
dance uses that approach anyway because it involves the upper body. It's loose and
fluid. That is where a contemporary choreographer like Cindy Cummings, whom
we are working with at the moment, comes into it. Cindy has a real sense of what
we are doing now. It's more improvisational stuff rather than being set in a contemporary way. We do a lot of improvisation. Cindy is actually learning Irish dancing
from us so that she can get the feel for what the feet are doing, and then make that
part of the body – rather than just doing a bit of an Irish step and then putting
movement on top of it. If we are combining the Irish with contemporary movement
it develops out of the footwork. Some of the footwork is very fluid and there are
turns out of it. The Munnix style isn't as percussive as modern Irish dancing in that
there aren't as many taps.

In our work, we ask questions such as when you do a certain move, what does
it do to the rest of your body? For our 2005 Dublin Fringe Festival show *rEvolution* we started with the traditional Irish step known as "the Blackbird". We experimented turning it backwards and dancing it backwards, which took a week to get
the hang of. But then by dancing it backwards, it threw the whole balance of the
dancer's body out – because Irish dancing is very balanced. The dancer's whole
body was moving because the balance was put way off. We said "Look at that, there
is something there. What can develop out of that?" Different types of moves came
out of that. We spotted things we never would have seen had we not experimented
in that way. So in Siamsa's work, every contemporary move comes from somewhere
in Irish dancing. That is the way we look at the dance here.

Dance is a big part of what Siamsa Tíre does. The shows are all presented and
told through dance and song. All have equal balance within a show. The 2005 *rEv-*

olution show was different because it was a dance experiment with multimedia. In Siamsa we have been developing dance for 20-odd years with different choreographers, like Jonathan Burnett, Mary Nunan, John Scott and Anne Courtenay. Since our foundation, in 1974, we have been consistently experimenting and trying different stuff. So we're not just an Irish dancing company, and our shows are not just Irish dance. As in the *rEvolution* piece, we are taking the Irish dance and developing it in a new direction. What we are trying to do is to keep the traditional Irish dance the way it is – not changing it too much, but just developing it.

Photo courtesy of Siamsa Tíre

rEvolution

Our style is untouched by competition Irish dancing, which features an immobile upper body. It's just the way it's gone, that there is this stiffness about it. Our style is more natural, in that the upper body moves fluidly with the steps.

We are lucky that in the late 1970s and early 1980s our founder, Fr Pat Ahern, filmed the old North Kerry dancers when they were in their '70s and '80s. We trace our dance lineage back to a very famous North Kerry dance master Jerry Molyneaux (1883–1967) – or Jerry Munnix, as we know him. He taught his own particular style. It was a very fluid, moving type of Irish dancing.

Our Munnix style is more like *sean nós*. But a lot of people think of *sean nós* as being from Connemara, whereas this is "old-style" Kerry. Some of the steps we use are maybe a hundred years old or more. Any Irish dancing we use then, we devise in this "Munnix" style.

What I see in a lot of Irish dancing today is from the knees down, and it is just quick. Whereas for us the whole body has always been part of the step – rather than just the feet – so the hands and the body become part of it. If you are dancing, it is what happens to your body naturally. So there is no

> *We trace our dance lineage back to a very famous North Kerry dance master Jerry Molyneaux (1883–1967) – or Jerry Munnix, as we know him. He taught his own particular style. It was a very fluid, moving type of Irish dancing.*

set movement of arms or upper body to the step, it's just a looseness, a relaxedness, a fluidity. That becomes part of the step. The upper body isn't disconnected, it's all one. In other "modernised" twentieth-century Irish dancing you see this rigid upper body that is doing nothing, and then the feet doing amazing stuff, but the way we look at it, it's the whole body. I don't think it was ever planned like that, it just naturally evolved that way. The reason it works is that the dance and the body are so natural. Rather than something that's stuck together, it's a natural progression.

That is why we brought contemporary dance into it. I suppose it has become more of a movement thing now than "contemporary". We did go through a phase of Martha Graham-style contemporary dance that involved some very set positions. Indeed, some early Siamsa productions juxtaposed a bit of Irish with a bit of contemporary, rather than incorporating them into each other – we have developed from that.

Clann Lir

We have always kept the traditional dancing. We've also gone all over Europe, incorporating folk dancing – from flamenco, with Maria Pages, to bringing a dancer over from Bulgaria who taught us some Bulgarian folk dances. Many European countries have folk groups that just stick to their folk dancing, the equivalent of the polka set. Siamsa Tíre however is about experimenting and trying different things.

We run a course in Tralee Institute of Technology where we teach this "Munnix" style of dance. In 1999 a professional Irish dancer took the course, learned the Munnix style with us, and saw the *Clann Lir* show, choreographed by Mary Nunan. She said there was no way that show would have worked with the modern side of Irish dancing, because it just doesn't have the fluidity of the Munnix style. According to her, modern Irish dancing would have been too robotic and jagged for these movements to have worked with it. In *Clann Lir*, we used the upper body when the swans began to dance – because we think of swans moving like that.

> *. . . modern Irish dancing would have been too robotic and jagged for these movements to have worked with it. In* Clann Lir, *we used the upper body when the swans began to dance – because we think of swans moving like that.*

Our founder, Fr Ahern, who retired as Artistic Director of Siamsa Tíre in 1998, is from a rural, farming background in Moyvane, County Kerry. Now in his seventies, he was always big into music and learned to dance in the Munnix style. Originally, he was into theatre, and developed a passion play. The way he always tells the story, when the passion play finished up, some of the future members of Siamsa had a party at which one of the dancers got up and did a bit of a step, another sang a song, and someone else played a tune. That sparked off the idea in Fr. Pat's head that "there is something in this, we should put something together". So they started rehearsing it, and putting it together. It kind of developed from there, kept going, then RTÉ came in and filmed it. Eventually they started putting it on as a show in Tralee over the summer.

It was Fr Ahern's brainchild, but put together by a group of them, who came up with the steps. This group included Liam Tarrant, a blacksmith who had been a pupil of Munnix. He actually dropped dead, aged 54, 30 seconds after dancing at the opening of Siamsa Tíre in 1974. But the story goes that Liam Tarrant got a milk churn – for

making butter – in Galway. There is a rhythm to that activity, and that became the rhythm for a work song around butter churning. They put a song to it, a tune to it, and there was a dance that went with it. That was the start of it. It became a story of how butter was made 150 years ago. So that would have been how things got going. It just developed from there.

Now we have our own theatre here in the centre of Tralee, and two training centres – one in West Kerry (Dingle), and one in North Kerry (Finuge), where we take in kids every year from the age of about seven or eight. They attend classes there for three years, audition again, and then come up to the theatre in

Liam Tarrant dancing at the opening of Siamsa Tíre, 1974

Tralee for extra classes, and may eventually become part of the company. All of us would have started like that. I was seven when I started in the training centre, and developed through that. By now I've been working here full-time for over 16 years. I went through the whole training system, and then became a performer. We've a cast of about 120, most of whom are part-time "community cast" in a *meitheal* system, who have their own jobs here in Tralee. At the moment we have a core group of five work professionals. They are Irish dancers, singers and musicians. Because of the way the company is set up, it's like a little family. People start so young. It's like an academy at this stage. We can take a kid in at six or seven, go through the training centres, the more advanced classes, and then do a BA in Theatre Studies at Tralee Institute of Technology, and eventually possibly get a job out of it.

Fr Ahern taught me a lot of singing and a bit of dancing as I was coming through. In the early days Jimmy Smith and Pat Hanafin were the Siamsa dance teachers.

Though Fr Pat certainly was mostly into the music, he would have had a very good knowledge of dance as well. Jimmy Smith taught me in the training centres. When I came into class in Tralee Fr. Pat would have been here as well. By then we knew the steps but he would have been making sure we had the style of it right.

While we've been experimenting a little with mixing contemporary and traditional for twenty years – with varying degrees of success – it's only really now people are thinking of incorporating contemporary dance into Irish dancing elsewhere. We had been working on it long before *Ding Dong Deder*ó – *Forging the Dance*, choreographed by Anne Courtenay in 1991. That didn't just come out of nowhere. For ten years prior to that we were bringing contemporary choreographers in – stuff that would have never been in the public because it was just our own development – to see where we could go with it. We might get ten contemporary choreographers in, but only one might work. From the other nine, though, you are going to learn something. It's not just the Anne Courtenays, or the Cindy Cummings, or the Mary Nunans, it is ten or fifteen years of work we have been doing before them, getting there. It's a slow progression, but I think that's probably better than just tacking it on.

The first time everything really seemed to click right was when Mary Nunan's 1999 choreography *The Children of Lir* (*Clann Lir*) allowed that upper body movement with the swans. Even going back to the 1991 *Ding Dong Deder*ó show, that certainly worked in its time, it was super. I was in that. The first time we worked with Anne Courtenay was two years earlier in 1989 with *Between Worlds*, to Micheal Ó Súilleabháin's music.

Clann Lir

Jonathan Burnett, a former soloist with the Irish National Ballet, had worked with us in a different style for *The Story of the Mermaid* in 1986. It went on stage here just a couple of times, and was a pure dance piece. Lovely piece, worked successfully, totally different than the subsequent shows, but still keeping the Irish dancing as a core.

Oileán

We had flamenco dancer Maria Pages here before *Riverdance*. Composer Bill Whelan did the *Seville Suite* for the 1992 Seville Expo. Before we went to Seville it was in the National Concert Hall, and the Concert Orchestra played the whole piece. Bill came up with the idea of putting dance at the end of it, with Irish dancing and Spanish flamenco, as the end of the piece develops into a meeting of Irish and Spanish music. So that night there was a piece done with Siamsa dancers. Then Fr Pat found Maria Pages and brought her over from Spain for a week to workshop with Siamsa. Again, just another experiment to see if we could link flamenco up with the Irish and how it might work. From that it was developed into something that was danced at the Expo in Spain in 1992, and later Maria Pages' performed her *Firedance* choreography in *Riverdance*.

What *Riverdance* does is super, but what gets to us is that so many people have tried to compare us. We do two totally different things. They are a big spectacular dance show, and totally different to Siamsa. We use our music, songs and dance to really tell a story. For us, showing off the dance, or the song, is secondary to getting into the story.

As the National Folk Theatre of Ireland our remit is to portray our traditions. We are trying to keep our traditions, but still move them forward into the twenty-first century – without stagnating. We don't want to be like most folk groups in other European countries. We keep our traditional dance as it is. We haven't strayed and gone with the modernisation of the Irish dance. We've kept it, and developed it in its own way. Being the National Folk Theatre – folk being the people – we try to tell the stories of the people.

For example, in 2003 we did a show called *Oileán* on the life of the people and the evacuation of the Blasket Islands. At the moment we are creating a show based around the time of the Famine – which is so much part of Irish history, life and the Irish psyche – set in a workhouse. There is a huge amount of local research involved.

While researching it, I came across this dancing master, Thomas Moore (1822–1878), or "Mooreen", as he was known, who died in a workhouse in Listowel. Someone sent Fr Ahern the 1878 workhouse death certificate, from which you can see that they are mostly farm labourers. Then, out of nowhere you have "Occupation: dance master", dead from "cold from exposure". Looking back at the history there was an O'Céirin (Kerrins) Dancing Master [late 1700s– early 1800s], which is – arguably – as far back as we can go in the Irish dancing history. He would have taught "Mooreen", who died in the workhouse, one of the people who inspires our story. It also ties in with our theme of how much dance would have died with that Dance Master? The whole idea of the new show is based on the notion that "OK – so much died – yes but look what survived as well".

Oileán

Photo courtesy of Siamsa Tíre

I'm directing the new show, *Tarmon*, and Cindy Cummings, who choreographed *Oileán* and *rEvolution*, is choreographing it. Also we have a writer for the first time – Michael Harding. Up to now we have always devised the shows ourselves. This time, Michael Harding came up with an initial storyline script, after which he came down for a week and we worked it out. He's down for a week now, after which he'll go away and re-write it. In the meantime we'll be working away. He'll come back down and we'll look at the whole thing again.

In the early days we por-trayed our stories through music, song, mime and dance. Mime and movement would have been a big element. Not using text means you can tour anywhere in the world and there is no language barrier. But on the other hand, it's very difficult to portray a big twist in a story through movement only – without being able to say it. With one sentence you can turn a whole plot on its head. But with movement only that's difficult. In Siamsa we train people to be dancers and singers. It wouldn't be formal acting training, but it's certainly part of it. There is non-dialogue acting in our productions. It varies from show to show. This show will be very character-based, as *Oileán* was.

We did a huge amount of research for *Oileán* as well – reading all the Blasket books like *An t-Oileánach* and *Fiche Blian ag Fás*. For *Oileán* the musical director got specific songs from the Blasket Islands and from West Kerry. We felt that if we were trying to tell the spirit of the island, we should use what they used.

When we are developing mythic stories, like the *Oisín* story and the *Clann Lir* story, the narratives are very set. *Clann Lir* was very dance-orientated, whereas with the *Oileán* story, and now this new piece as well, we are looking more at the human characters.

Before I became acting artistic director last year, I was dance master in the company. We had a contemporary class each morning as a warm-up. Or Joanne Barry, one of our performers who has an MA in Drama might give us an hour of a drama workshop – because though it's part of it, dance is not our main thing. Music and singing are also part of our ethos. While dance would be the one we have most developed, it is not all we do.

Folk Theatre Studies, which I teach at Tralee Institute of Technology, has been going for 11 years. It was instigated by Fr Pat and Siamsa's former manager, Martin Whelan. Music and dance are part of the course. The dance element includes contemporary and traditional Irish dancing, as well as the theory and history of dance. We do European folk dance, and encourage the students to develop their own way of using Irish dancing. It's not just teaching them steps. They are learning about dance in a broader sense. There is also stage-craft, lighting, sound, sales and marketing and theatre management. It helps if you know about lighting and the practical side of theatre. Another subject called *Saíocht* goes into civilisation and history – for example the effect the Famine has had on the Irish psyche. Folk theatre itself then would be the thing that ties everything together. At the end of each year they do a project and at the end of fourth year they do a full-length show themselves, and write their thesis on that afterwards.

Photo courtesy of Siamsa Tíre

Rehearsal for Tarmon *(2006)*

Siamsa Tíre is funded by the Arts Council, and our season goes from the end of April to the end of September with nearly full houses for the five months, six nights a week. The theatre is hired out to other groups during the winter. There are 25 or 30 people in each show, five of whom would be professionals.

We are very proud that we do keep our traditions, and keep focussed on what we are trying to do – even though we do experiment. Fine, modernise, but it's crucial that we do hold on to the core tradition.

Note
[1] Carolyn Swift, *The Irish Times*, 7 April 1999, in her unpublished manuscript "Dance in Ireland".

Chapter 8

Chapter 8

Wild Geese

Traditionally, dancers had to go away to complete their training, to find kindred choreographers, or simply to spread their wings. Contemporary dance is, after all, an international art form, and by its nature an import-export business. Michael Keegan-Dolan of Fabulous Beast Dance Theatre trained at Central School of Ballet in London, and had his working base there for many years. In the classical ballet world, Monica Loughman from Santry, trained at Perm State Ballet school in Russia from the age of 14, after which she became the first ever Western European to join the company.[1] In the contemporary dance world, Ríonach ní Néill, who also has her PhD in Geography from UCD, danced with Bremen Dance Theatre and is coming back to Dublin to put on a show at Project Theatre.

In this chapter, we listen to two extraordinary journeys our dancing wild geese have taken, bringing their Irish moves to the international stage. First, from Longford, Marguerite Donlon, now director of her own Donlon Dance Company in the Saarlandisches Staatstheater Saarbrücken, Germany, tells her story of how, from local *Slógadh* competitions, to a dresser at the English National Opera, to a soloist in the Deutsche Oper Berlin she got to where she is today. Classically trained, Donlon is known for incorporating Irish dancing footwork into her contemporary dance choreography, which is now part of the German contemporary dance landscape.

Then there is Finola Cronin, who began her dance career in Dublin with Joan Davis in the 1970s, and found herself, via The Place in London, performing with Pina Bausch's Tanztheater Wuppertal for ten years, before returning to Ireland in the mid-1990s to become dance specialist at the Arts Council.

For these brave, adventurous spirits, following their instinct and making it up as they went along paid off dividends. Imitate at your own peril, however.

Marguerite Donlon
Choreographer

*F*rom Longford, where she first began to dance, Marguerite Donlon like many had to travel abroad to hone her talents and to find an outlet for them. From performing at the English National Ballet to becoming soloist in the Deutsche Oper Berlin, Marguerite gradually made the transition to choreographer, creating works for Nederlands Dans Theater NDT 2, the Stuttgart Ballet and the Vienna State Ballet, among others. Marguerite is now artistic director of her own Donlon Dance Company in Saarbrücken's Saarlandisches Staatstheater. Here she shares the somewhat unorthodox route that took her there.

Ballet was something I always wanted to do. But as there was nothing else but Irish dancing in Longford, I was happy with that. It was at that stage that I started to incorporate some arm movements into the Irish dancing because I found it rather stiff, with the arms so tightly down by the sides.

Then I was very fortunate that a South African woman, Anica Louw, married an Irish farmer, Philip Dawson, and returned to live in Longford, where she started to teach ballet. It was quite funny because the advertisement she put in the newspaper said she was looking for children who were under twelve years of age. So when I called her and told her that I was 15, she said, "Oh no, you are too old." I think it was one of the only things I ever begged for in my life, trying to convince her that she should take me. She did, and that was the first step in getting into dance.

Anica was also starting out – it was her first time teaching. She gave me a great love and understanding of movement and dance of all kinds. We also did African dancing with her. Then I did some Royal Academy of Dance exams. Anica told Dorothy Stevens, a Royal Academy of Dance teacher, about me, and it was decided that if I was even to consider a career in dance, I should go to a proper school. Dorothy Stevens said, "I'll take her." So off I went to England when I was 17. I began from the beginning, learning all the techniques and doing every exam imaginable related to dance. I worked hard. I knew at that age there was only one chance; 17 is old to be starting. With Dorothy I did everything: jazz, tap, modern. I also did O Level history of ballet, and my A levels, because I wasn't convinced that I was going to make my career as a ballet dancer. So it was intense. I don't think I've ever worked so hard in my life.

Peter Schaufuss saw me while I was taking class with the English National Ballet, who were on tour. The teacher, Kevin Hagan, and Peter Schaufuss decided to offer me a contract. Actually, they didn't have a contract to offer me at first. But they brought me down to London, where I learned everything with the company, did class every day, and had parts to learn in the various ballets.

They knew I didn't have any money, so they arranged to get me a little job as the dresser for the London Festival Hall Christmas season. This confused the other dancers who asked, "What are you? Are you a dancer, or the dresser?" One day Peter called me to the studio, and presented me with a contract. I stayed with them for about three and a half years. Within that time I danced and learned even more. I went from *corps de ballet* to soloist quite quickly. It was strange because I came in there with no background. I didn't go to the Royal Ballet School, I didn't know all the famous teachers. I didn't know who was who in the dance world. But I loved what I was doing and kept going. Then Peter Schaufuss left and became the director in the Deutsche Oper in Berlin. He invited seven dancers with him, and I was one of them. That's how I ended up in Berlin.

I did my first choreography before I learned ballet – for the dance section in a *Slógadh* competition in Ireland. I read a lot of books, and saw things on TV. My mother was very active in the household. She never learned dance but she saw all the Hollywood movies as a child, and was passionate about movement. She danced as she cleaned. I used to think she was a film star.

Photo: Todd Rosenberg/Hubbard Street Dance

Patrick Simonello (upright) Tobin Del Cuore, Massimo Pacilli, Julia Wollrab and Jamie Meeks in Reverse Deconstruct *by Marguerite Donlon*

When I went to England I not only danced the classics like *Swan Lake* and *Onegin* but worked with and danced in pieces by people like Christopher Bruce and Michael Clarke. When I went to Berlin I worked with choreographers like Stephen Petronio, Meg Stuart, William Forsythe and Jiri Kylian, each with their own style. So there was a vast amount of information coming in. But I think the Irish roots were a very strong influence on me. There is a lot of Irish-related footwork going on in my work, and use of black humour. Many of the critics in Germany talk about "Donlon's black Irish humour".

The first semi-professional piece I made was *Celtic Touch* in '92, in the young choreographers' platform, *Unter den Linden* at the Komisches Oper in Berlin. I went around to all the Irish pubs in Berlin looking for the perfect Irish band to perform with me on stage. Several pints later I found them. Funnily enough, it was made into a documentary. Eoin Moore from Dublin was studying in the film school in Berlin, and he did his final film, *Child of Light*, on the making of my first ballet. So the two of us were starting out in our own professions. It was shown on RTÉ a couple of years ago. It was very contemporary movement, with a lot of Irish footwork. From there on I did a piece every year. Even if there wasn't any choreographic platform arranged, I would still get some dancers together and do a piece.

Photo: Bettina Stoess

Meritxell Aumedes Molinero and Lee Youn Hui in Chocolate

I was still very busy with being a dancer and loving it. In 1998 I choreographed a piece called *We Three Sheep*. That was the one that made a lot of people interested in my work – not just in Berlin. From this piece I got invited to competitions, and won a couple of prizes with it. Then I got invited to do a piece with Tanzensemble Cathy Sharpe who have been to Ireland many times. That was my first piece for a professional company. I did a piece for the big stage at the Deutsche Oper, and then a piece for Vienna State Ballet. It kind of started to roll from then on.

It was at this point that I started to call it Marguerite Donlon Dance Company. But all the time I was still dancing. Then there came a point when I thought, "Okay, I always wanted to stop at the top of my dance career. Now is the time to stop." I didn't want to dwindle down. I felt I'd done everything I really wanted to do as a dancer. So I dedicated myself to choreography from around 2002. I still dance from time to time in my own work or if there's a special choreographer I feel inspired by.

I work with composers nearly all of the time – contemporary composers of acoustic and electronic music. But I also work from time to time with orchestras. I created a piece in Berlin in 2003 which was a mixture of Stravinsky played live, combined with newly composed electronic music by Sam Auinger. I tend to not use classical romantic music. If I do use classical music it's more like Ligeti, Stravinsky, Bach or sometimes Baroque. But I usually mix it with composed music.

Critics often comment on the Irishness in my work. I think as a contemporary choreographer you are something of a channel. At the same time, when things get too serious I tend to go, "Oh no, God, please, things are getting too deep and meaningful." It's not that I don't value the depth of work and the seriousness of what I am trying to say, but I think there is usually another way to say it. Whether you call that Irish or not I don't know. As for the footwork – it's also mixed very much with a lot of the stuff I learned. Peter Schaufuss was a fanatic about footwork. The kind of thing I do is more like disfigured Irish footwork. It's thrashed footwork. No perfect fifth positions. I don't do perfect fifth positions.

> *Critics often comment on the Irishness in my work. I think as a contemporary choreographer you are something of a channel. At the same time, when things get too serious I tend to go, "Oh no, God, please, things are getting too deep and meaningful."*

After I decided to stop dancing full-time with the Deutsches Oper Berlin, and began to freelance as a choreographer, friends said, "Are you sure you should do it? It's very difficult as a freelancer." But suddenly I got the invitation from Nederlands Dance Theatre, and then Chicago, Hubbard Street Dance Company, then Stuttgart Ballet and it just went on. It was amazing actually. I took it as a sign to go ahead and follow my intuition.

Then the Saarlandisches Staatstheater Saarbrücken called me. They had been looking for a new ballet director. I almost said no. I had just started freelancing and I didn't think I wanted to go back into a Staatstheater situation. Staatstheaters can sometimes be a little restricting because of the system: You either have to have an open-minded Intendant (main director) or a lot of fight. But I feel that fighting within the system which is meant to support you is nothing but a waste of time. The mentality usually is, "Well, we've done it like this for 20 years so that's how we'll continue." I didn't want to do that. But they asked me to come and talk with them, so

Photo: by Bettina Stoess

Hitami Kuhara, Ruben Reniers and Nicola Kohlmann in Be Bob

I did. I was highly impressed with their openness and the fact that they were absolutely genuine about what they were saying. They gave me the feeling that, yes, I could do everything I wanted to do. So that's how this position came about. I was very close to saying "no" but then I realised that these opportunities don't come by every day.

Since coming to Saarbrücken I have been able to realise a lot of my ambitions, work on movement language, collaborate with other artists and build up a wonderful company. I have experimented with doing story ballets like *Carmen-private* (told from a female's point of view) and *Midsummer Night's Dream*. It was a lot of fun actually. We have a company full of strong personalities and I thought it would suit them very well.

Photo: Bettina Stoess

Toby Kassell in Different Directions

All my dancers have a classical training and background. It's very phy-sical, very moving, very dance-y, but also very fast and dynamic. We also use the voice in various ways: singing, talking, whatever it takes. But no, I wouldn't say it borders on dance theatre.

So far the company has been to the Santa Barbara Dance Festival in California, the International Festival in Seoul and Korea, Luxembourg and the international *Tanzmesse* in Duesseldorf.

Next year we have been invited to Canada, Korea, Luxembourg again and various festivals and theatres in Germany. We were to do a dance film of *Taboo or Not* in 2004 in Ireland, with the involvement of RTÉ. I thought it should be done in Ireland, creating surreal situations in the landscape with bizarre characters, but unfortunately the Irish involvement fell through. It did happen though, with ARTE and was filmed in the Völklinger Hütte – a huge iron factory between 1890 and 1990, now a World Cultural Heritage Museum.

Unfortunately, every time I'm home in the summer, everyone else is on holidays. I've met Liz Roche and John Scott, but I don't know their works, and they don't know mine.

Finola Cronin
Dancer

*H*ow does a native of Clontarf end up being a key performer with one of the most renowned, and zaniest, Dance Theatre Companies in the world – Pina Bausch's Tanztheater Wuppertal? Here Finola Cronin, who did just that, recounts the unlikely path that led her via Wuppertal to perform on the world's most presti-gous stages, from La Scala in Milan to Brooklyn's Academy of Music and the Paris Opera, before returning back home where as well as lecturing at UCD's Drama Studies Centre, she is now dance specialist at the Arts Council.

I started to dance at a very young age with Patricia Joan McCarthy in Clontarf. She was a wonderful teacher. I used to think she was very exotic, with her hair in the style of Alicia Markova, and also very elegant. I did a little Irish dancing, but it was ballet that I loved. I suppose I needed to dance, as dancers do. It's a kind of voca-tion really.

The extraordinary thing was that at the age of 18 I felt I'd already missed the boat in terms of wanting a career in dance. The only avenue I knew to a career in dance was to be a classical ballet dancer. But for that you have to go away and start training very intensively from the age, ideally, of 12. By 15 or 16, you have to be real-ly working very seriously. That option wasn't open to me here in Ireland. I certainly didn't even think about going to the Royal Ballet School. So I had kind of given up on the idea of ever being a dance per-former.

Then, in my late teens, I started classes with Terez Nelson, who had come to Dublin from the States where she had worked with Martha Graham. The Graham dance technique opened a whole new vista to me.

Through Terez Ne-son I met Joan Davis, a

Finola Cronin (front right, flower in hair) in 1980 . . . a piece by Pina Bausch

key figure in contemporary dance in Ireland. I had seen her perform as a member of her company. I worked very closely with Joan when she began to teach and subsequently performed with her company at Project Arts Centre, around 1977. All that we see here today comes, in some way, shape or form, out of Joan Davis's work.

Working with Joan opened up the possibility of doing another genre of dance – fulfilling the dream to dance and be a performer. To think that was possible was an enormous boost. Joan helped sponsor my very first series of contemporary classes at the London School of Contemporary Dance. She came with me and we did various different courses. When we came back we shared our information and our knowledge with our other colleagues, Karen O'Callaghan and Pamela Harris, the other two members of Dublin Contemporary Dance Theatre.

It seemed like a natural progression to study in the London School of Contemporary Dance. So that's what I did. Getting in a full-time dance school with access to a tradition and lineage to Martha Graham, the key figure in modern dance in America, and in the world subsequently, was an enormous gift. I worked there with figures like Jane Dudley, who had worked with Graham; Richard Alston, who had worked with Merce Cunningham; Naomi Lapeson; and Robert Cohen – all outstanding teachers.

Joan was building up her company in Dublin then. There was also Irish National Ballet Company, which was based in Cork. But I felt I needed to test the waters and see where I fitted into a more global place in dance. I didn't particularly want to go away – I would have loved to have had the influences and the range of opportunities here in Ireland. In fact Joan did facilitate dance teachers to come from abroad to teach us here. But I needed to spread my wings, and see how I could work in a different environment.

> *But I felt I needed to test the waters and see where I fitted into a more global place in dance. I didn't particularly want to go away – I would have loved to have had the influences and the range of opportunities here in Ireland.*

Soon after studying in The Place I realised that I would have to get a job, and work full-time as a dancer. While dancer friends of mine were teaching and doing other jobs to support themselves, I didn't want to do that. I decided to live on very little and only dance, and be open and ready to take any job opportunities that came my way. I heard of an agent in Germany and when I eventually travelled to meet him, he told me that there was a job going in Coburg. So I landed up in Coburg, a place I hadn't even heard of, and to be honest I immediately asked myself, "What am I doing in this place?"

Coburg had an opera ballet company with a resident choreographer, and a small company of about 12 dancers, and it turned out to be a golden opportunity. The choreographer choreographed all the musicals, the operas and the operettas, as well as her own work. So we were performing maybe 25 nights out of every month.

This was just the experience I needed to get used to the stage, and to the idea that dance was a job. Sure, there were creative things about it, but it was also a way of earning a living. To be able to earn a living as a dancer was very important.

I was introduced to that hugely comprehensive state-subsidised system in Germany. That world of resident opera companies, ballet companies, speaking theatre companies, and lots and lots of theatres, is completely different to what I was used to here or in the UK.

A few years later I came back to London because I wasn't sure I wanted to stay in Germany. I ended up with an invitation from two different Viviennes to join their respective companies: Vivienne Lorraine, a ballerina in London who was starting a ballet company and Vivienne Newport, who was coming out of a very unknown place for me then, the tradition of Pina Bausch and *Tanztheater*. I opted for Vivienne Newport, who was beginning a new company. The thing that really attracted me was that at the audition, after all the conventional technical elements of the class, she asked me to just walk across the room. While I was doing that, Vivienne asked some questions and began layering the actions of a simple walk with different emotional or character motivations. Some sort of door opened and I thought, "This is very interesting . . ." It wasn't dancing but it seemed so exciting.

The tasks were more to do with a mental association than mime – something very pedestrian; for example: "Walk across the room now and imagine you are very tired"; or, "Imagine that it's raining". This did open a huge door. Being asked to do something I hadn't learned, I thought, "My goodness, the possibilities here are endless." I could manage with my skills, but it wasn't something that I would have to technically learn and master. It was another aspect of what I could do.

> *The tasks were more to do with a mental association than mime – something very pedestrian; for example: "Walk across the room now and imagine you are very tired"; or, "Imagine that it's raining". This did open a huge door.*

This was 1981 – long before I had heard of devised theatre or improvisation. That might have been familiar if you were working in drama, but it was certainly unheard of in dance. I was immediately taken with this notion that you could be pedestrian, and make very human movements, but as a dancer you have a skilled body to do these human movements. Vivienne had worked with Pina Bausch in Wuppertal and, in the main, was adapting Pina's work process, but not necessarily her aesthetic, into her work.

Vivienne would set us tasks that might range from creating small dance movements to creating a scene, like a day at the beach. We would enact it, write it down in a notebook and be very precise about it. Vivienne would then shape this material. For the first time I had to sing on stage. There was singing, speaking, uttering, laughing, talking, joking and acting. I loved it. It was so challenging, and so satisfying to do. I really felt I was home. I had found my genre. This was my place.

We worked constantly in Vivienne's company, based at Theater am Turm in Frankfurt, creating 11 full-length works over a four-year period. I then auditioned for Pina Bausch and got into the company. It was a hugely different environment from working in Vivienne's chamber-size company. In Wuppertal, there were about 30 performers, of 17 different nationalities. It was on a different scale and, even then, in 1985, there was an enormous repertoire.

Pina's company is really an ensemble of principals but initially I learned group work or *corps de ballet* roles from the mid-1970s, the Gluck operas, *Iphigenia auf Tauris*, *Orpheus und Eurydice* and *Le Sacre du Printemps*. This was more the pure dance work – I also then began to get roles from the more avant-garde material she was doing in the 1980s: *Arien, 1980 . . . a piece by Pina Bausch, Auf dem Giberge* and *Bandoneon*. I had an enormous workload, which was wonderful, but very daunting as well.

The first piece that I contributed to making was *Viktor*, a co-production with Teatro Argentina in Rome where we went on location for about three weeks in 1985. Pina's method of creating work is terribly rigorous. Like Vivienne's, it begins with questions. But because of the numbers or performers it is extraordinarily time-consuming. It would take at least three and a half to four months to make a piece.

One scene (in *Viktor*) was inspired by a carpet auction Pina saw while out and about being shown the hidden secrets of Rome. She was fascinated with the speed at which the auctioneer was taking and accumulating the bids. So she asked us who

Finola Cronin (second from left) in Ahnen *(Ancestors)*

could do this. Melanie Lien, an American dancer, thought of the American cattle auction. I immediately thought of the way I heard the cattle auctions on radio for I don't know how many years. I tried to do it. Antonio Carallo did it in Italian. Of these three versions, mine was selected, and went into the piece.

It's something I really had to concentrate on, and speak as quickly as I could, auctioning off various items that were on a table in front of me. Lots of people came in from off-stage carrying props that looked like they were being auctioned. People were also being carried backward and forward, as if they too were being auctioned. For example, performer

Helene Pikon draped over a chair with wheels, is rolled onto the stage looking like an enormous spider. There were all sorts of strange things coming on stage – a big mix of commodities. I was the person with the microphone in this big picture, auctioning them off. This scene is repeated throughout the work and also forms the closing moments when all performers eventually come onstage to slowly make their way downstage towards the audience, as if they are all being auctioned.

The next piece I collaborated on was *Ahnen* – which loosely translates as "Ancestors" – in 1987. We rehearsed in a big old Wuppertal cinema called the Lichtburg with two enormous cupboards full of costumes, and lots of props. For one scene Pina asked us to create our national dance. Now when she says something like that you can take any aspect, do completely wacky things with it, or completely serious things.

In response, I found a black woollen dress that had a funny skirt, but was very tight and didn't allow much movement. I put a check scarf across my shoulder and down my body as if it was a sash. I found safety pins, strung them together, and hung them on my lapel (the medals!). Then I just did 1,2,3,4,5,6,7 – that basic Irish dance step that traverses – across the room and back again.

I also put on a hair net. That was inspired by the fact that when I was a child studying ballet, you had to have your hair in a particular way with a pink ballet band and a hairnet – pulling the hairnet around your ears and clipping it in place, so nothing would move. I thought that would fit the image. Of course, this was all pre-*Riverdance*.

Because I couldn't move much, this evolved into a scene where I came on stage and danced and danced as if I was holding my breath. After a bit, two colleagues came onstage and put me on a stretcher and carried it off, as if I had asphyxiated myself.

While Irish people who saw the scene did take a delight in that piece, the audience wouldn't have realised that I was trying to do Irish dance. I don't think even now, since *Riverdance*, that they would know. It was just a very in-joke in Ireland, how we considered that Irish dancing didn't move too much above the hips!

In the creation process, Pina would take all the scenes, bring them together and create work block by block. Then she'd rub it all out, and start all over in some other place, creating another block. Eventually, like a huge jigsaw puzzle, it would come together. Sometimes, even after the premiere it still wouldn't be right, and we'd all be

In the creation process, Pina would take all the scenes, bring them together and create work block by block. Then she'd rub it all out, and start all over in some other place, creating another block. Eventually, like a huge jigsaw puzzle, it would come together.

back in the studio pulling it together again. That was an invaluable lesson in rigour, attention to detail and time.

I worked with Pina for nearly ten years, until 1995, and still continue to guest with her – which is fun. The last time I was there was two years ago.

If Pina had been working in Paris, Rome or Dublin I would still be working with her. But I had been living in Germany for 15 years, and was a little tired of being homesick, because I always missed Ireland. So I decided to come back.

As a way back into Ireland, because I had been away for so long, I went to the Drama Studies Centre, did my MA in Drama in 1997, and I'm still in UCD.

Coming back, it was difficult initially to see how I would fit into the scheme of things. I didn't want to begin a company. After being part of an ensemble for so long, I wanted to work in a more isolated way. Being in UCD gave me an opportunity to think about teaching. It also gave me a chance to begin developing my own work, and to work as a choreographer. I could look at my own craft in terms of choreography.

In 1999 I was appointed dancer-in-residence at UCD. The idea was put forward by the Drama Studies Centre to Gaye Tanham, who was Dance Officer in the Arts Council. It wasn't the first residency in a university in Ireland, but it was a first for UCD. There was precedence in terms of UL, and at Project Arts Centre. That was hugely beneficial for me and allowed me access to rehearsal space in UCD, along with a little funding for performance research.

Though dance has hugely developed here over 20 years, our young talented dancers still have to go abroad for training. For example, when I left in the late 1970s there was Irish National Ballet and the beginnings of Dublin Contemporary Dance Theatre, and then Dublin City Ballet came on stream. A lot of that disappeared at the end of the 1980s. Out of those ashes came the further surge through the 1990s. Now, it's a small but potent community of dance artists. In my opinion dance presents among the most creative work in the performing arts in Ireland. From such a small group of people, there has been a lot of very innovative work.

Note
[1] Documented in her book *The Irish Ballerina* by Monica Loughman, with Jean Harrington, Dublin: Maverick House, 2004.

Appendix

Performed Works

W.B. Yeats's **Four Plays for Dancers** – *At the Hawk's Well* (1917); *The Only Jealousy of Emer* (1919); *The Dreaming of the Bones* (1919); *Calvary* (1920) – which each ended in a dance, preceded the Abbey School of Ballet. For further information see Yeats, W.B., *Four Plays for Dancers*, London: Macmillan, 1921; and *The Collected Plays of W.B. Yeats*, London: Macmillan, 1952.

Abbey School of Ballet

The ballet formed one part of the evening's entertainment. Most were performed with one or two plays. The programmes for the eleven performances were as follows:

30 January 1928

Part One

Venetian Suite, Respighi

The Romantic Lady: Ninette de Valois
The Sophisticated Lady: Vivienne Bennett
Two Unsophisticated Ladies: Marie Nelson
and Freda Bamford
The Minstrel: Eileen Murray

A Daughter of Eve, Arensky

Ninette de Valois

Beauty and the Beast, Ravel

Beauty: Marie Neilson
The Beast: Vivienne Bennett

Pastoral, Schubert

Cepta Cullen, Doreen Cuthbert

Pride, Scriabin

Ninette de Valois

Part Two

Rhythm, Beethoven

Marie Neilson, Vivienne Bennett, Freda
Bamford, Michael O'Sullivan, Rachel Law,
Eileen Murray, Margaret Horgan

Mexican Dance, Valverde

Vivienne Bennett

Dance of the Peasant, Liadov

Ninette de Valois

Fantaisie Russe, Rebikov

Ninette de Valois, Marie Neilson

Part Three

The Curse of the Aspen Tree, arr. Kennedy-Frazer

Freda Bamford, Michael O'Sullivan, S. Spratt, Kate Curling,
Freda Beckett, Eileen Murray, Margaret Horgan

---

16 April 1928

Part One

Thème Classique, Chopin

Ninette de Valois, Marie Neilson, Frances James, Chris Sheehan, May Kernan, Margaret Horgan, Doris Nolan

Silhouette, Grieg

Doreen Cuthbert, Cepta Cullen, Toni Repetto-Butler

The Goldfish, Debussy

Marie Neilson, Frances James, Sara Patrick, Doreen Cuthbert

Solo Piano: Hilda Shea

Part Two

Serenade, Boccherini

Ninette de Valois

Prélude Orienale, Gliere

Frances James

Les Buffons, Liadov

Sara Patrick, Cepta Cullen, Rachel Law, Eileen Murray, Freda Beckett

Yarabe Tapatto (Mexican), arr. A Partichela

Ninette de Valois

The Awakening, Ravel

Marie Neilson

Part Three

Rituelle de Feu, Manuel de Falla

The Maiden: Ninette de Valois
Chorus of Sun Worshippers: Marie Neilson, Frances James, Sara Patrick, Chris Sheehan, May Kiernan, Margaret Horgan, Doris Nolan, Eileen Murray, Rachel Law, Freda Beckett
Solo Piano: Hilda Shea

24 September 1928

Théme Classique, Chopin

Ninette de Valois, Sara Patrick, Doreen Cuthbert, Margaret Horgan, Chris Sheehan, May Kiernan, Doris Nolan

Divertissemente

A Daughter of Eve, Arensky

Ninette de Valois

Idyll, Schubert

Doreen Cuthbert, Cepta Cullen

Dance of the Russian Peasant, Liadov

Ninette de Valois

Les Buffons, Liadov

Arthur Hamilton, Rachel Law, Thelma Murphy, Muriel Kelly, Mariequita Langton

The Faun, Arthur Hamilton

Elves: Doreen Cuthbert, Cepta Cullen, Toni Repetto-Butler, Jill Gregory, Anne Clarke, Geraldine Byrne

Shades: Ninette de Valois, Sara Patrick, Margaret Horgan, Chris Sheehan, May Kiernan, Doris Nolan, Rachel Law

Music by Harold R White

Costumes designed by Rosalind Patrick

Choreography by Ninette de Valois

29 April 1929

Divertissemente

Turkish Ballet Suite, Lulley
(The Would-be Gentleman)

Sara Patrick, May Kiernan, Margaret
Horgan, Doris Nolan
Choreoegraphy by Sara Patrick

Pride, Scriabin

Ninette de Valois

Jack and Jill

Jack: Toni Repetto-Butler
Jill: Eileen Hare or Muriel Kelly

Fantaisie Russe, Rebikov

Ninette de Valois, Sara Patrick

Prelude, Chopin

Chris Sheehan, Doreen Cuthbert,
Cepta Cullen
Choreography by Sara Patrick

Serenade, Boccherini

Ninette de Valois

Idyll, Schubert

Jill Gregory, Geraldine Byrne

Rout, Arthur Bliss

Poem by Ernst Toller, trans. by Ashley
Dukes
Ninette de Valois, Sara Patrick, Chris
Sheehan, Margaret Horgan, May Kiernan,
Doreen Cuthbert, Cepta Cullen, Thelma
Murphy
At the piano: Julia Gray, Hilda Shea
Vocalist: May Doyle
Costumes and Setting: Hedley Briggs

Choreography (unless otherwise stated)
Ninette de Valois

14 May 1929

Les Sylphides, Chopin

Chris Sheehan, Cepta Cullen, Doreen
Cuthbert, Eileen Murray, Rachel Law,
Muriel Kelly, Mariequita Langton
Choreography by Ninette de Valois

Prelude, Schubert

Sara Patrick, Margaret Horan,
May Kiernan
Choreography by Sara Patrick

13 August 1929

(De Valois was choreographer, and played Fand in Yeats's *Fighting the Waves* on
the same night)

Tambourine

Chris Sheehan, May Kiernan

Waltz, Johann Strauss

Polka

Thelma Murphy, Muriel Kelly, Rachel
Law, Ninette de Valois, Hedley Briggs

Pavane

Margaret Horgan, Doreen Cuthbert,
Mariequita Langton
Singer: John Stevenson

Tybolese, Schubert

Ninette de Valois, Sara Patrick, Hedley
Briggs

Choreography by Ninette de Valois

19 November 1929

Waltz, Johann Strauss
Thelma Murphy, Doreen Cuthbert, Cepta Cullen

Jeune Paysanne, Dunhill
Sara Patrick (chor: Sara Patrick)

Movement Perpétuel, Poulenc
Ninette de Valois, Sara Patrick, Hedley Briggs
Choreography by Ninette de Valois

9 February 1931

Les Jeunes Paysanne, Dunhill
Doreen Cuthbert, Muriel Kelly, Evelyn Murphy
Chor: Sara Patrick

Air on G String, Bach
Thelma Murphy, Margaret Horgan, Doris Nolan

Russian Court Dance
Ninette de Valois

Pas de Trois Classique, Tchaikovsky
Jill Gregory, Eileen Kane, Toni Repetto-Butler

Sunday Afternoon, Somerville
Doreen Cuthbert, Cepta Cullen
Chor: Sara Patrick

Prélude Orientale, Gliere
Ninette de Valois

When Phillida Flouts Him, Julia Gray
Sara Patrick, Frances Robert, Thelma Murphy, Doreen Cuthbert, Joan Crofton, Muriel Kelly, Evelyn Murphy, Eileen Kane
Chor: Sara Patrick

(Choreography by Ninette de Valois unless otherwise stated)

6 December 1931

Thème Classique, Chopin
Thelma Murphy, Coreen Cuthbert, Cepta Cullen, Eileen Kane, Jill Gregory, Muriel Kelly, Audrey Smith

Dance Studies

1. The New Hat, *Grieg*
Geraldine Byrne

2. At the Ball, *Strauss*
Ginette Waddell

3. Solitude, *Grieg*
Cepta Cullen

4. He Loves Me, He Loves Me Not, *MacDowell*
Eileen Kane

5. Variation, *J.S. Bach*
Thelma Murphy

6. Tyrolese Dance, *Schubert*
Victor Wyndham, Cepta Cullen, Audrey Smith

7. The Water Lily, *Mac Dowell*
Muriel Kelly

8. Serenade, *Boccherin*
Jill Gregory

9. Russian Court Dance, *Zwerkov*
Doreen Cuthbert

Fedelma – a Mime Ballet in One Scene

Fedelma: Doreen Cuthbert
The Son of the King of Ireland: Victor B. Wynburne
The Hag: Nesta Brooking
Doves: Molly Furley, Muriel Kelly, Eileen Kane, Audrey Smith
Ravens: N. Curtin, R. Francis, J. Reynolds

Choreography for Dances and Ballets, unless otherwise stated, by Ninette de Valois;
Music by William Alwyn; Costumes by Dolly Travers-Smith

---

25 July 1933
(De Valois played The Guardian of the Well in Yeats's *At the Hawk's Well*)

The Drinking Horn A Ballet by Arthur Duff	*Bluebeard* A Ballet Poem by Mary Davenport O'Neill
The Elf: Vera Bryans	
The Knight of the Well: Robert Francis	Sister Ann, Illina's sister: Ria Mooney
The Flute Player: Bartholemew Lynch	Cyril, a manservant: Joseph O'Neill
Dancers: Christine Kane, Mabel Rockett,	Illina, Bluebeard's seventh wife: Ninette de
Marjorie Pearce, Eileen Mayne, Fanny	Valois
O'Meara, Tess Dillon Kelly	Baron Bluebeard: J. V. Wynburne
The Youth: Toni Repetto-Butler	Attendant: Toni Repetto-Butler
The Girl: Jill Gregory	Illina's two brothers: Robert Francis,
Choreography by Ninette de Valois;	Bartholemew Lynch
conducted by the composer	The Ghosts of Bluebeard's former wives:
	Chris Sheehan, Doreen Cuthbert, Muriel
	Kelly, Cepta Cullen, Thelma Murphy,
	Margaret Horgan
	Choir: Misses K. Roddy, C. Kenny, Betty
	Burne, M. Fanning
	Programme produced under the direction
	of Arthur Shields
	Music by JF Larchet; Choreography by
	Ninette de Valois

---

30 July 1934
De Valois played The Queen in Yeats's *The King of the Great Clock Tower*

Note:
All of the above programme information is taken from Robinson, Lennox, *Ireland's Abbey Theatre: A History, 1899–1951*, London: Sidgwick and Jackson Ltd., 1951. Courtesy of Pat Laffan.

Dublin Contemporary Dance Theatre 1979–1989

1978

Duo (chor: Joan Davis)

Vertical Man (chor: Joan Davis)

1979

Ishmael (chor: Joan Davis)

Energies (chor: Joan Davis)

Triplet (chor: Joan Davis)

Clearing (chor: Marsha Paludan)

1980

Blue (chor: Ruth Way)

Two Fables (chor: Joan Davis)

Kites (chor: Ruth Way)

Passing Time (chor: Ruth Way)

Rachmaninov (chor: Joan Davis)

Solo I (chor: Joan Davis)

Doina (chor: Royston Maldoom, Scotland)

1981

Amerindance (chor: Robert Connor)

Action Painting (chor: Joan Davis)

Grey Gentleman (chor: Judy Cole)

Just Stories (chor: The Company)

Malice in Funderland (chor: Ruth Way)

Seabreak (chor: Loretta Yurick)

Solo II (chor: Joan Davis)

*Casting Cool Changes (*Karen Callaghan, Ireland/New York)

Rules of the Game (chor: Kedzi Penfield, Scotland/USA)

*Acid Rain (*chor: Jerry and Sara Pearson, New York)

Rebel (chor: Ingard Lonnroth, Sweden)

1982

Anna Livia (chor: Joan Davis)

Missed and Moving Hearts (chor: Loretta Yurick)

Spinoff (chor: Joan Davis)

Solo III (chor: Joan Davis)

The Classical Ideal (chor: Jerry Pearson, assisted by Sara Pearson, New York)

Firestone (chor: Richard Haisma, New York)

1983

Inside Outside (duet, Robert Connor and Loretta Yurick)

People (chor: Joan Davis)

Search (solo, chor: Mary Nunan)

Wake...re...em (35 min, chor: Robert Connor)

Tango Echo Bravo Romeo November (chor: Martha Bowers, New York)

1984

Lunar Parables (full length, chor: Jerry and Sara Pearson, New York)

Freefall (chor: Mark Taylor, New York)

Ancestral Light (chor: Loretta Yurick)

Coupled Reflections (chor: Robert Connor and Loretta Yurick)

Inside Outside (solo, chor: Robert Connor)

Minnaw (chor: Joan Davis and Mary Nunan)

Sand Dance (chor: Mary Nunan)

1985

Almost Home chor: Marta Renzi (USA, New York) Music: Van Morrison

Telecom Erring (chor: Robert Connor)

Polyester Pyjamas and Things Like That . . . (chor: Mary Nunan)

Eireann go Brea (chor: Karen Callaghan/Loretta Yurick)

1986

Single Line Traffic (chor: Yoshiko Chuma, New York)

White Line (chor: Mark Taylor, New York)

Of a Feather (chor: Joan Davis)

The Longest Night (35 min) (chor: Loretta Yurick)

Continuum (chor: Joan Davis)

1987

Simon Says Duet (chor: Loretta Yurick; music: Paul Simon)

Sojourn (chor: Robert Connor)

Hey! solo (chor: Joan Davis)

Moves and *Dreams of a Boy Child,* solos (chor: Paul Johnson)

Don't Ask me to Choose (chor: Jenny Kavanagh)

Heaven Somewhere (chor: Scott Clarke, England/US)

1988

Into the Night, full length programme comprised of five works:

Celtic Night (chor: Randy Glynn, Canada; music: The Bothy Band and others)

Bread and Kerosene (chor: Dairine Davison)

Later that Day it all Came Back (chor: Art Bridgman and Myrna Packer, New York)

Agony, Romance and other Cosmopolitan Pages (chor: Robert Connor and Loretta Yurick)

Ancestral Light (see 1984) (chor: Loretta Yurick)

Warning Dawning (chor: Jenny Kavanagh)

Bloomsday: Impressions of James Joyce's Ulysses; Full length work. (chor: Jerry Pearson, US)

1989

Modern Daze, full length work (chor: Nina Martin, New York)

Dance Theatre of Ireland

Choreographies

(choreography by Connor and Yurick unless otherwise stated)

1989
La Beauté des Fleurs (chor: Pierre Doussaint/Isabelle Dubouloz)
Remnants

1990
Freedom's Gait
Full Moon

1991
Touching the Moon (chor: Janet Smith)
Weigh the Heart against a Feather

1992
Dances in Dreams
Enough

1993
BYTE!
Fuchsia

1994
Trembling on a Limb

1995
Bonefire
Angel Land
Licks its Lips and Chews its Gums (chor: Liz and Jenny Roche)
Hopelessly Helixed (chor: Jerry Pearson)
Deserts d'amour (chor: Dominique Bagouet)

1996
Deseo (chor: Blok and Steel)
Body Travels Time

1997
Jours Etranges (chor: Dominique Bagouet)
Like Water Flowing East

1998
Tombs

1999
Made to Measure (chor: Rui Horta)
Soul Survivor

2000
Only Human

2001
Cha-Cha-Cha d'Exil and A Question of Distance (chor: Charles Cre-Ange and Philippe Saire)
Evidence

2002
Prism
RE:Lease Me (chor: Niamh Condron)
The Simulacra Stories (chor: Joanne Leighton)

2003
As a Matter of Fact

2004
Between You and Me (chor: Philippe Saire; Will Dorner; Marie-Francoise Garcia; Alexandre Iseli)

2005
Watermark

Mary Nunan

Daghdha Dance Company (Choreographies by Mary Nunan)

1991
Through an Eye of Stone

1993
Territorial Claims

1993
For Company

1994
Like Writing on Water

1995
Fictional

1996
On Earth as it is in Heaven

1996
Aerdha

1997
Here Then – Elsewhere Now

1998
Chimera

1999
Far Flung

Daghdha Education Programme (Choreographies by Mary Nunan)

1991
Homing In
Heartscore

1992
On Time with Pigs

1995
This Way Up

1996
Tales of the Unexpected

1997
Just In Case

1998
Little Red Riding and the Wolves of
Progress Gone Wild

1999
Feels like Thunder Looks like Rain

Independent Choreographies

1996
On Earth as it is in Heaven
Commissioned for the Lyon
Conservatoire

1999
Clann Lir for Siamsa Tire

2001
On the Water's Edge, Myriad Dance
Company

No Knowing, duet for for Daghdha
Dance Company "2x2x5" production
under Yoshiko Chuma

2002
Claim Reclaim, solo in collaboration
with Ferenc Szucs (cellist)

2003
Yellow Room, as a collaborator under
the direction of Yoshiko Chuma

Dance for Camera
1997: Screen Adaptation of *Territorial Claims*

Solo Programme
Currently devising Solo programme entitled *God Series*
2004: God Series # 1 bach and #2 reid
2005: God Series #3 wolf

Irish Modern Dance Theatre
(www.irishmoderndancetheatre.com)
Choreographies (by John Scott unless otherwise stated)

1991
Beneath the Storm

1992
Invisible Territory
Rhapsody
Rough Notes and Dance Points

1993
Dance for Another Place
Thunderstorm

1994
Ruby Red

1995
Palace of Emptiness (Chor: John Wiseman)
Slam
Macalla

1996
You Must Tell the Bees (with text, "Widda", by Tom Mac Intyre)
Perfect State

1997
Nous – the loss of the winds (Chor: Fabrice Dugied)
Just Bodies

1998
Intimate Gold
That Place Those People (Chor: Sean Curran)
Real Pearls

1999
Wishing Time

2000
Off the Wall

2001
Rough Air

2002
Missed Fit (Chor: John Jasperse)
Left and Right
Last Supper

2004
like Silver
"It is better to . . ." (Chor: Thomas Lehmann)
Fall and Recover (with the Centre for the Care of Survivors of Torture)
Friezes

2005
RrrrrrrrrrrKILLKILLKILL . . . (Chor: Chris Yon)
The White Piece

CoisCéim Dance Theatre
(www.coisceim.com)

Choreographies (by David Bolger unless otherwise stated)

1995
Straight with Curves
Dances with Intent (Co-chor: Diane Richardson)

1996
Dragons and Tonics (Chor: Liz Roche)

1997
Ballads
Back in Town
Hit and Run

1998
Seasons (Chor: Muirne Bloomer, Allan Irvine, Liz Roche)
Toupées and Snare Drums (script: Gina Moxley, Peacock Theatre co-prod.)

1999
Dish of the Day

2000
Boxes (co-choreographed with Sean Jeremy Palmer)
When Once is Never Enough

2002
Hit and Run (dance-film, co-produced with Rough Magic Films)
The Rite of Spring

2003
Swept
Mermaids

2004
Chamber Made (co-created with Katie Read)

2005
Knots (Chor: Liam Steel)
Nutcracker
Out of Harm's Way (Tanztheater Freiburg/Heidelburg)

David Bolger's Opera Theatre and Film Choreography

Orfeo ed Euridice (Opera Ireland)
Hurl (Barabbas the Company)
The Synge Cycle, Sive and *Sharon's Grave* (Druid Theatre Company)
Sophie's Choice (Royal Opera House, London)
A Dash of Colour (Special Olympics, Dublin, 75,000 people)
Dancing at Lughnasa (TNM, Montreal)

The Coast of Utopia, The Relapse, Love's Labour Lost (Royal National Theatre, London
Martin Guerre (Cameron Mackintosh, UK and US)
Big Maggie, Tarry Flynn, The Colleen Bawn and *The Secret Fall of Constance Wilde* (Abbey Theatre)
Film choreography of *Dancing at Lughnasa* with Meryl Streep and directed by Pat O'Connor

Rex Levitates Dance Theatre
(www.rexlevitates.com)
Choreographies (by Liz Roche)

1999

Interrupted Light (Aerowaves International Platform, Dublin)

Peeling Venus (Diversions Festival, Temple Bar)

2000

Blush (Dublin Fringe Festival Commission)

The Salt Cycle (Diversions Festival, Temple Bar)

2001

Trip Down (Festival de la Nouvelle Danse, Utzes, France)

Over the Rainbow (The Gallery of Photography, Dublin)

2002

Their Thoughts are Thinking Them (National Gallery of Ireland)

Senses (collaboration with Maiden Voyage Northern Ireland, premiered at Lyric Theatre Belfast)

2003

Bread and Circus (Project Arts Theatre commission)

2004

Cross Purposes (Mermaid Arts Centre commission)

Catalyst (collaboration with The National Ballet of China)

Resuscitate (mentored by Rosemary Butcher, International Dance Festival Ireland)

2005

Six Frames – Memories of Two Women (Chor: Rosemary Butcher)

Proximity (St. Patrick's Day Festival commission)

2006

Sweet Apollo

Fabulous Beast Dance Theatre
(www.fabulousbeast.net)

Choreographies (by Michael Keegan Dolan)

1995
Farmyard Fantasia Documentary

1996
Ariodante (opera)
The Oedipus Plays (theatre)

1998
The Good People
Sunday Lunch
Manon
Idomeneo
Ephemera (ballet)

1999
Fragile
Alcina (opera)

2000
The Flowerbed
The Ashgirl (theatre)

2001
The Christmas Show
Pique Dame (opera)
The Love for Three Oranges (opera)

2002
Macbeth (opera)

2003
Giselle
Manon (opera)
The Duchess of Malfi (theatre)

2005
The Bull

Barabbas
(www.barabbas.ie)

Plays

1994
Half Eight Mass of a Tuesday
Macbeth

1995
Sick Dying Dead Buried Out

1996
Strokehauling

1997
The Whiteheaded Boy
Out the Back Door

1999
Hupnouse

2000
Barabbas . . . the cube
God's Gift

2001
Nightmare on Essex Street
Moby Dan
Dog

2002
Temple of Clown
Blowfish

2003
Hurl
Blowfish

2004
A Midsummer Night's Dream

2005
Luca
Tanks a lot!

Joan Denise Moriarty

Some Important Dates:

1947: Founded Amateur Cork Ballet Company, which performed bi-annually at the Cork Opera House

1954: Founded Irish Theatre Ballet

1973: Formed Irish Ballet Company, later to be the Irish National Ballet

Colin Dunne
(www.colindunne.com)

Choreographies

1995-1998:
Riverdance – The Show:
Trading Taps (with Tariq Winston)
Firedance (with Maria Pages)
Heartbeat of the World (with Maria Pages)
Heartland Duet (with Jean Butler)

1999
Dancing on Dangerous Ground (with Jean Butler)

2002
HeadFoot (for Daghdha, part of Yoshiko Chuma's *10,000 steps*)

The Arrival of The Queen of Sheba in Galway (premiered Jubilee Auditorium, Edmonton, Canada)

Piano One (premiered Jubilee Auditorium, Edmonton, Canada)

Oh So Virtuoso (premiered Charleston City Ballet)

Bar480 (premiered Vail International Dance Festival)

2003
The Yellow Room (contributing choreographer, for Yoshiko Chuma)

2004
The Shaugraun (Abbey Theatre)

2005
Rashers and Sausages (shown at Sean Nós - Nua Nós, St Johns Church, Limerick)

The Bull (for Fabulous Beast Dance Theatre)

Carna (with the Irish Chamber Orchestra, written by Bill Whelan)

Jean Butler
(www.jeanbutler.com)

1994-7 :
Eurovision and Riverdance: The Show

Riverdance solo piece and original duet with Michael Flatley

Countess Cathleen (except for Russian ballet segment)

Heartland Duet (with Colin Dunne)

1998

Reel Beatrice (music by Sharon Shannon)

Spanish Point (with Donal Lunny and the Kodo Drummers)

2000

Dancing on Dangerous Ground (with Colin Dunne)

2004

Her Riyal Waggedey Toes

Blue

Greyage

Back in 5

2005

Does She Take Sugar in her Tea?

White

Two pieces of choreography for Takarazuka Company in Japan

Breandán de Gallaí

Choreographies

Breandan choreographs for various plays and theatrical productions, and has choreographed for *Riverdance* TV appearances

1999
Trasnu (for the opening of An Grianan Theatre, Letterkenny, Co. Donegal)

2005
Celtic Dreams (contributing choreographer, Cork City Ballet)

Ongoing
Balor (www.balor.com) (90 minute dance show incorporating contemporary, classical, and Irish dancing)

Siamsa Tíre
www.siamsatire.com

Some Key Siamsa Tíre Productions in Choreographic Development:

1986
The Story of the Mermaid
(Chor: Jonathan Burnett)

1989
Between Worlds
(Chor: Anne Courtenay;
Music: Micheál O'Súilleabháin)

1991
Ding Dong Dederó, Forging the
Dance (Chor: Anne Courtenay)

1992
The Seville Suite (Music: Bill Whelan;
Chor: Maria Pages and Siamsa
Dancers)

1999
Clann Lir (by John Sheehan;
Chor: Mary Nunan)

2000
Oisín (by Oliver Hurley)

2001
Samhain (by Oliver Hurley)

2003
Oileán (by Oliver Hurley;
Chor: Cindy Cummings)

2005
rEvolution (Collaboration with Cindy
Cummings and Andrew Duggan)

Finola Cronin
Choreographies

1997
The Chirpaun (by Tom MacIntyre,
Peacock Theatre)

1999
Cúirt an Mheán Oiche (by Tom MacIntyre, Peacock Theatre)

1999
Faust (MA Drama Studies Centre
UCD production)

2001
Work in Progress Project Cube

2002
The Murder Ballads (A Tanztheater
Cabaret, Kilkenny Arts Festival)

Women in Arms (Storytellers Theatre
Company & Cork Opera House)

Collaborations

1981-1985 (Company Vivienne Newport Mist) *Hinter der Scheune überfrisst sich ein Ochse* *Trigger* *Persicare* *Weder den Tag noch die Stunde* *Damals* *Ertrinken* *Valeska Gert*	**1985-1995** (Tanztheater Wuppertal) *Tanzabend 2* (Co-production Madrid) *Palermo Palermo* (Co-production Teatro Biondi Palermo) *The Plaint of the Empress* (film) *Ahnen* *Viktor* (Co-production Teatro Argentina Rome) **1995** (Lyric Theatre, Hammersmith, London) *A Crocodile Looking at Birds*

Marguerite Donlon and Donlon Dance Company (www.donlon.de)

Productions List

1992
Celtic Touch

1994
We Three Sheep (Deutsche Oper Berlin)

1999
Stew (Cathy Sharp, Basel)
Patch of Grass (Deutsche Oper Berlin)
Lokus (Donlon Dance Co)

2000
Taboo or Not (Vienna State Ballet)
Different Directions (Donlon Dance Co, Berlin)

2001
Reverse Deconstruct (Hubbard Street Dance Company, Chicago)

2002
Bebob (Nederlands Dans Theater 2)

Move (Saarbrücken)
Somewhere between remembering and forgetting (Stuttgart Ballet)

2003
Poetic Licence (Berlin Ballet)
Chocolate (Saarbrücken)
Carmen – private (Saarbrücken)

2004
Blind Date (Saarbrücken)
Beauty (Saarbrücken)
Summer Nights Dream (Saarbrücken)

2005
Strokes through the tail (Hubbard Street Dance Company, Chicago USA)
In Memory of . . . (Saarbrücken)
On Top (Saarbrücken)
Eros (Saarbrücken)
The Red Shoes (Staatliche Ballett Schule Berlin)

Dance Films	**Installations (2001-2004)**
1999: *Locus*	*Hitomi @ Home*
2004: *Carmen (ARTE)*	*Bubbles over head*
2005: *Taboo or Not (ARTE)*	*Strange Incounters*
	Entre Files
	Upside down Room
	Kitchen Dance (video)

Index